W9-BNB-149

"If you love movies and are committed to a conscious world, you absolutely must read this book. Stephen Simon produces paradigm-shifting movies that change not only individual lives but also shape a new world consciousness. He has dedicated his life to bringing spirit to the screen; in this book you will get to see the challenges he faced in doing so. In addition to being a gripping read, the book also has a very practical side to it: Stephen's far-ranging exploration turned us on to dozens of undiscovered movies that we've now put on our 'must-see' list.

"Buy this book, keep it close at hand and consult it often—it's an essential reference guide to the dawning of a new consciousness."

—Gay Hendricks, Ph.D., and Kathlyn Hendricks, Ph.D., authors of *Conscious Loving* and *The Conscious Heart*

"Stephen Simon is a unique individual, soulful, passionate, wise, loyal, and fiercely determined to explore the world of spirit and its connection to our lives. The film we made together was a journey I will always remember. I know you will find this book to be the same."

—Ron Bass, Academy-Award-winning screenwriter for *Rain Man* and screenwriter of *What Dreams May Come*

"Stephen Simon's *The Force Is with You* heroically defines a new movie genre: spiritual and transformational films—here is an author who has been there. Want to know why some movies affect us so? Look here!"

—James Redfield, author of *The Celestine Prophecy* and *The Secret of Shambhala*

THE FORCE IS WITH YOU

MYSTICAL MOVIE MESSAGES THAT INSPIRE OUR LIVES

STEPHEN SIMON

WALSCH BOOKS
an imprint of
HAMPTON ROADS
PUBLISHING COMPANY, INC.
www.hrpub.com

Cover design by Marjoram Productions

Hampton Roads Publishing Company, Inc.
1125 Stoney Ridge Road
Charlottesville, VA 22902

434-296-2772
fax: 434-296-5096
e-mail: hrpc@hrpub.com
www.hrpub.com

If you are unable to order this book from your local
bookseller, you may order directly from the publisher.
Call 1-800-766-8009, toll-free.

Library of Congress Cataloging-in-Publication Data
Simon, Stephen, 1946-
The force is with you : mystical movie messages that inspire our lives
/ Stephen Simon.
p. cm.
ISBN 1-57174-349-9 (alk. paper)
1. Motion pictures--Moral and ethical aspects. I. Title.
PN1995.5 .S59 2002
791.43'653--dc21
2002011664

ISBN 1-57174-349-9
10 9 8 7 6 5 4 3 2 1
Printed on acid-free paper in the United States

Is the universe communicating with us?
Are we telling ourselves something?
Either way . . .
There are mystical messages in movies.

This book is dedicated to my four daughters—
Michelle, Tabitha, Cari, and Heather—
For teaching me the meaning of love and for
Their infinite patience in raising me.

Table of Contents

Acknowledgements

Remember when you were a kid and your parents caught you and a friend trying to do some crazy stunt like a backyard science experiment? Taking responsibility for wild flights of fancy is not exactly one of our strong suits when we're children, so most of us immediately gave all the "credit" for the idea to the friend who was with us, or any living creature within sight. That's how "the dog ate my homework" got started. Not exactly an advanced spiritual practice but, then again, we were kids and most of us have grown considerably since those days; therefore, I just want to say from the onset here that NEALE DONALD WALSCH MADE ME DO THIS!

Neale had been talking to me for weeks about writing this book and, frankly, I thought he had taken leave of his senses. I had never written anything more complicated than my marketing list every week, and even that was constantly revised by my daughters—so it wasn't exactly a solid foundation on which I could build. Neale was relentless. He really felt I should just sit down and write and, truthfully, he's a hard guy to turn down. Neale has been a friend and an inspiration to me for a few years now. Our company Metafilmics is working with Neale on filmed versions of his *Conversations with God* books, and I've come to know and deeply respect not only his work but also Neale as a really great guy.

Finally, one day, Neale wouldn't take no for an answer again, and I thought to myself that maybe I should pay closer attention. Who was I to challenge his "sources"? He gave me a schedule and some great writing tips (like always end the writing day in the middle of a sentence so you know where to start the next day), and I started to write. He told me the book would come out of me in two months. I started the first draft in April, and finished it slightly less than two months later.

Forget E.F. Hutton. When Neale talks, I listen. And so do a lot of other people. He inspires me, and he inspired this book, and for both, I am eternally grateful. Any tips on the stock market, Neale?

As you have already seen, this book is dedicated to my four extraordinary daughters. Without their love and the mirror that they hold for me, I would be lost.

Thank you and much love to my parents, Harriet and Armand Deutsch. To you, Mom, for always letting me know how much I am loved, and to you, Dad, for your incredible decency, wisdom and dignity.

To my "kid" sister Susan Granger, thank you for the unconditional love. You are my eternal hero.

To our Texan Mary Poppins, Blanca Chapa, thank you for coming into our lives when you did. You are an extraordinary role model and a gift from the universe. Without you, I never would have been able to raise such wonderful young women.

To the amazing Lisa Schneiderman, thank you for your guidance and for opening my eyes and heart.

To Dr. Stephen Renzin, with deep appreciation for the past forty years—you are the kindest and best friend in the universe.

To Lee Stein, Kip Hagopian, Ron Bass, Nick Thiel, Jane Sindell, Michael Dellar, Don Granger, Greg Mooers, Dyanne Aponte, Nancy Walsch, Robert Evans, Tara Walsch, Paul Roth, Anthony Benson, Melissa Giovagnoli, Beverly Dennis, and Harris Schoenfeld for your enduring friendship, guidance, and generosity. If not for all of you, I wouldn't have been able to make it this far.

To my spiritual guide and dear friend, Richard Matheson, thank you for trusting me with your brilliant books and for giving me the opportunity to learn at the feet of a master.

To my mentor and teacher, Ray Stark, thank you for giving me my first job, teaching me, guiding me, inspiring me, and for allowing me to begin my career with a living legend.

To Gay and Katie Hendricks with deep gratitude for sharing and keeping the faith.

To Barnet Bain, thank you for the adventure and the mirror.

To Robert Friedman, for believing in me and this book . . . and for being the ultimate mensche of the publishing world.

To Annie, with gratitude, for leading me back to the rivers of believe.

To Arielle Ford and Brian Hilliard, thank you for your guidance, friendship, and love.

To Andrew Fogelson, thank you for your support and your insights.

To Lisa Gerrard, thank you for the extraordinary artistry of your CD "The Mirror Pool." I must have played it several hundred times as the muse music behind this book and it sounds new every time.

To Chuck and Amanda Weber, thank you for being my constant inspiration.

And to those of you who have communicated with me about the films with which I have been involved over the years—thank you for giving me the strength and inspiration to not only write this book but to live my life with your own hopes and dreams within my heart.

Foreword

If you love movies, you're going to love this book. If you love life, you're going to adore it. And if you love a good story, get set, because you're about to hear some great ones.

I call these the Stories of Stories. They are the stories of the *making* of stories, and of what some of our most popular stories have had in store for *us*—whether we knew it or not.

This particular story is going to be told by a wonderful friend of mine—who also happens to be one of the master storytellers on our planet—Stephen Simon.

Working with the wonderful tool of film, Stephen is responsible for bringing to the world two of its most special stories ever, *Somewhere in Time* and *What Dreams May Come*. I, along with millions of others, found myself instantly captivated and forever entranced by the first, and the second took my breath away.

As producer of these films Stephen brought pure magic to the screen, and to my life. I carry these stories within me always. You know you've been told a good story, I mean, a *really* good story, when you can't let go of it. And these two are stories that the heart cannot forget, carrying messages that only old souls could imagine, but that all souls resonate with deeply.

When I first saw these movies I wondered whether their extraordinary messages were being sent consciously and deliberately, or arrived on the doorstep of my mind as mere after-products of the movie-making process—unintended outcomes of what were simply commercial ventures. Then, as I traveled my own surprising life path, I chanced to meet the producer of those films—something I never in a million years thought would or could happen—and I got to find out.

I asked.

No, they were definitely *not* unintended outcomes.

Stephen (and his co-producer on *Dreams,* Barnet Bain) was *very* much aware of the incredible nature of the messages he was sending with these films, and *made them for that reason.*

Here was a conscious filmmaker, who was choosing consciously to help *shift the consciousness of the planet* with his life work. I am proud to now list Stephen Simon among my close friends. Not because he is a Hollywood movie producer (he allows that to impress you for about three and a half minutes), but because he is one of the courageous members of our human family: someone who has chosen to be a messenger, someone who has chosen to make a difference, someone who has chosen to see a brighter world and a grander truth and a wider vision, and who seeks to share it with all of us—not so that we can see how special *his* world is, but so that we may be inspired to bring that specialness to our own.

This is life-changing stuff I'm talking about here. These films have messages that change inner realities—and those kinds of changes alter outer experiences, and can shift the collective experience of the planet.

One day as I was talking with Stephen about all this, we began a quick thumbnail review of how many other movies we could think of that contained real mind-bending, consciousness-shifting messages, and before too many minutes had passed the list had grown very long.

Starting with *Matrix* (a very recent and vivid example) and moving right on to other contemporary films such as *The Kid* (one of my personal favorites), *Pay It Forward, Field of Dreams, Cocoon, Frequency, Groundhog Day, Star Wars, The 13th Floor, Ghost,* and many others, then on to older movies like *Defend-*

ing Your Life, Resurrection, The Ghost and Mrs. Muir, The Razor's Edge, and countless more, we impressed ourselves with the vastness of the inventory of truly meaningful movie messages we were able to catalogue with just a moment's thought.

Neither of us was particularly surprised by this, however. We both understood that important and timely messages are constantly being sent *to* life *about* life, and that the performing arts—including the high-impact medium of movies—were among the chief means by which the Universe was sending them. Entertainment, it turns out, is a great delivery system.

"You know, Stephen, you ought to write a book about that!" I suddenly blurted. "I'm sure that people are aware, as we are, that there's more to many movies than meets the eye. Wouldn't it be great to have an 'insider' from Hollywood reveal to us how this is being done? And maybe even point out to us some of the mystical movie messages we may have missed?"

"Oh, I don't know," Stephen hesitated. "I'm a movie producer, not an author. That's your stage."

"Hey," I insisted, "if you can talk, you can write! Besides, who better to tell this story than someone who's been *making* these stories and *sending* these messages?"

He thought about it for a moment, and I pressed the advantage. "Stephen, the world needs to hear about this. We need to have a compilation of what we've been telling ourselves—an all-in-one-place, entertaining, breezy but important look at the messages movies have been sending us. And you're just the person to do it. In fact, you're the *perfect* person to do it."

"Hmmm," he smiled, "maybe you're right."

"So *do it.*"

"God, I don't have *time* to write a book," he backed off again. "This is crazy!"

"Are you kidding me? You can write this in eight weeks. *You know everything there is to know about this.* Everything that *we want to know* about this. C'mon, Stephen, stop keeping secrets. Take us inside. *Tell us everything.*"

Now even he was starting to see the possibilities.

"If I do it, you've got to write the foreword," he bargained.

"Sold!" I chirped, and we shook hands on it.

"Eight weeks, eh?" he mused.

"That's it. Eight weeks. Two months and you've got a book. It's already all in your head. Just put it down on paper."

Well, okay, so he didn't finish it in eight weeks.

It took him ten.

What do you want from me, I should predict the hour and the day?

The point is, the guy has been a great fan, and thus a great student, of filmmaking long before be became, himself, a great filmmaker. Who better to tell us these stories of stories?

Thanks, Stephen, for getting the message that your own latest message was supposed to be a message to us about the messages sent to us by the movies. *I love this book.* And I love you, pal.

—Neale Donald Walsch,
author of Conversations with God

"If you build it, they will come."

—*Field of Dreams*

Introduction

Magellan's Ships

Is it possible that certain movies contain spiritual messages that either we or the Universe transmit by way of our own collective subconscious and unconscious minds?

I think the answer is yes.

There are those who have said that if beings from other civilizations or dimensions were trying to help us evolve, they would do so by utilizing entertainment as their chief teaching tool. Even the most gifted teachers among us have done so. Storytelling has always been the preferred tool of shamans and great teachers. It is no accident that Confucius, the Buddha, and Jesus were all gifted storytellers.

Today's great storytellers are novelists, publishers, lyricists, musicians, screenwriters, and filmmakers.

As we evolve as a species, we hit certain key moments in that evolution when old ways are discarded and new maps of behavior are forged. Movies are the most electrifying communications medium ever devised and the natural conduit for inspiring ourselves to look into the eternal issues of who we are and why we are here.

The realization of this connection electrified my senses. Could this entertainment in the form of the movies be, in some cosmic way, reflecting to us in those darkened theaters the deepest questions, challenges, and yearnings of our humanity? Could movies be fashioning a metaphoric pathway to the forgotten secrets of our very existence?

If the answer is yes, why has no one seen this before?

I think I know.

Let me tell you—what else?—a story. It is the story of Magellan's trip around the world in 1519. Magellan's fleet of massive high-sailed ships would sail into the bays of primitive islands, and the natives would go wild with fear upon seeing these huge vessels. It would take weeks for the priests aboard to calm the natives and get to know them.

One day, the fleet sailed into the bay of an island, and to the amazement of all aboard, the natives onshore paid no attention whatsoever. They simply went on about their daily chores without the slightest shred of concern for these foreign invaders. Picture blasé New Yorkers on a lazy Sunday afternoon. These islanders were just not interested.

When Magellan's crew got into their longboats and neared shore, the natives finally did react, and with even greater terror than had been witnessed elsewhere. They ran screaming into the interior of the island, and it took weeks and endless search parties to first find and then assure them of their safety. When the priests ultimately calmed the natives and learned their language, they realized something extraordinary. These particular natives were so primitive that they didn't react when the ships came into the bay—because they actually couldn't physically perceive them! The ships were so far beyond their consciousness that they literally could not see them.

Metaphysical films and the messages within them are the Magellan ships of the movie industry today.

Film technology today has become so advanced that there really is no limit to what we can see on screen. We are rapidly approaching a time when all the outer experiences of human imagination will have been thoroughly mapped by the technical wizardry of the filmmaking process.

There is another landscape, however, that has only begun

to be mapped—our inner world, where we weave dreams of who we might be as a humanity when we operate at our very best.

Magellan's ships—this time carrying the cargo of our deepest questions and hopes about ourselves—are now sailing into the waters of the mass consciousness of human awareness. Movies are part of the mainsail. I believe that it is now up to those of us on the shoreline to see with new eyes . . . to a distant horizon of evolution that is just now reflecting the first rays of dawn.

"Life is like a box of chocolates.
You never know what you're going to get."

—Forrest Gump

CHAPTER ONE

Recognizing a New Genre

I believe that the universe is sending us messages through movies—or, maybe, we are sending those messages to ourselves.

Or both. It's a matter of perception. Some of you will feel more comfortable with the notion that the messages are coming from outside of ourselves and others will feel more empowered by perceiving their origin as coming from our own consciousness. As a collective consciousness, the human race from time to time reaches critical mass on certain issues or challenges. This point of critical mass is almost never a conscious one. Usually, we only recognize what has happened when we can look at it in retrospect.

Is it possible that *before* that critical point occurs, the issue gets expressed in a movie or a series of movies that act as beacons for our awareness and, in fact, creates critical mass?

The movies discussed in this book reflect an emphatically affirmative answer to that question. These films, however, are not meant to be an all-inclusive list. I can already anticipate the hue and cry from individuals who see films other than those listed herein as being worthy of inclusion. I know that I'm leaving out films that might qualify as being within the parameters of this discussion. There are several reasons for these omissions.

First, despite my efforts to the contrary, I simply may have inadvertently overlooked some films that could be included. Mea culpa. My philosophy regarding the movies that are included and those that are excluded is aptly summarized by David Picker, a producer who used to run Paramount Pictures. David had a wonderful philosophy about the pictures that he both made and rejected: "If I passed on all the pictures I made and made a lot of the pictures I passed on, I think it would have wound up the same."

Second, I have purposely omitted certain films that I know could be included because of my own lack of resonance with them for various reasons. There is a cliché that one should never try to tell a joke unless he personally thinks it's funny. It's hard enough to make people laugh. I'm following that guideline here. If I don't personally resonate to the message, I'm not going to try to explain it, because I know I won't do it justice. That also is one of the reasons I was never a very good film executive. Devil's advocates make terrific executives. If I don't feel it in my heart, I can't sell it.

Third, I have not included many foreign films for two reasons. I am simply not familiar with a lot of films made in this category, if they have not had major exposure in the United States. In addition, I want most of the films in the book to be those that have been readily accessible to most viewers and readers in America.

Fourth, I am focusing mostly on films of generally broad appeal and recognition. Although I have included a few rather obscure films, I have tried to focus more on films that a wider number of readers may have seen.

Fifth, I'm excluding certain films simply because they don't quite seem to fit, even though they had enormous impact on me. For example, Lindsay Anderson directed two fantastic films within five years of each other—*If* in 1968 (Malcolm McDowell's entry onto the acting scene) and then its "sequel" *O Lucky Man* in 1973. They're fascinating movies but, try as I might, I couldn't quite figure out where to put them.

Many of these films were box office successes, and some were not. Over the last thirty or so years in Western society, how much money a person or project makes has gone from being *one* of the measurements of success to being almost the *only* such yardstick. If your only goal is to make money and you fall short, then I guess that you might consider that experience a lack of success. In these pages, success is measured in a completely different manner. If the movie has a message in it that pertains to our inquiry, then it is a success and deserves to be so noted. Some of the most extraordinary films ever made, such as both *2001* and *It's A Wonderful Life* were not initially successful at the box office.

I have organized the films in this book by category, rather than in chronological order because I believe that a chronological listing would imply an overarching method to our collective consciousness in which I do not believe. I don't think that there is some kind of umbrella, worked-out plan here. I think that we are evolving as a species and working things out as we go. I believe in free will, destiny, *and* God! A paradox, yes? As a metaphysician, I find myself living more and more of each day in that powerful space in between the seemingly contradictory poles of paradox. The more determined I am not to solve but rather just to resonate in the internal conflict of a paradox, the more powerful the insights and ultimate resolution become.

As to which films to put in the various categories, I can only say that my beard has several more gray hairs in it as a result of that dilemma. Some movies such as *The Matrix* and *Final Fantasy* could easily fit under more than one heading, while others such as *Crouching Tiger, Hidden Dragon* almost defy categorization. In those numerous cases where films fit in more than one category, I have included the primary discussion of the film in the chapter in which I feel the film most appropriately fits, and that is where it is listed in the table of contents.

Remember the sequence in the original *Rocky* in which Rocky explains to Adrian his expectations of the upcoming fight with Apollo Creed? He wants "to go the distance." No one believes he even belongs in the ring with Creed so, for himself, he just wants to have the experience of trying and not quitting. That is called "managing expectations." In *Rocky*, it was a brilliant idea because the audience did not go into the fight with the unreasonable expectation that Rocky had to knock out Creed for them to be satisfied.

So, let's manage our own expectations right here and now.

This is neither a scholarly work nor a scientific exploration. I am not qualified for either of those disciplines and I make no pretenses about being able to "prove" anything. I do not delude myself into thinking that I am right and everyone who disagrees with me is wrong. I am not a metaphysical missionary; that is, I'm not out to convert anyone. I'm a film producer who loves movies and has made some movies in this genre, and I simply have a point of view about spiritual themes in films. I want this book to be fun, thought-provoking, personal, and, I hope, inspirational and empowering. *I am personally sick and tired of all the doomsday scenarios that seem so prevalent in our modern world, and I think that the spiritual messages in movies are actually leading us to a bright and beautiful future.* If the observations in this book resonate with you, perhaps they can be considered insights. If they don't, they're just my personal opinions.

If that doesn't manage (manipulate?) your expectations sufficiently, I look forward to hearing from those of you who have particular favorites that are not discussed in these pages. And I'm sure I will. Chapter 16 outlines the way in which you can elaborate on your own experience of the spiritual messages in the movies we discuss—and in the movies we have omitted.

Why am I writing this?

We're at a crossroads both in society and in our industry. There is such a yearning for meaning and hope in the world, for stories that challenge us to be our best, to lift up our hearts to the skies and encourage us to become the people we were born and have evolved to be. Storytelling has always lifted our sights and our spirits. We have struggled long enough. We have died enough. We have lived through enough pain. We want to be at peace with both ourselves and our world.

The spiritual experience in the arts can open wide the doors of perception. Unfortunately, the internal mechanics of our industry have become such that storytelling has all but faded from view. This is no one's fault. No one is to blame. It has just happened (and we'll look at a lot of the reasons later on in this book).

There is a great opportunity to return now to a classic type of storytelling in this unrecognized genre of spirituality. There is a new awareness and receptivity to stories that look into the very depth of how our souls can be awakened and nurtured. In so doing, we can create space for the recognition of the beauty and power of the messages in these films and then, to quote one of my favorite lines in *The Lion in Winter*: " . . . in a world where a carpenter can be resurrected, anything is possible."

So much of this is a matter of faith, of belief. For about four hundred years, Western society has generally placed its faith in science as the final arbiter of disputes. "Can you prove it?" has come to mean "Can you take it into a laboratory and scientifically demonstrate it?"

Just for fun here, let's look a little bit at scientific proof nowadays.

☆ Today, quantum physicists can actually prove that the chair you're sitting on, or the bed you're lying on, while you read this book is not "real." All physical objects are very loose amalgams of atoms that really defy space constrictions. Our consciousness orders that they be solid.

☆ You know the old question about whether or not there is a sound of a tree falling in the forest if there is no one there to hear it? Many quantum physicists today will argue that there is no sound and, in fact, if there's no one there to observe it, there isn't even a tree or a forest!

☆ Science has already proven to itself that the expectations of the observer actually influence the "objective" result of the experiment.

☆ Science today has proven that light itself is a wave pattern until it is observed, and then it becomes particles; that is, perception of it changes its form.

Now, does laying all that out necessarily mean anything to a skeptic? Absolutely not. Nor would a passionate theologian be able to make any better progress with someone totally committed to a scientific viewpoint. In fact, that *is* the point: We see what we want to see.

Before the "Renaissance" four hundred years ago, the pendulum had been stuck in the exact opposite direction. The church was the arbiter of what was "true" and people were expected to accept pronouncements from the church as "gospel." So it was absolutism at both ends of the spectrum—either total and blind faith in religious dogma or the same kind of faith in scientific methods.

Part of the fascination of modern life today is that the pendulum seems to have settled finally somewhere near the middle. There is still great faith in things spiritual, and deep respect for science, but neither has a dominant position in Western society as a whole, particularly in America. We are squarely in that paradoxical "space in between" of which I have already spoken. For those of us on spiritual paths, that "twilight zone" provides the ideal human petri dish for exploration.

So many of us today are less concerned with "proving it" to the world (our egos) and more concerned with journeys of discovery (our soul's call to adventure). This book is, I hope, a reflection of the latter. I started leading (I don't consider myself a teacher) seminars on this topic in 1995 because the subject matter fascinated me personally and I thought it would be fun and inspiring to examine it with a large group. It is said that we teach what we most need to learn. I've learned a lot from the last seven years of leading seminars on this subject matter. This book is an extension of that process. I find all this personally fascinating and, for me, there is great inspiration and wisdom in the movies mentioned in this book.

I do not delude myself into thinking that only spiritual/evolutionary messages are contained within films. Films have a way of illuminating several different landscapes of our psyches. The best recent example of that may be *Traffic* which brilliantly portrayed the real doubts (which I believe are growing) about our so-called war on drugs.

While messages in films have indeed been a staple of Hollywood almost since the inception of movies themselves, spiritual messages have created a genre unto itself that has not yet been recognized as such. That is what's new here. We're not reinventing the wheel. We're recognizing a new brand name. While other genres have their own internal mechanisms and messages, the spiritual journeys of the last century of films have not been chronicled. Until now, the genre hasn't even been acknowledged as such. These spiritual, evolutionary whispers are the ones that fascinate and motivate me.

As of now, none of the studios or production entities in Hollywood acknowledges spirituality as its own genre. They are just flat-out afraid of it or they don't see it at all, often both. Perhaps this book can be the beginning of a collective conscious decision to bring these modern ships of Magellan into the public harbor and recognize them as their own genre. With that recognition, the issues of the new spirituality alive today in our world will be thrust powerfully onto a more international stage and will be produced with the internal integrity of the material intact.

I believe that spirituality is in and of itself a genre of film *that has been around for decades but has never been recognized as such. "A Magellan Ship." This book is my attempt to share my belief in both the existence and viability of this genre; moreover, it is my belief that these films hold the key to the next century in entertainment.*

After almost one hundred years of filmmaking, most of the outer world has been mapped. It is the new frontier of the inner world that provides the greatest opportunity for discovery, awe, and wonder.

What do *all* of these films have in common?

They contain illuminating aspects of the single most important question that we ask ourselves:

Why are we here?

"How many more simulated worlds like Earth are there?"

—*The 13th Floor*

CHAPTER TWO

Reality and Time

Both spirituality and quantum physics today are questioning the so-called reality of the world around us. *As the mantra of the sixties was to "question authority," the mantra of the current decade is to "question reality." We are coming to realize that this life we live may indeed be an elaborately designed illusion in which we play out the evolution of our consciousness. The huge question then is, of course, an illusion designed by whom and for what purpose? God? Ourselves? A different consciousness? All or none of the above?*

It's a tremendously challenging concept to grasp because it calls absolutely *everything* into question. Is there a precedent for this belief? If so, that might make it easier to explore. Is there any aspect of our daily life that we have taken for granted that has already been proven to be an illusion?

Yes.

Time.

Time travel has a basic fascination for us because it allows us to suspend the rules under which we operate every day and fantasize about what could have been and what could be; moreover, I think it resonates in our hearts because we now do know that *time itself is an illusion.* It is not real. *That's* one theory that has been scientifically proven by no less a light than Albert Einstein.

The illusion of time is a difficult concept for a lot of people and I'm not going to even attempt to lay out the scientific proof of the theory. Simply stated, Einstein discovered that past, present, and future all exist simultaneously and that it is only our consciousness that dictates where we are on that spectrum at any given time. Quantum physics has accepted this fact for more than thirty years. As a further example, all the work in space science today has led to the inescapable conclusion that interstellar space travel would *have* to involve some type of technology that would manipulate our traditional theories about time and space.

It is no wonder then that traveling both backward and forward in time is a favorite plot device for the movies. Most of us are fascinated with the concept. What if we could go back and see, maybe even change, the past? What if we could see what our future holds?

Somewhere inside all of us, we either know or sense the inherent power of the possibilities in all this, and that's why time travel seems to have such a special place in our imaginations.

Now that we know, even from a scientific perspective, that time is an illusion, what about the concept of reality itself? If even time is not real, what then?

*A recent and growing group of films embody dazzling leaps of faith about the human experiment we call life. All of the films in this "reality" group have been made in the past five years. At their core, they present profoundly revolutionary perspectives on the nature of reality itself. For me, the fact that they have actually been made at all—and that one of them won the Academy Award as Best Picture of 2001—is a very hopeful and positive sign that we are indeed beginning to ask some very important questions of ourselves that we have not even approached before. The fact that four of them (*Vanilla Sky, Beautiful Mind, Waking Life, *and* Mulholland Drive*) were released in a single three-month period at the end of 2001 clearly reflects our growing fascination with the questioning of reality itself . . . and that bodes very well for the future.*

To paraphrase Shakespeare: "Something wonderful this way comes . . . "

Reality?

The Matrix

The Matrix is a brilliantly conceived and executed metaphysical action-thriller. On the surface, it is a fast-paced, visual effects-laden action movie. Underneath the surface, there is a breathtaking metaphysical message that is almost unprecedented in Hollywood big-budget moviemaking. For that reason alone, just getting *The Matrix* made at all is an historic event.

Just think about it. Here is a film that asks its viewers to accept the conceit that the life they are living is not real. That there is no objective reality. That we live in an elaborately constructed experiment (although here it is designed by machines), in which we are mere players. This kind of thinking, minus the disempowering machine aspect, is at the very dew line of metaphysics. The fact that it got expressed in *The Matrix* with fantastic critical and commercial success says a lot about where we are as a humanity at the turn of the century.

There are enough people alive today who share this concept about the nature of our existence that the process gets exposed in both *The Matrix* and *The 13th Floor* (which will be discussed next), two films with the very same astounding concept. To me, that says we are signaling our readiness to move toward a whole new openness to the questions of our very existence.

After all, the entire core of *The Matrix* is that we are living in an illusion, that the entire fabric of our day-to-day life is an elaborately constructed illusion. Is that not the entire core of metaphysical thought? The fact that this film got made with a major star (Keanu Reeves) from a major studio (Warner Brothers) demonstrates how far we've evolved in just the past twenty or thirty years. This concept is so daring and so threatening to the status quo (within the film industry and in society as a whole) that we need to closely examine exactly how extraordinary its depiction in a mainstream film really is.

First of all, this kind of spiritual message is anathema to Hollywood movie studios, to both production and marketing executives. To mainstream Hollywood, these movies do not even qualify as a distinct category. Mention "spirituality" in a studio meeting and the executives' eyes glaze over. They quickly change the subject or just directly reject the very notion as "non-commercial." I don't want this to sound like a rant against these people. It's not. Contrary to a lot of public perception, most of the people who work in Hollywood are decent, well-meaning people who really would like to do the right thing on a daily basis. They are good people.

The challenge is simply that the new spirituality that has become so prevalent in the world has not yet consciously penetrated the corridors of power in Hollywood. Magellan's ships are still off the radar in the film business. This is not unusual for our industry because, traditionally, Hollywood movies have reflected trends already rooted in society rather than leading society into examining new thought. That is neither good nor bad. It just is.

Our industry always seems like "the last to know."

The publishing industry has certainly caught on. "Visionary books" are the fastest growing sector in the history of the publishing business. The growth rate in 1999 was twenty-five percent and the trend is continuing. "One Spirit" is the biggest and fastest growing book club in the history of the industry. *The Celestine Prophecy, Conversations with God,* Deepak Chopra's books, Richard Bach's books, etc. are huge international hits. These books are not just successes. They are mega-best-sellers all over the world, selling by the tens of millions. Many of us remember the days when the only way you could get a book on this subject matter was in new age/metaphysical bookstores. That is, if you even had a store like that in your city at all. Today, walk into any mainstream bookstore in any city and there are large sections—usually near the front of the store—exclusively devoted to visionary titles.

The music industry has also embraced this visionary/inspirational/new age concept. Only a few years ago, finding this kind of music was a real challenge everywhere. Music stores often didn't carry the category at all and, if they did, it was in one bin in the back of the store, and you were lucky if anyone in the store could even tell you where that bin was. Today, huge companies such as Wyndham Hill and Higher Octave turn out best-seller after best-seller. Artists such as Yanni, Kitaro, and Enya (and even some artists with *two* names) are mega-million best-selling acts. Just in the last few years, albums from such mainstream artists as Madonna and Jewel have been spiritually-themed and went platinum (more than one million units sold). Walk into any music store today and ask for the new age section and *every* clerk knows where it is. Even much of the music for teenagers contains deeply spiritual themes. Acts like Staind and Linkin Park are recording and selling music that speaks directly to the souls of our kids. If you despair over much of the music for teenagers today, listen to lead singer/songwriter Aaron Lewis of Staind.

But the movie industry? Not yet. The movies get made—every once in a while. They are not, however, perceived as spiritual films. They are looked upon as comedies, adventures, action films, etc., which *may* have a spiritual theme or message but they are not marketed as such; moreover, even when they succeed (and they usually do), there is no follow-up. Take a look, for instance, at an action movie like *Die Hard*. When that film was a huge success, it not only spawned several distinct sequels, it also generated dozens of imitators in the genre. Now look at the worldwide success of a film like *Ghost*. Where was the follow-up? Not sequels per se, but films like it? Answer—there were none. As usual, the industry perceived *Ghost* to be another "one-off," movie business slang for an anomaly. Just a unique film that "happened" to connect to an audience. Coincidence. Accident.

Movie marketers today are still afraid of distinguishing these films as being what they are. Eventually, that will change and the genre and its vast audience will be recognized separately, but as it hasn't happened yet, the success of *The Matrix* is fascinating indeed and very illustrative of the issue of non-recognition.

Remember the marketing campaign for *The Matrix?* Was there even an indication about the core concept? Not at all. It was a very cool-looking action/suspense thriller, right? By the way, there is absolutely nothing "wrong" with that per se. The movie was not misrepresented in its marketing, so this was not false advertising. It is just incomplete. The movie was sold for what the surface was, and that worked. My own experiences with the marketing engines of the industry lead me to believe that the marketers themselves may not have really even focused in on the underlying theme of the film. I know from my own discussions with some of those involved in the process that the studio executives didn't focus on this aspect at all. The filmmakers were brilliant in the way they constructed the film, because it obviously worked on an experiential, visceral level as an action film. In fact, in many ways, it is a very traditional, violent action movie with extraordinary visual effects. (The same company—Mass Illusions/Manex—that pioneered the painted world sections of *What Dreams May Come* created the effects for *The Matrix* and deservedly won Academy awards for their efforts on both.)

The underlying spiritual message was left for the audience to discover and that's great. The movie got made, and the message is there: Reality is subjective rather than objective.

At some time in the future, the movie industry will catch up to both the world culture and their publishing/music counterparts and then these movies will be identified for what they are. For now, it's terrific that *The Matrix* made it through the process.

As to the film itself, the entire spine of the story is the mystery surrounding what the matrix really is and why the powers-that-be in the society are so determined to eradicate those who would dare to find it. A wonderful metaphor for daring adventurer/mapmakers everywhere who seek out the mysteries of life without regard to the attendant personal risks. Neo, the main character played by Keanu Reeves, is a man in search of something that he cannot identify. He doesn't know why he is so driven to find Morpheus, played by Laurence Fishburne, but he is obsessed with the quest.

When Morpheus actually contacts Neo and they meet, we find that the matrix "is all around us, the wool that has been pulled over your eyes to blind you to the truth. You are living in a prison of your own mind. You can't be told what the matrix is. You must see it for yourself."

While it is not empowering to be painted as the victim of a hoax, that is not the key to the power of the concept, nor is the ultimate explanation: the world Neo thinks he is living in is not real. He thinks it's 1999. It's actually at least 200 years later. In the interim, humanity had pioneered an advanced form of artificial intelligence that then "spawned" a whole race of machines that depended, we thought, on solar power to exist. They started to take over the world so, thinking we had the answer, we "torched the sky" to cut off their power. Undaunted, they found a way to take energy from our very bodies and also invented a new way to harvest their own human beings.

As Morpheus explains to Neo: "The Matrix is a computer-generated dream world built to keep us under control, so we can actually be an energy source to continue to power their machines."

On one level, this portends a dark, cataclysmic future followed closely by a cruel hoax. Sounds pretty nihilistic, right? So why do I find it so exhilarating? It questions the very nature of reality. Ignore the reasons they create to justify it and the concept itself is achingly beautiful and radical.

What is real? The critical message of the film is that we simply have no way of knowing.

When Neo ultimately is taken into the matrix, he finds that the life that he was living was nothing more than an elaborately conceived program. The matrix is not the "real world." The real world is something completely different. Sentient machines seek out those who discover the secret and are seeking the location of the only "real city" left. Called "Zion" (interesting name?), it is located near the core of the Earth and we never see it in the film (Matrix 2 and 3 are coming). The rest of the plot revolves around Neo's slow realization that he is "the one" destined to save humanity. Prophesied by an oracle, he is the reincarnation of the first man who began to discover the truth about the matrix. So we have a messiah in this new world as well.

As I commented earlier, questioning the very nature of

what we call reality is both a powerful message and a dazzling leap forward in the movies.

The 13th Floor

Interestingly enough, another film with the very same core concept also opened within a year of *The Matrix* but with totally opposite box office results.

The 13th Floor is a much more avant-garde version of the same concept and is, unfortunately, a movie with which many of you may be unfamiliar. It came and went very quickly. Although the core concept is the same as in *The Matrix*, the delivery vehicle is vastly different. While *The Matrix* was cleverly designed as a mainstream action movie, *The 13th Floor* is a dark, brooding character drama that centers on an experiment within a computer program. When the financier of the project is murdered, his protégé becomes the prime suspect and, in search of "the truth," he goes into the computer program himself. Inside, the programmers have created a three-dimensional world of Los Angeles, circa the 1930s.

Although the plot gets a bit convoluted, the crux of the story is that two of the "humans" within the program become aware that they are not "real." Once out of the computer, the main character goes on to discover, in a wonderful moment reminiscent of the energy of a *Twilight Zone* episode, that the world in which *he* is living is not "real" either. When he confronts the woman he knows is from the world "above" his, so to speak, he is told that there are thousands of simulated worlds, but that his is the only one that tried to simulate others themselves.

When two movies with the exact same central conceit come into being at the same time, it is my sense that there must be something powerful at work in the universe. As we enter this new century, our curiosity seems to be peaking about who we are and what this experiment we call life might be all about. When that type of energy reaches critical mass, it gets expressed in the world—for me, in the movies. This is not to say that the filmmakers of either *The Matrix* or *The 13th Floor* were consciously expressing this critical mass of energy; in fact, the conscious intent is somewhat irrelevant. Both films got made and released and, for those of us who try to be attuned to these messages, their existence in the world is an exciting verification that we are indeed moving forward.

The clear message of both films is that we are questioning the very nature of "reality." When we do that, we courageously step into the unknown and thus open ourselves to the limitless power of our own innocence.

A Beautiful Mind

The (deserving) winner of the 2001 Academy Award for Best Picture, *A Beautiful Mind* may not, on the surface, seem to fit in this category . . . or, to some, even in this book. After all, it is a story about mental illness, yes? The "true" story of brilliant mathematician John Nash, his descent into schizophrenia, and his remarkable ability to ultimately cope with his demons. So, for our purposes . . . and as the old ad used to say, "Where's the beef?"

For me, *A Beautiful Mind* represents far more than a story about one man's demons; rather, it is an extraordinary illustration of the very bone marrow of this chapter: What is "real" and what is "illusion"?

The movie itself chronicles the saga of Nash's life (brilliantly portrayed by Russell Crowe) from his early days as a student at Princeton to his ultimate triumph over his illness and the winning of the Nobel Prize. As this is not a book of reviews, I'm not going to spend any more time here detailing the plot because what fascinates me in the film is the "gimmick" on which the entire story turns.

We see Nash and his roommate at Princeton develop a strong bond of friendship that lasts beyond their graduation, and we also meet a shadowy FBI agent who recruits Nash to help decipher complicated war codes. His roommate eventually returns with a young niece who charms Nash. Then, abruptly, Nash has a breakdown and we, the audience, discover that the roommate, the FBI agent, and the little girl are simply figments of Nash's imagination. That they don't "exist" at all. Never did.

What a great movie surprise this is! I was completely stunned by this twist . . . as were many, if not most of us, who did not actually know the true story. Those people sure looked "real," didn't they, to Nash and to us as the audience? Nash interacted with them as though they were completely "real." Even on medication, he continued to encounter them. They never disappeared. Even as he wins the Nobel, they are "there." At a distance to be sure, not even engaging him anymore, but still there. *It was only his ultimate acceptance that these entities were representations of his subconscious that allowed him to be able to cope in the world. Isn't that a perfect metaphor for the process of engaging all of our own inner beings and, yes, even demons?*

When we are meditating . . . or just thinking . . . encountering the world . . . we all hear those inner voices that tell us how to interpret the events that unfold every day in our lives. We also have certain triggering encounters that strike deep into the chords of our souls and remind us of key moments in our lives, both happy and tragic. Such daily experiences produce different responses from us. The memory of a deeply traumatic childhood event can completely catch us off guard and, all of a sudden, we are responding, not as adults, but as the child who originally lived the triggering experience. Those voices of the differentiated aspects of our being are as real to us in those moments as those of our co-workers, families, and friends. Often, in fact, they seem even more real, more insistent. We may even feel compelled by them to act in certain ways that we know are contra to our nature. "The devil made me do it," yes?

It is only when we can differentiate those voices and compulsions that we can function from a place of true peace within ourselves. Let's use one simple example. Say you were raised by a parent who had a horrible temper and was constantly yelling at you when you were small. That kind of energy coming from what seems to a child as this huge and scary person can be terrifying, even traumatizing. Somehow, you get through it, but you have a real problem with anger being directed at you from others. Time passes, you grow up, and, in most ways, you function well in the adult world. Except when someone directs anger or rage at you. Then, without even being conscious of why, you get intimidated, frightened, and you feel your inner child telling you to "Be quiet. Don't talk back. If you do, you'll get hurt, maybe even die." So, as an adult, you somewhat automatically revert to childlike behavior. Your inner child has taken over and is determining your responses.

Much of the processing we do as adults on a spiritual path is focused on recognizing these moments of feeling compelled by childhood experiences. We learn to step outside of them, recognize them for what they are, and refuse to engage in the behavior that those frightened entities seem to demand of us. When we can do that—in the moment—we feel a great sense of peace because we have conquered a fear. We still hear the voices, but we can recognize them for what they are and not engage. And, for me, that is the central and empowering message of John Nash's triumph.

☆☆☆

The question I'm about to pose as it regards our next two movies is considered to be truly blasphemous in most mainstream film conversations:

Is confusion such a bad thing?

The word "confuse" is actually quite neutral. Most dictionaries provide such definitions for the word as "to make unclear or indistinct." There is nothing inherently "bad" in that, but "confusion" seems to have taken on a very negative connotation over the past several centuries. As a species, we may have been born in doubt, questioning everything before us, not knowing; however, the modern era, commencing with the scientific revolution of some four hundred years ago, seems to have moved "confusion" over to the very negative side of the ledger. It almost seems that a decision was made for us that uncertainty was too dangerous a concept for society, so all the answers needed to be clearly defined for us to feel safe. Fortunately, much of the growth in new thought over the last forty years has started to bring the whole discussion of "confusion" back to a more neutral, even positive position. Most metaphysical/spiritual training now actually extols the virtue of uncertainty—the paradox of that place "in between." There is great power in "not knowing" and great wisdom in being in the place of "about to know."

Einstein often spoke of the inability of any human to understand the universe simply by the use of our logical mind. So many of our concepts of "reality" have been called into question in the past fifty years that it was inevitable that films would step up to address our growing understanding that life is not nearly as simple and easily explained as the scientific era would have had us believe. In chapter 5, we discuss the concept, in films, of an afterlife in film but it is worthwhile to note here that people who have survived near-death encounters relate tales of experiencing their lives in a totally non-linear manner, jumping back and forth in time and place. It seems that enough of us—a critical mass—are ready to accept that life is more than just a straight line from birth to death, and movies are beginning to reflect that acceptance back to us.

Both *Vanilla Sky* and *Mulholland Drive* are purposely confusing. Their narratives are non-linear and we must pay very close attention throughout, so as to have even a chance of having some understanding of what is unfolding in front of us. This caused both films to be considered by mainstream Hollywood as "underachievers" at the box office; nevertheless, that can be discounted by the Magellan Effect we discussed earlier.

For me, both films are fascinating and brave adventures into the unknown.

Vanilla Sky

Released in 2001, I think that this will emerge as one of the most underrated films of the last decade.

Like *Mulholland Drive*, its "plot" is almost impossible to

describe in typical terms. On the surface, its story revolves around David Aames (Tom Cruise), a young heir to a publishing fortune who lives the fantasy life of a young, rich, handsome (this *is*, after all, Tom Cruise) playboy. He has a sex buddy named Julie (Cameron Diaz in an underappreciated and heartbreakingly vulnerable performance) who ultimately becomes so obsessed with him and his lack of commitment to her that she commits suicide by driving her car off an embankment with both of them in it. Aames is horribly disfigured and maimed in the accident but survives.

Now that is just about all one can reasonably say for certain about the plot of the film. The rest is conjecture and depends wholly upon one's own experience of the events that unfold thereafter.The rest of the film truly unfolds as if it were a dream, jumping back and forth between seemingly contradictory and unconnected moments.

Aames has met a mysterious and beautiful woman named Sofia (Penelope Cruz), with whom he becomes fascinated just before his accident. After the accident, he encounters her again, in several different ways, some of which are obviously dream settings and some of which seem to be really happening. We also experience an intercutting narrative with a sympathetic psychologist named McCabe (Kurt Russell), who is interviewing Aames in jail where he is being accused of murder. Just who he murdered is another mystery because it appears at one moment to have been Sofia while, to Aames himself, it seemed like Julie. The film's third act involves a cryogenic facility where Aames seems to have made a pact to be frozen until some point in the future . . . which may or not be what we actually encounter at the end of the film.

Whew!

Confused?

Good. Welcome to the new millennium, where we seem to be making ourselves comfortable with the notion that the very act of "not knowing" is a powerful place to be.

Everyone interprets *Vanilla Sky* in a slightly different manner. It was the subject of my first "MovieMystic" column back in March, 2002, and the comments I received on individual interpretations were fascinating—almost no two were exactly alike.

There is one key scene in the film that deserves mention here and a special place in the pantheon of landmark spiritual films.

At one point in the film, Aames is so confused that he seems to be losing touch with any vestige of his own sanity. He is approached in a bar by a mysterious man who tells Aames that he is creating the entire life that he seems to be living at the moment. To dismiss the whole notion, Aames flippantly says, "Well, if that's true, I wish all these people would just shut up!" Whereupon, every person in the bar immediately falls silent and just stares at David. *Never in film has there been a better envisioned example of the notion of each individual creating his/her own reality!*

See the film for yourself. More than once. Have friends over. And prepare yourself for some fascinating conversation.

Mulholland Drive

David Lynch is one of the great, original, totally unique American film directors. Whatever one might think of his work (*Elephant Man*, *Blue Velvet*, the amazing *Twin Peaks* television series), you know you are watching a Lynch film from the very first frame. His films are all about mood . . . style . . . and attitude. Plots never seem to be as important as the experience itself. So, when he turns that prodigious talent in the direction of a film about the experience of life—and death, the results are mesmerizing.

For many viewers, *Mulholland Drive* makes *Vanilla Sky* as easy to understand as a Roadrunner cartoon. The film almost seems like an homage to the line in the Beatles' immortal "Strawberry Fields": "nothing seems real." And you can just sense Lynch's utter glee in creating that kind of mood.

Again, the straightforward elements of the "plot" do not take long to explain. A young woman (Laura Elena Harring) seemingly escapes a murder attempt by surviving a car crash on Mulholland Drive. (That street, by the way, winds through the hills in Los Angeles that separate the San Fernando Valley from West Los Angeles. With views of the entire L.A. area—on a rare clear night—it has always been the ultimate passion spot in L.A. to go, park, and "connect," so to speak.) Suffering amnesia, she wanders into a seemingly vacant apartment, where she soon encounters Betty (Naomi Watts), a perky newcomer to L.A. who has come to search for fame and fortune as an actress. Together, they decide to find out who the woman (who just takes on the name "Rita") really is.

OK. But even that much may not be accurate because the rest of the film plays out in a completely non-linear manner and there is no really accurate way to describe what happens in simple terms. It has typically Lynchian, random off-beat characters, a Spanish version of Roy Orbison's immortal "Crying" that you'll never forget, steamy sex, and enough twists and turns to make a roller coaster envious.

Lynch won't talk about his own take on what the film is really about, and Hail David! for that. If you haven't seen it, you might want to stop reading right here and rent it . . . . because I'm going to give my interpretation of what the film seems to me to be about. Not what the film is about. Only what it says to me. For those of you who haven't seen the film, stop here and go on to *Waking Life*.

Ok? Here goes.

For me, the film has one historic precedent: *Jacob's Ladder* (chapter 5). I think that the entirety of the action in *Mulholland Drive* takes place in the mind of the Naomi Watts character (Betty) in the very instant of her death. She relives all the key moments that brought her to that last moment, and, as we have previously discussed, that kind of experience is totally non-linear. She jumps back and forth in time, confuses herself with her lover, and experiences what really amounts to a fever dream in the moment of death.

Now, that being said, I'm fairly confident that anyone's take on what "really" happens in either Vanilla Sky *or* Mulholland Drive *is somewhat beside the point. As the lines in an REM song goes: "life is a journey, not a destination." Once we accept that, and surrender our need for everything to make logical sense in the moment, we embrace the beauty of our soul's adventure in life.*

Waking Life

Most of the world missed this film. It was released in just a few art theaters in the fall of 2002 and then, despite brilliant, glowing reviews, it disappeared rather quickly into the world of DVD and video. It think it will have a long life in those ancillary markets because it is a breathtaking, utterly metaphysical inquiry into the question of what is more real: our "waking life" or our dream life?

Even the form of this film is unconventional and daring. Director Richard Linklater actually shot the footage in live action and then overlaid animation on top of the live footage, creating an eerie, surreal feel to every frame. This process creates an innovative atmosphere for the action of the film that, truth be told, is nothing less than a psychological/spiritual inquiry into the meaning of life itself.

There truly is no story per se to the film, so an analysis of it cannot be done in traditional terms.

It opens with a young girl telling a young boy that "dream is destiny," and the film then plays out that theme. The boy dreams he is floating out into the ethers, and the rest of the film explores his various waking and dream states, leaving the audience in constant wonder as to which is life and which is dream. Along the way, he encounters a variety of philosophers, teachers, musicians, and even criminals who have something to say about the experiment we call life. What he comes to realize is that he has no more reason to believe that his waking life is any more real than his dream life.

As with *Oh God* (chapter 6), the film is most memorable for some of its dialogue, which is light-years away from any mainstream dialogue that one might imagine. Some of you may remember the film *Mindwalk*. Well, in comparison, *Mindwalk* is kindergarten and *Waking Life* is graduate school!

Consider these observations from various characters in the film:

"Your life is yours to create. It's always our decision who we are."

"Words are just symbols. When we feel understood, we feel spiritually connected, and that's what we live for."

"Maybe all of life is just a dream. Dreams are real as long as they last. What if the same thing can be said of life?"

"There is no difference in our neural system between experiencing something and dreaming something."

And, along the way, there are extensive discussions of lucid dreaming, a state in which the dreamer can actually be conscious of being in a dream and begin to exert influence over what transpires in the dream.

The most striking line in the film, for me, occurs near the end of the film, and it accurately summarizes the overall optimistic tone of the film:

"This is absolutely the most exciting time that we could have picked to be alive . . . and things are just starting."

We are definitely not in Kansas anymore.

Sliding Doors

This movie has one of the most subversive metaphysical concepts yet put on film: what if we live separate realities at the same time? Remember, that's not a flight of fancy. It's Albert Einstein.

Helen (Gwyneth Paltrow) gets fired from her job in London and goes to take the tube (train) home. At that point, she somehow splits off into two parallel versions of herself. Exactly how this happens is not explained. We simply see her jump aside to avoid a little girl on a stairway and miss the sliding doors of the train by inches (hence, the title). Then we see the same scene literally rewind and she doesn't have to swerve to miss the child and makes the train by inches.

In the version where she boards the train, she sits next to James (John Hannah), a very nice man who unsuccessfully tries to cheer her up. She gets home in time to find her boyfriend Jerry actually in the act of cheating on her. She leaves and goes to a bar where she runs into James again. After a week or so of grieving, she cuts her hair and dyes it blonde (making it easier to distinguish between this Helen and the one who remains brunette), and eventually opens her own business and falls in love with James. In the other version, she misses the train, doesn't catch her boyfriend "in flagrante delicto" and goes through a lot more misery until she ultimately is confronted with the affair anyway.

In both versions, she becomes pregnant.

At the end, the blonde Helen is hit by a car and the brunette version falls down a stairway, putting both in the hospital. Surprisingly, the blonde version dies and the brunette, having finally broken off with Jerry, leaves the hospital. In the elevator, she too meets James and we see that they will be together in this reality as well.

Separate simultaneous realities. Time is an illusion, so "scientifically" this is possible. Metaphysically, this concept is very viable. It is often said that we have infinite versions of ourselves, and it is our consciousness that determines which version we consciously inhabit. Small moments in life can make the entire difference as to how that particular reality plays itself out. What's particularly fascinating and affirming about this film is that she winds up with James no matter what she does in the interim.

The message here is that we will indeed make the connections to those people with whom we have a committed destiny, no matter what barriers we might encounter. In our dark nights of the soul, that is a message to truly be cherished.

Time

Somewhere in Time

Using films that I have produced as examples in this book presents an interesting challenge. I do not want this to be a self-serving, ego-centered exercise, yet, at the same time, I feel that I would be remiss if I did not include discussions of these movies where I honestly believe that they deserve to be included.

What is reality anyway? What supposedly is "now"? How many times have you awakened from a dream and just known —not felt or hoped—actually *known* it was more real even than a waking state? If reality and time are subjective, can you time travel simply by "hypnotizing your mind?" To quote Professor Finney in this film,"now *that is* a question." Einstein's answer would, I think, be a more unequivocal "yes." If consciousness is all that determines our perception of time, it only stands to reason that our consciousness can bend time as well. As I've already mentioned, even "science" has proven that time is an illusion, so it is entirely possible that time travel can take place by utilizing no more than one's mind. For those who have experienced a past life-regression, for instance, that is precisely the experience that it enables.

In *Somewhere in Time*, Richard Collier (Christopher Reeve) falls in love with the portrait of an enigmatic young woman named Elise McKenna (Jane Seymour) that he finds in an old hotel. Finding out that she was an actress who played in the hotel theater in 1912, he becomes obsessed with her and researches everything about her. He soon sees a picture of Elise as an old woman and realizes that it was this old woman who gave him a watch many years before and mysteriously asked him to "come back" to her. He also finds out the old Elise died the night she gave him the watch. Further research at the hotel uncovers a 1912 hotel register, where he discovers that he indeed was there in 1912 at the hotel.

Richard Matheson came up with the notion that Richard Collier could remove all reminders of the present from his room, dress in 1912 clothing, carry 1912 money (except for one damn penny), and hypnotize his own mind into a journey to 1912.

Who is to say that time travel could not happen in such a simple manner?

Richard finds Elise in the past, where he discovers that she has indeed been expecting him. ("Is it you?," she asks when he first approaches her.) They fall in love despite the meddling of her overprotective manager (Christopher Plummer), and are sure they are facing an idyllic future when he finds a 1979 penny in his 1912 suit, which he inadvertently left there when he hypnotized himself into the past. As Elise is left holding his watch, he is then hurtled back to 1979 where, in a weakened and heartbroken condition, he literally dies of a broken heart and is reunited with Elise after death.

Some have observed that Richard's journey to 1912 was all in his mind, a dream state from which he is awakened by the jarring discovery of the 1979 penny. Could be. Also could it not be that his 1912 experience was the "real" one and that everything else was a dream?

One of the great mind teases of the film is the question of where the watch originated in the first place. Did it begin in 1979 and get taken to the past or did it begin in the past and get brought by Elise into the present?

Our ability to find a soul mate wherever they might be, either in time or in the life-after-life continuum, is the underlying message of the film

For more insights into that issue and the rest of the *Somewhere in Time* story, please refer to chapter 14.

☆☆☆

It has always been a standard convention of time travel stories that one must not do anything to change the events of the past because of the supposed certainty of dire results. The past is immutable in this theory, and all we can do is make matters worse for ourselves if we try to change it in any way. After all, this is one of the prime directives of the Enterprise in *Star Trek*, so it must be right. . . .right?

Maybe. Maybe not.

Is this interest in changing the past just a natural occurrence as the baby boom generation ages and begins to look back, or is it an indication that we are more consciously aware of the potential of being able to go back and change things from our past?

Part of the new thinking in the whole human potential/new age/spiritual/meditative wave of the past thirty or forty years has been to look at the experiences we had as children in a new way. As we now know that time is an illusion, there is a very widely accepted, if controversial, concept now that our inner child is actually a real being still living within us. This theory holds that meditation can take both that child and us back to early traumatic experiences and consciously change them within the meditative process. Once the experience is changed, the child can be changed, and the scars created by the original event can be healed.

Is this a consensus concept? Can anyone "prove" the actual existence of an inner child? Absolutely not; however, the existence of bacteria was only a theory until the microscope was invented. Proven or not, this theory has made its way deeply into the consciousness of millions and millions of people and is an intriguing potential catalyst for these next three films in which the past is indeed changed. That alone would have been considered "blasphemous" even in film philosophy up until recently so this change signifies again that something indeed is going on below the waterline.

There is a powerful message in this next group of films about being able to alter past events so that both the present and the future can be more positive.

Back to the Future

Certainly the "grandfather" of the modern movies in this arena is the 1985 film *Back to the Future*. The film is so popular that I'm not going to spend a lot of time detailing the plot. Basically, Marty McFly (Michael J. Fox) goes back in time through the use of a souped-up Delorean created by the quintessential mad professor Emmett "Doc" Brown (Christopher Lloyd). McFly winds up changing a critical moment in his parents' past so that his Dad (Crispin Glover) stands up for himself and his future wife (Lea Thompson) on the night of the senior prom. In the "original" past, he had not done so and had become somewhat of a lifelong wimp.

Back to the Future does end with the hint that Marty's changing of the past has indeed caused some problems for Marty himself in the future, but his Dad has become a different man and his Mom respects him in a way she did not originally feel. The significance of this film is that it was the first mainstream blockbuster film to really suggest that we can go back and change the past without causing disastrous results.

The Kid and *Frequency*

In *The Kid*, Bruce Willis plays image consultant Russ Duritz, who personifies slick, cynical L.A. stereotypes. In other words, he needs to get a personality transplant. He is given the opportunity to do so when he encounters the eight-year-old version of himself (who, by the way, decides that he grew up to be a "loser" when he discovers that Willis is unmarried, forty, and doesn't fly jets or own a dog).

The key to the film is that Willis gets to tag along with his eight-year-old alter ego until he encounters a playground incident that clearly influenced his whole life. In the original incident, he got beat up by the school bully and didn't put up a fight. This time, he coaches his younger self to fight back, thinking that this will change the future. He soon realizes, however, that a far more important event happened that day. His father becomes enraged that young Russ has caused his mother to come to school to pick him up after the fight. He berates Russ and tells Russ that his mother is dying and that Russ has to stop crying and grow up. The adult Russ realizes that he shut off his emotions in that moment, and that indeed was the cause for where he found himself in life, not the playground fight, as he thought it was.

This realization leads to the climax of the film where both the adult forty-year-old Russ and eight-year-old Russ meet their seventy-year old counterpart—who has married, has a dog, and flies a jet! We also discover that this future Russ is the one who has led his forty-year-old self on this journey.

Russ does change an event in the past here (the playground incident) that leads to a new awareness; consequently, he shifts his current consciousness, allowing the creation of a whole new future.

The film symbolizes our ability to manifest our deepest yearnings at whatever moment in which we determine that we will do so. Just one instant of self-awareness can trigger the realization of all the dreams of a lifetime. And that is a powerful message of hope.

In *Frequency*, John Sullivan (James Caviezel) plays a cop whose fireman father Frank (Dennis Quaid) died years earlier in the line of duty. Rare sunspots cause a communication glitch which allow father and son to communicate via an old radio. John figures out a way to save his father from dying in the fire, but that time warp creates a situation where his mother (Elizabeth Mitchell) gets murdered. Without delving into the complexity of the story, the point here is that somehow both parents live and James gets to experience both of them in his current life.

The message of these films is fascinating and comforting. We seem to be terrified to repeat the past, particularly if we have experienced real trauma as children. Physical, sexual, and emotional abuse may be the most difficult obstacles for people to overcome in adulthood. Such experiences are daunting, devastating, painful, and wrenchingly confrontative challenges. They rob individuals of self-esteem, without which life becomes a seemingly endless struggle. These encounters become rooted in our memories and greatly inhibit us from moving forward.

In addition, even those of us who escape such traumatic experiences as children are often still inclined to look to our past to excuse our current behavior. "Mom didn't love me." "Dad intimidated me." "I was unpopular in school."

There is something beautiful and comforting, therefore, in a message that encourages us to believe that we can revisit these experiences and at least see them differently. Even more important, we might actually be able to "re-shoot" those horrific past experiences, and change them, maybe not in the literal, physical manner of these movies but meditatively. If we choose these meditative realities to be more "real" than the original experience, then why can't we thus alter those painful memories?

Can we consciously move "outside the Matrix" to affect and even change what occurs inside the Matrix? Can we change the traumatic events of our past?

The message of these films answers those questions with an emphatic yes. Thus, we can begin to imagine that our past pain can now be transformed into hope.

"May the force be with you."

—*Star Wars*

CHAPTER THREE

Visionary Adventures

One of the heroes of my youth was Bobby Kennedy, whose most remembered quote is: "Some men see things as they are and ask why. I dream things that never were and ask why not?" I could not think of a more appropriate definition (adding "women," of course) for this category of films.

True visionary films look at worlds we have not yet encountered (in this lifetime, anyway) and reflect hopes and dreams about those very worlds yet to come.

One of the most intriguing aspects of the traditional nature of what most people call visionary films is that they almost exclusively seem to envision dystopian futures: the world after a huge disaster like nuclear war, asteroid hits, rampant pollution, etc. It is almost as if we, as a humanity, have sense memories of civilizations that turned out badly—Atlantis, etc.—and we are projecting our fears about that collective past into our future. We don't seem to have a paradigm in our experience for what it would look like if we didn't either self-destruct or become prey to some natural disaster (not that those are mutually exclusive occurrences). Even *Star Wars* takes place after the Empire has basically overrun the universe and sent the Jedis into hiding.

Sifting through the history and mythology of humanity's past reveals the underlying reasons for this prevailing dystopian perspective.

On Earth, we have undergone a series of natural disasters (usually involving pole shifts and massive meteor strikes) that, from time to time, have destroyed life on this planet as we knew it. In addition, our memories are seared with the self-destruction of Atlantis and the rise and fall of great empires such as the Romans, Greeks, Mayans, Sumerians, and Egyptians. Simply put, we have not "made it work out" yet. For those of us who believe in the cycles of life, death, and rebirth, there are thousands of years of both sense and experiential memories stored in our cells of previous attempts that turned out disastrously.

It is interesting to note here that all the doomsday prognostications about the end of the world are at hand right now. For decades, if not centuries, Armageddon enthusiasts have pointed out that the Mayan Calendar ends in the year 2012. Most of the prognostications about our destiny from the great seers of antiquity, and also the more modern ones like Nostradamus, seem to come to an end in the next ten years. (I guess that kind of ups the ante on old expressions like the Chinese proverb of "may you live in interesting times," doesn't it?) The dystopian visionary films that comprise the bulk of the films in chapter 4 deal with various versions of those "end times."

How many films can you think of, that are set in a utopian future, which envision a world where life has worked out well without having to go through Armageddon or a pole shift or some similar disaster? If you find *even one*, please let me know. I'm still looking.

That's certainly one way to look at all this.

There is, however, another way.

There is another school of belief that looks upon this time frame in a radically different manner. Maybe those prognostications all end now because none of those seers could truly predict what was going to happen now and hereafter (no pun intended). Many of us who are alive today believe that we remember times and civilizations in which we did not succeed in manifesting the beautiful worlds of our imaginings. Maybe the seers of our past saw this critical mass of people being born in the mid-twentieth century, coming to this life with a very new and simple commitment not to repeat the mistakes of the past.

Many of us are looking for ways to model optimal futures without having to pass through the gates of hell to get there. This possibility represents a sea change in the old doomsday scenarios. In this new and optimistic philosophy, we can look at the predictions of the "end of the world" as being metaphoric reminders, not future predictions. The world we know can indeed end, not in Armageddon, but in a new and exciting evolution in consciousness. Seen in this light, the future is promising, exciting, and hopeful.

Recent breakthrough films such as *The Matrix* are beginning to illuminate this brave new world into which we are heading, both cinematically and culturally. The films in this chapter straddle that barrier between utopian and dystopian futures. Even though they are somewhat structured around struggle, they also contain very hopeful and positive statements about who we might be as humans when we are operating at our very best.

2001: A Space Odyssey

2001 raised the concept of movie messages and metaphors to an art form and, for me personally, is the pre-eminent film in this entire genre.

Stanley Kubrick directed *2001* and I believe that he was the greatest filmmaker of the first century of movies. Certainly, Frank Capra and Steven Spielberg are extraordinary directors too, but no one can come close to Kubrick when it comes to vision and singular artistic audacity. Starting with *Paths of Glory*, every Kubrick film was an event unto itself: *Lolita*, *Dr. Strangelove*, *2001*, *A Clockwork Orange*, *The Shining*, *Barry Lyndon*, *Full Metal Jacket*, *Eyes Wide Shut*. Film classes need only study those films and they will understand what movies can be when a true visionary is in charge. He was the master, pure and simple.

Kubrick made *2001* in the late sixties (it was released in 1968), when a whole new and radically different generation was changing the international dialogue and thought processes about our place in both the world and the cosmos. The beginning of the whole new age movement had taken root in "California consciousness" during that decade and in the late fifties. The ideas were being incubated all over but were centralized at the extraordinary Esalen Institute in Big Sur, California, where most of the early thinking and philosophy was getting crystallized. *2001* was released just as the whole new world of consciousness was beginning to ask questions about who we might be as a humanity, and the questions were getting asked and framed in new ways. There was a new curiosity about why we are here, how we came to be, and where we might be going: rethinking the past, re-examining the present, and reinventing possible futures. This was the human crucible of thought and imagination that was bursting forth into the world when *2001* opened in 1968.

Its opening images (under the graphic of "The Dawn of Man") actually visualize the moment in our evolutionary past when we first conceived of using a weapon on each other. We see a family of apes casually foraging for food with wildebeests right along side, living in harmony with one another. Then, the next morning, the family of apes awakens to a terrifying sight—right in their camp stands a huge monolith, seemingly made of marble or stone, perfectly rectangular and obviously made "elsewhere." The apes react with fear and anger and cautiously approach the monolith, finally daring to touch and then marvel at the smooth surface of the mysterious structure. The "touching" of this monolith becomes the moment that Kubrick intends as the "dawn of man." We see the apes touching the monolith in wonder and then look up into the sky to see that the structure seems perfectly aligned with both the sun and the moon as an ear-piercing sound emanates from the monolith. At that moment, something is transferred into the psyche of the apes that very quickly transforms their thought processes. A "link" is made between the dry bones of dead beasts lying about and using those bones to actually kill other animals. We actually see an ape as it plays with a bone, and then, as it starts smashing other bones, we see it visualize smashing live creatures. The ape quickly kills a wildebeest to feed the ape family. It is not long before these apes figure out how to kill a rival ape leader with one of these bones.

There are those who have long hypothesized that "the missing link" between ape and man is not a creature yet to be found, but rather was intervention by those not of this planet at that time; this opening sequence can be viewed as the holy grail of that philosophy. For Kubrick, that quantum shift happened when apes learned how easy and profitable it was to kill other creatures. And the inspiration for this new thinking was a futuristic monolith purposely placed in their midst to stimulate "the dawn of man." A chilling and provocative notion. A disturbing but intriguing message about the birth of our modern humanity, and only the first in a staggering series of messages and images from this miraculous movie.

At the end of this opening sequence, the ape that has just killed another of his own kind for the first time, tosses the bone into the air and Kubrick does a breathtaking transition into a spacecraft. At that point, Kubrick and his effects team proceed to set a new standard for visual effects, showing us the vastness and challenges of space (including a wonderful brief encounter with a zero-gravity toilet) in a startling new way, incongruously underscored by classical pieces of music like "Thus Spake Zarathustra" and Strauss waltzes. Again, the past meeting the future.

We then discover that "something" has been unearthed on the moon that could possibly destabilize the entire world if its discovery becomes widely known. We know only that it has been purposely buried there for a very long time.

As we follow the members of the expedition to the moon, we see a large excavation that centers on a single object—the same monolith from "the dawn of man." As our now "evolved" space-suited scientists touch the monolith, they and we hear the same ear-piercing sound emanate from the monolith that the apes had heard so many eons before. This sets in motion the heart of *2001,* which is the journey aboard a spacecraft whose mission it is to try to find the origin of the mysterious monolith.

We quickly find out that the scientists have determined that the sound we heard from the monolith was a high-powered radio signal aimed at Jupiter, so a huge scientific mission is launched to go to Jupiter to discover the source of the signal. The ship itself is run by a powerful on-board computer known to the crew as HAL, by far the most famous character in the film. HAL was the forerunner of the supercomputer of today. In 1968, remember, computers were the size of storerooms (such as the one in the 1968 film *Colossus: The Forbin Project*). We were about to enter the computer age. The age of information. The revolution in technology that would mark our transition from an industrial age to the information age. A massive, quantum shift in the way humans communicate, store knowledge, and evolve. In HAL, all those aspects were personified by Kubrick for the first time. A computer that could actually run a ship, play chess, communicate with the crew, and also do sophisticated psychological analysis of the humans it was programmed to assist.

HAL represents all the dreams and whimsical imaginings of people at that time who were seeing the coming of a new age; moreover, HAL also became the vehicle for expressing our greatest fears about computers. What if they become independent entities who supersede their own programming and "take over"? As a society, we were still only at the far edge of considering these issues. As a film, *2001* personified all that and more. Kubrick also throws in the fact that the majority of the crew has been cryogenically frozen to be "thawed" only when the ship reaches its final destination, another new concept in society in 1968.

The crucial dramatic conflict in *2001* occurs when HAL informs the crew that he has picked up a malfunction in a crucial guidance system, that the system will cease to operate and must be repaired or replaced. In a breathtaking glimpse of what actual space walks will look like thirty years later, the pilot removes the particular object to bring it aboard. Upon closely examining it, the pilot, Dave (Keir Dullea), informs HAL that he can't find anything wrong with it, a development that HAL finds "curious" and the pilots find very disturbing. The decision is made by all to put the unit back and wait for it to malfunction the way HAL predicted. The pilots try to mislead HAL into thinking they are in agreement, but they lock themselves in a pod where they think HAL can't hear them so they can speak their real concerns to each other. They even "test" to see if HAL can hear them by asking him to rotate the pod. When there is no response, they speak freely, confident that HAL can't hear them. They note that the HAL 9000 series has never made a mistake and it concerns them greatly that this might be the first such incident. If so, they would lose faith in HAL's cognitive skills, forcing them to decide to disconnect HAL's brain functions if the projected malfunction does not occur, leaving only the "motor" skills intact to run the ship. Presciently, they ask each other how HAL might react to that eventuality, as no HAL 9000 has ever been disconnected. As they continue to speak, Kubrick accomplishes a directorial tour de force by cutting outside the pod, stopping all sound, and seeing that the glowing red eye of HAL's computer "face" is actually watching the lips of the crew as they speak, cutting back and forth in such a manner that we, as the audience, know that HAL is reading their lips and knows what they are planning. Anyone who saw this film in a theater will always remember that moment (unless, of course, they attended under the influence of a "controlled substance," which became, by the way, a well-known phenomenon surrounding this movie, for reasons soon to be described herein).

As one of the pilots (Gary Lockwood) departs the ship to re-install the defective part, HAL takes over and actually severs the pilot's lifeline, sending him hurling into space to die (which he does). The other pilot rushes into a rescue pod without his space helmet to retrieve his friend, and HAL won't let him back in. This is a distillation and projection of everyone's deepest fears about computers. Not only can we lose our jobs to them, we can actually lose our lives.

Through sheer ingenuity, the surviving pilot gets back into the ship and, with HAL pleading with him to reconsider, finds his way inside HAL's huge brain complex and begins to disconnect HAL's higher functions, leading to the only really classic dialogue in the film, all from HAL:

"Dave, what are you doing? I'm afraid."

"Dave, please stop. My mind's going. I can feel it. Please, Dave . . . "

At this point, we are informed that this mission is to discover what the monolith might actually be and represent.

As we reach Jupiter, the most famous and thought-provoking sequences of the film begin, under the mystical subtitle, "Jupiter . . . and Beyond the Infinite."

"Dave" departs the mother ship in one of the pods and, as he seemingly nears the surface of Jupiter, he begins a journey which has come to be known as "the light show," a phantasmagorical three minute journey into a universe of lights, strobing colors, mysterious images, and eerie music (the "ultimate" acid trip, as it came to be known). There are those who would literally sneak into theaters at the very end of the film, completely zoned out on whatever hallucinogenic substance they could find, just to sit through this sequence. It's pretty trippy even when you're doing nothing stronger than the liquid Coke in your hand. For those of you who did this, no explanation is necessary. For those who didn't, no explanation is possible.

As Dave begins this part of the "odyssey" (interesting choice of a title word, isn't it?), we also see the monolith floating near the mother ship. It is as though we know that the next great step in the evolution of humanity is at hand. The monolith symbolizes that. It is present at paradigm shift moments in humanity. It is also a link to worlds beyond, not only the extraterrestrial realms but also the worlds of consciousness "beyond the infinite." To devotees of the film, the monolith has come to represent evolution, humanity, extraterrestrials, consciousness itself, and perhaps even God. To me, there is truth in all those projections. The image has haunted me for the last thirty-four years. Almost as much as the final image of the film. Almost.

After Dave passes through the light show, is he still alive and arriving on Jupiter? Or has he passed through to "the other side"? The surface of the planet looks surreal, pastel colors, odd shapes. It's as though we are watching humanity pass into a new frontier. An in-between realm of awe and wonder.

Suddenly, the pod has stopped and we are in the most visionary and, I think, extraordinary single sequence ever filmed. That's a big statement, I know, but how many other eight-minute sequences can you name on which whole courses in both philosophy and cinema can be based?

The pod has come to "rest" in a very cold, sterile, yet curiously ornate room with the feeling of both antiquity and sixteenth-century French art mixed together. As the sounds of the pod disappear, we hear faint noises outside the pod in this odd room. Are those the faint sounds of apes we hear? Is this a connection to the "dawn of man" from the opening sequence?

Suddenly, Dave, still in his spacesuit, is outside the pod walking around in this "room," with only the sound of his own breathing. Where is he? What is he? He sees his reflection in a mirror and he has aged considerably since he entered the pod for the ride to Jupiter.

New sounds begin. From another room. Who can possibly be there? As Dave maneuvers his way to a doorway, we see someone else sitting at a table. We and Dave are shocked and frightened. As Dave's breathing becomes more pronounced, we abruptly cut to the man at the table who seems to maybe hear the breathing—but the man at the table is Dave himself and, when he laboriously turns around to see where the noise is coming from, space-suited Dave is gone. We have jumped time frames and are in a new reality because there is no rational way to view the events that are unfolding.

Dave continues to slowly eat at the table. He is much older, his movements slower. As he reaches for a glass of wine, he knocks it over, shattering it on the marble floor. As he leans over to inspect it, he glances to his right where, in a startling new cut, we see a man lying in a bed. We quickly realize that this is Dave, too, much older, bald, dying. As this old man begins to draw his last breath, his eyes focus on something at the foot of the bed. He slowly raises his hand to try to touch it . . . and we cut to his point of view. At the foot of his bed stands the monolith.

At this moment, we begin to hear the strains of the classical music which has become the signature for *2001* and we are in space again. Something is moving through space, toward earth, bathed in light. A bubble of light and, in it, the fetus of a child. A child with an angelic face. A child still in the womb. And, unlike any previous child in any womb, his eyes are wide open. Huge, compelling, and wide open. ("Interesting" that Kubrick's final film would be entitled *Eyes Wide Shut*, isn't it? Just a coincidence, I'm sure.)

This new star child is making its way to Earth with its eyes wide open and full of love. Cut. End movie.

I will never forget my feeling at the age of twenty-two, sitting in the Cinerama Dome in Hollywood, seeing that last sequence. I literally could not get up out of my seat. I was too stunned to move. And I was not alone. All around me, people sat in their seats, not knowing quite what they had seen, but knowing that it had transcended what we had come to traditionally accept as a "movie." "What the hell was *that*?" I wondered.

I got up, went outside, bought a ticket for the next show, and saw it again. Different audience, same reaction. Not from everyone. Some people were bored and/or just unfazed by it. But some of us were literally transformed. That was my formal introduction to spirituality in this lifetime. Nothing was ever the same again.

It took a lot of years and a lot of thought for me to begin to formulate my own version of the transcendental significance of the last sequence. Mine is a purely personal take. I'm sure you have your own. There is no absolutist "truth" in the perception of art but, for whatever it might be worth, here is my interpretation of the end of *2001*.

For me, that sequence symbolizes nothing less than a vision of the next evolutionary phase of humanity. The "dawn of man" evolves "beyond the infinite."

There is no question that Dave dies in that sequence, either on the descent to Jupiter or in the room itself. I believe that his body dies in the light show, and that the room is a symbolic representation of both his soul's perception of that death and its own transformation into a new form. His mind is flashing forward to his last moments. The room has no sense of reality to it at all, and Kubrick makes that disconnect very clear from the opening shot in the sequence where the pod itself is actually in the room.

Dave transforms as the monolith stands before him. *Dave's rebirth is symbolic of the emergence of a new kind of human being into the world, and his new form heralds the dawning of the next step in our journey. His transformation into a beautiful star child, returning to Earth with eyes wide open and full of love, is a dazzlingly visual message that embodies the new consciousness that was dawning in the world of 1968.*

2001 represents a quantum leap in many ways. Certainly, the technology presaged the advent of a whole new era in visual effects and in our ability to visually create worlds beyond our own. Take a look at *Star Wars*, *Close Encounters*, and the Star Trek phenomenon. All took *2001* and built on it.

More important, Kubrick gave so many of us in the world our first visual glimpse at the magic of metaphor and spirituality on screen. It gave me the courage to envision myself contributing to the film dialogue with other stories that could contribute to expanding this new language of film.

For me, *2001* is the holy grail of this entire genre. There were other films before it and many after it; however, to me, it is the watershed film.

Star Wars

Star Wars is on the cusp of this phenomenon. While its story does occur after generations of interstellar warfare, it is also a powerful and amazingly spiritual journey.

First things first: what makes *Star Wars* such an encouraging and powerful experience in this genre is the whole message of "the force."

Let's remember that the film was released in 1976, eight years after *2001* and right in the midst of the ferment of spiritual thought in the seventies. Ever notice how many extraordinary landmark books in this arena were originally published in the 1970s? *Illusions* by Richard Bach, Frank Herbert's *Dune*, *The Education of Oversoul 7*, *Zen and the Art of Motorcycle Maintenance*, not to mention *Bid Time Return* and *What Dreams May Come* by Richard Matheson. There was literally an explosion of titles that have proven over the years to be classics in this genre; moreover, as the successor decade for us baby-boomers to the turbulent sixties, the seventies were a time of deep soul-searching and, for many, a rethinking of core values. As an old friend of mine (film director Floyd Mutrux) once commented to me "We fought the battles of the sixties and thought we won. In the seventies, we realized that we had only just begun."

Into this ferment then enters "the force" and a classic battle between good and evil—again, within ourselves and out in the world. Luke Skywalker (a spiritual Indian name if I've ever heard one) is the classic hero with a destiny. Orphaned, left to himself, he feels the calling of his future but doesn't know how to manifest it. Again, in the great tradition of spiritual practice, "when the student is ready, the teacher appears." In the *Star Wars* trilogy, Luke has three great teachers—Obe Wan Kenobee, Yoda, and his father Darth Vader. He is taught the balance between the light and the dark.

In the famous sequence in the first *Star Wars* where Luke first meets Obe Wan, he learns the history of the universe, his family, and his tradition. Quite a lot for a young boy to have to absorb. It is in this sequence that Obe Wan explains the force as "the energy that binds us, that guides us, that is everywhere at once." It is explained to Luke that Darth Vader "got seduced by the dark side of the force." If this film did nothing more than this, it would be remembered forever as a classic in this genre. What an unbelievably simple and cogent way to describe the powers of the universe that are expressed within each one of us.

Darth Vader becomes privy to the powers of the cosmos that are balanced in nature in perfect harmony between the dark and the light. Each are acknowledged with equanimity by the universe. For humans, this is part of our evolution: to acknowledge all sides of our nature and to choose to pursue the power of our beauty, to attain our greatness without losing sight of our frailty and vulnerability. Unfortunately, Darth Vader can't stand the light, and becomes forever enmeshed in the dark.

The climactic confrontation in the first *Star Wars* film puts Luke in a position that literally "forces" him to transcend the "illusion" around him and trust in a power beyond his ordinary senses. This sequence has brought us one of the most famous phrases in the history of movies:

May the force be with you.

Luke has to drop a bomb into a very small opening in the Empire's Death Star so that he can thwart the Emperor's plan to destroy the resistance to its rule. The timing of the drop and the space into which it must fit is so precise that even his on-board computer can't quite get it right. As he nears his last chance to save the day, he hears his mentor's voice telling him to "Trust the force, Luke. Reach out with your feelings."

"Trust the force." Three words. A powerful lesson for Luke, of course, and an even more powerful message for all of us, phrased so simply with so much depth.

One of the big challenges we face as a species is our ability to trust what we cannot see. I distinguish trust here from blind faith in that, to me, trust is earned and blind faith is actually a lack of trust. Blind faith, whether demanded or offered, is given with no basis in our experience. For example, if two people have known each other for a long time and one of them promises to do something for the other, one's dependence on that promise being kept is a matter of trust that has been built up through similar experiences over the years. If, however, you meet someone for the first time and depend upon them honoring a promise they make to you, then that is blind faith and even perhaps martyrhood.

So Luke has been brought far enough along in his training as a Jedi that he can, with justification, trust the force. I find that to be a powerful metaphor because I believe that we as a humanity are in search of trusting something beyond our ordinary senses. Classic religions originally demanded blind faith from their followers with the only justification being "God's will." Science then came in and used laboratory results as a justification for trust, and it has worked for almost four hundred years. Recently, however, science has discovered within itself that the intent of the experimenter has a powerful impact on the results of the experiment. Purely scientific answers have been brought into question by scientists themselves.

As spiritual beings, we search now for the power within ourselves. The great paradigm shift that author/philosophers like Neale Donald Walsch, James Redfield, and Richard Bach have brought to the forefront of world thought today is the notion that, while there certainly is a power in the universe we know outside of us as God, the power within us is the connective tissue to our core spirituality. The crux of the whole new age movement of the past forty years has, in essence, been to recognize, acknowledge, accept, and tap into our inner connectiveness to the universe. There may be no more elegant way to phrase this new consciousness than "the force is with you"; hence, the inspiration for the title of this book.

Luke is being urged to close his eyes and trust his own inner connectiveness to the power of the universe and his unique place within it. *This is a crucial distinction.* It is not giving the power away and praying that the independent power outside of himself will smile benignly and grant his wish. It is saying you have the power within *yourself,* Luke, to allow this to happen by connecting with the forces inside and outside of you.

This powerful spiritual message at the end of *Star Wars* is, for me, what makes the message of the movie so inspiring.

The NeverEnding Story

I guess I could say that the title says it all and end it on that. There's too much beauty and soul in this amazingly empowering movie to even consider being so flippant about it; however, it is one of those films which is so direct in its message that it basically requires only a brief recitation of its story to understand its eloquence and power.

Bastian is a young boy who is chased by a group of bullies through the streets until he finds sanctuary in an old bookstore. There, he finds a book called *The NeverEnding Story,* which he takes with him and immediately begins to read. The story within the book centers on a crisis in a magical kingdom called Fantasia that is being obliterated by a force called "the nothing." Soon, the entire kingdom will be eliminated. The empress of Fantasia is dying and calls upon a young boy named Atreyu to save the kingdom. Atreyu accepts the quest and goes off on a journey to solve the challenge of "the nothing."

As Atreyu gets deeper into the quest, Bastian begins to be aware that he too is part of the story, although he doesn't understand how or why. When Atreyu faces a particular danger in the book, Bastian screams aloud and Atreyu actually hears him, a fact that startles them both.

Atreyu endures many trials of his faith and courage. Joined by a huge flying dragon named Falcor, he is told to "never give up, and good luck will find you." He survives a challenge that threatens to destroy him and is told that "you must feel your own worth or you can't pass by," and then, "you must face your true self." He survives both challenges and is told by an oracle that the only thing that can save Fantasia is to find a human boy beyond the boundaries of Fantasia who will give the empress a new name and save the kingdom; however, Fantasia is being torn asunder even faster than he had feared.

Ultimately, he comes face to face with a fierce animal that is actually a personification of the nothing, where we finally discover that Fantasia is truly the world of the human imagination. As such it has no boundaries and is the "place of the dreams and hopes of mankind." The reason that the kingdom is being destroyed is that people have begun to lose hope and forget their dreams and it is that emptiness which is the nothing that is destroying the world. "People who have no hope are easy to control, and whoever has the control has the power."

At that point, Fantasia actually disintegrates, leaving only small fragments that fortunately include the ivory tower where the princess still lives. Atreyu believes he has failed but the princess says that he has indeed brought the human boy with him and that it is Bastian who now actually begins to accept that he is indeed the boy for whom the princess is searching. She tells him that he is already part of the never-ending story. As he is sharing the adventures of Atreyu, others are sharing his adventures, and on it will go just as long as he speaks her name. Finally convinced, he shouts her name and finds himself in her presence. All that is left on Fantasia is one grain of sand that she places in his hand. His imagination then recreates the entire kingdom just as it was, and he goes off on his own adventure with Falcor.

The message here certainly doesn't require a lot of interpretation, does it? It goes right to the heart of our human ability to dream the world in which we live and then manifest it. Reality creation at its simple and exquisite core.

Simply put, the message is that "the nothing" is all that can destroy us. Not war or technology or meteors or any other apocalyptic threat. Just "the nothing," our lack of hope. If we keep hope alive and dream all that our consciousness can imagine, nothing can destroy us. We are all a part of this never-ending story and, as long as we maintain that conscious awareness, our humanity can and will prevail.

Another exquisite aspect of the whole film for me is that it focuses on the hearts of children.

There is so much pain today around the world of our kids. All we need to do is look at issues like the tragic violence that has erupted in our schools and the shocking rate of teenage suicide to know that our children are coming into a world that terrifies and intimidates many of them. Kids killing kids. The drug and alcohol problems, but most of all, the despair that so many of them feel. It is mirrored in much of their music and some of their heroes. This new generation of kids has chosen some pretty high hurdles to clear in this lifetime.

Some look at all that and see only its darkness. I see its light. Our kids have a lot to overcome, but all you have to do is spend time with them and you find that they are up to the task. They are smarter, more aware, more sophisticated about the world around them than ever before. They are indeed a new generation, one whose responsibility it will be to take the next steps into a future that I personally believe will be the personification of our most beautiful dreams rather than our nightmares. As the more public tragedies exhibit a dark side to being young today, there is also a balance of light in the hearts and souls of so many of these extraordinary kids.

Having four daughters has exposed me to a lot of young people over the past twenty-six years, and I believe completely that they will overcome all these obstacles. They are looking for inspiration and hope, and many of them find that in music and movies. Sure, a lot of the music is about fear and anger but much more of it is about finding a way through the maze. They're seeking, just as we all have, but they're doing it at a lot younger age than most of us ever considered.

Just imagine who our children can evolve into being when they get older—as long as they keep hope alive. And that is the central message in *NeverEnding Story.* Keep hope alive by keeping our imaginations awake and vibrant.

There is an old Indian saying that says that we don't inherit the land from our parents. We borrow it from our children.

I believe that.

I also believe that the future of our evolution is truly in the imagination of our children and that both we and Fantasia are in very good hands.

Raiders of the Lost Ark

From a pure entertainment viewpoint, *Raiders* is about as perfect an adventure film as can be conceived. Steven Spielberg was at the height of his creative commercial directing powers with *Raiders,* and no one who saw it will ever forget the experience. It was an adrenaline rush from start to finish and would be a landmark film even without the powerful spiritual messages within it. I often use *Raiders* in my seminars as the textbook example of how to structure a screenplay and, most particularly, how to explain the rules in a film.

For our purposes here, however, *Raiders* is very relevant both for its use of the mythology of destructive power and also for the message it leaves with us in the very last shot of the film.

When Indiana Jones (Harrison Ford) is asked to explain the Ark of the Covenant to government representatives, his blend of fact and fiction not only convinces the people *within* the movie of the lore surrounding the ark, he also convinces us in the theater that the lore is historical fact when, in actuality, much of it was made up.

The ark is portrayed as having the power to obliterate anything in its path. What's important is that we know that the ark contains the power of God and that "an army that carries the ark before it is invincible." The illustrations we are shown seem to indicate that the great light that emanates from the ark literally disintegrates anything in its path. Its power can be used for good but, if misused, will lay waste to all around it.

What does that sound like? A perfect metaphor for nuclear

power and weaponry, isn't it? The power of God, certainly. Can it not also be taken as a metaphor for the great powers that humans have attained in histories now mostly forgotten? The misuse of the nuclear powers generated by the great crystals of Atlantis is mentioned often as the key ingredient for the last destruction of that civilization. (There has never been a movie that really addressed Atlantis. Sure, there were a couple of sword and sorcery attempts, but they were simple adventure films that used Atlantis as a background but never really addressed it as the extraordinary civilization that it was. Disney's animated version *Atlantis* is very entertaining—and it portrays crystals as powerful Atlantean images—but, as a children's film, it really does not pertain at all to the lost civilization that Plato introduced back into the modern world.)

If we have misused these great powers in the past, it is very easy to see why we so strongly resonate to the fear of letting the ark fall into the wrong hands. Even in the "right" hands, it has led to the fall of great civilizations. Whether it is the power of God or a metaphor for the misuse of power by humans, putting the ark in the hands of a dark force would naturally frighten us. And what darker force to use than Nazis who are the nadir of the base impulses of our dark side?

It's as though we are cautioning ourselves to remember that power has both light and dark sides and we need to remember what happens when the dark side is unleashed.

Another extraordinary aspect of *Raiders* as it relates to this book is the way it parallels *2001.* In both films, great discoveries are made which could, if made public, completely change our perception of who we are and might be in the process of becoming. In *2001,* the existence of the monolith is kept secret for the same reason that the ark is crated up and hidden in storage at the end of *Raiders:* the "powers that be" decide that the public can't handle such revelations, so they are kept secret and private.

The "government" is an omnipresent oppressor of information in a lot of these movies, isn't it? What is that really about?

Why is this eventuality such a key and omnipresent message in so many movies? Why are we so afraid that major revelations will be kept from us, or are we afraid that we can't handle them—or both?

What exactly is government anyway? Isn't it just an agreement that we have made with ourselves to protect us from anarchy and chaos? There is no such thing really as "the government" as an inanimate being that makes independent decisions for us like some impersonal computer. The government is a group of people no different from any of us who have, for various reasons, chosen to work in what is known as the public sector. Certainly some seek government service for reasons of job safety with good benefits, while others like the idea of having power and influence. Still others decide on such a career because they really want to make a difference in the world. Taken all together, why do we have such a fear about what those people represent in us that the "government" serves as such a useful and universal villain in film?

I believe that the dark shadow part of the answer lies in our distrust of ourselves.

The concept of the dark shadow side of human nature is deeply embedded in Jungian thought. I am neither a therapist nor an expert on Jung, so the following distillation of shadow theory is not meant to be clinical nor couched in scientific certainty. (For a wonderful and more complete explanation of the shadow phenomenon, I heartily refer you to Debbie Ford's wonderful book entitled *The Dark Side of the Light Chasers*.)

For us lay folk, the shadow side of our personality contains all those hidden, unexpressed angers, frustrations, and rage that we never felt were safe to express. For instance, say a young boy is beaten up by a bully. The child is humiliated, frustrated, and full of rage and impotence. He wants to fight back but knows he can't win so he pushes all those feelings into his shadow self, to be held there either in perpetuity or until it is safe to express them, or your boss berates you for nothing in particular, but you're afraid to get fired so you just take the abuse and those angry feelings get put into your shadow. At some point, the shadow gets "full," and that's when the real danger arises. Either we face all these things consciously and accept them as part of us or they get expressed back at us in the world around us. If we continue to deny the shadow, we can split off, and become ultimately dangerous, to ourselves and to the world around us (often, this forms the crux of "middle age crisis"). In truly advanced cases, we become so shut down to the shadow that we can perpetrate horrible crimes and succeed in utterly denying them to ourselves. Case in point: Albert deSalvo, the infamous Boston Strangler. When finally confronted with the truth of his crimes, he went into a fugue state from which he never really emerged.

Thankfully, our light shadow is a beautiful balance to this dark shadow and we will examine that more closely in the introduction to our discussion of "Enhanced Abilities and Sensibilities" in chapter 8.

The government, then, proves to be a useful way for us to project our shadow fears out into the world. We have deep fears that we have mishandled power in the past and we are very uncertain that we can handle it now; therefore, we create a villain that is just us in another guise and use that villain as our enemy. You know the old phrase: "We have seen the enemy and it is us"? That's my take on why the government works so well as a villain. We're not really sure that we can handle information that could shake us out of our complacency, and we sure as hell mistrust the way we have used power in the past, so we just create another manifestation of ourselves, call it government, and blame it. Simple. Fear-based, but simple.

The other part of the answer lies within our light shadow yearning for knowledge and evolution. The integrated and visionary aspects of our being know that we are here for a purpose. We don't consciously know what that individual or societal purpose might be, but we strive to look beyond the next hill to see what we might find.

When we see the ark being hidden in a government warehouse at the end of Raiders, *we are both relieved and angered. Relieved that it has been kept out of the hands of those disintegrated parts of us that could use it inappropriately, but also angered because the fearless and mapmaking qualities of our souls want to have a new try at handling these powers and revelations. The courageous nature of our integrated self believes that we can handle these revelations, either now or in the very near future.*

When a movie taps into these deep fears and passionate longings, it stays with us forever; hence, the lasting legacy of *Raiders*.

Lost Horizon

This is the first Frank Capra film we have covered. The two Capra movies that we're looking at are this one and, of course, *It's A Wonderful Life* (chapter 11).

Frank Capra believed in people and in their innate goodness. His films were always optimistic about the basic human condition. He was a genuinely compassionate and hopeful man whose career was played out during very challenging times in the world—the 1930s and 1940s. Even in the face of depression and wars, Capra remained true to his faith in our basic goodness as a species. Unfortunately, there has never been anyone else quite like him.

Lost Horizon (released in 1937) is another one of those films that could fit under several different chapters. I'm putting it here under adventure because of its depiction of an epic journey to find a fabled land known as Shangri-La.

Shangri-La. The word itself is now listed in most dictionaries because it has become so commonly used as a synonym for a lost paradise. Utopia. Our fascination with a paradise that exists outside the rules of time and space is as deeply engrained in our culture as our myths about a great flood, and it doesn't take a rocket scientist to know that the Garden of Eden lies at the root of this yearning. Eden, of course, represents many things in our consciousness but none more pure and simple than as the archetypal symbol of our innocence. Before temptation. Before evil. Before greed. A time and a place where we were at one with God and ourselves.

Ronald Colman plays diplomat Robert Conway who crash lands in the mountains of Tibet and is guided to an idyllic hidden paradise called The Valley of the Blue Moon. He soon learns that his plane "crash" was no accident. He has been brought to Shangri-La by Chang (Sam Jaffe), the High Lama who sees in Conway the idealistic dreamer who can succeed

Chang. The High Lama is 200 years old, but in Shangri-La, the aging process is very different.

Chang tells Conway that the overriding concept of Shangri-La is "be kind." What a powerful message for us in 1937 because, due to the depressed economic times and the unrest in Europe, kindness was in very short supply.

Conway is talked into leaving by his brother who has fallen in love with a girl he's met there, and Conway goes with him (not terribly convinced as a character or convincing as a plot device). Once outside the protection of Shangri-La, his brother's girlfriend reverts to her actual chronological age and literally withers away instantly.

The last sequence in the film is narrated by a character named Lord Gainsford, who was in Tibet to help find Conway. He tells of rumors of Conway being spotted from time to time trying to climb the mountains, babbling on about a place called Shangri-La. At the end, he proposes a toast right before we actually see Conway find his way back to the entrance to Shangri-La.

The last lines of the film and its underlying message are:

"Here's my hope that Robert Conway finds his Shangri-La. Here's my hope that we all find our Shangri-La."

Crouching Tiger, Hidden Dragon

Crouching Tiger, Hidden Dragon opened in the United States in late fall, 2000 to very little fanfare. It was, after all, a Chinese film with an entirely Asian cast and subtitled in English. The conventional wisdom for that kind of film is very simple: open it in a few cosmopolitan big cities with histories of strong art house patronage from middle-aged adults and hope for the best.

From the beginning, however, it became very obvious that, no pun intended, *Tiger* was a very different animal altogether.

Critics went berserk for it, and that certainly helped establish an identity for the film right away; however, it was young audiences who showed up quickly at a film that the conventional wisdom viewed as an art film—and in huge numbers—and their interest immediately signaled that something unique was afoot.

Tiger is a dazzlingly original film. The basic story revolves around Li Mu Bai (Chow Yun Fat), a famous warrior in feudal China who wants to retire but still feels that his work is unfinished because he has not yet avenged the murder of his mentor. His magical Green Destiny sword gets stolen and he discovers that the thief is Jen (Ziyi Zhang), a young female protégée of his mentor's killer. He shares an unrequited love with Shu Lien (Michelle Yeoh) and both of them try to befriend Jen and find her mentor. Jen is from noble birth but has always lived on the edge of her world and has actually been charmed and then seduced by Lo, a young desert warrior. Ultimately, all four lives intersect and the warrior gets his revenge but dies himself as well.

That, quite simply, is the story, but the power of this movie lies in its heart, visuals, and spirituality. The film is steeped in mysticism and constantly crosses the barrier of what most people consider to be reality. The breathtaking martial arts sequences defy any ordinary sense of human actions. For instance, the most beautiful of all the sequences takes place in the treetops of a forest. There is no sense of gravity whatsoever as the warrior and his young adversary fly from tree to tree and branch to branch to branch. What makes the film so special is that the audience just goes along with it. No questions asked. As with the mystique that is at the core of all martial arts, the characters have an unshakable belief in the reality in which they live these ancient arts.

The core message of the film is contained in a story related to Jen by Lo when they are in the desert alone together.

Lo tells Jen of a mystical mountain where wishes come true. Lo tells her of a young man who was concerned about the health of his parents, and he jumped from the mountain. "He just floated away, never to return, but he knew his wish had been granted. Anyone who dares to jump from the mountain, God will grant his wish. If you believe, it will happen. A faithful heart makes wishes come true." This prophecy foreshadows the last shot of the film as Jen, realizing that she has caused the death of Li Mu Bai, dives off a bridge on the mountain, and quite literally floats into eternity.

Daring to jump from that mountain is both a message and a metaphor for where we are today as human beings. Standing with our toes on the edge of a precipice, we are comforted to know that "a faithful heart" will not only prevent us from falling into the abyss, it will also enable us to cross a bridge of belief to our destinies.

"Looks like we've just been asked to save the world."

—*Armageddon*

CHAPTER FOUR

Floods, Fires, Earthquakes, and Riots

The joke (and often sad truth) has become that floods, fires, earthquakes, and riots are the Southern California version of the year's four seasons.

They are also an appropriate distillation of most dystopian visionary films.

Why are there so many films that posit that the only way we can get to the future is to go through disaster first? As previously noted, I believe that the answer lies in our sense memories as a species that have only experienced either catastrophe or decay. We have trouble envisioning positive futures because we have not in our past been able to evolve into one; therefore, filmmakers have taken their "inspirations" from our fears and created the next set of films at which we are going to look.

All of these films contain cautionary messages about the ways we have destroyed ourselves in the past—technology, overpopulation, pollution, nuclear power, violence, natural disasters, loss of freedom—and serve as reminders of what we are committed to avoiding this time around.

Taken just at face value, the messages of the films in this chapter could be perceived by doomsday "enthusiasts" as frightening; however, I experience them very differently.

Once you have faced a fear head-on, it loses its power. If a warning light comes on in your car letting you know that you need oil, you stop at a gas station and add oil to the engine. The warning light then goes out. When seen from that perspective, the messages of the movies in this chapter are actually about empowerment; that is, they exist to remind us of our understanding and promise to each other and ourselves that we will not allow any of these doomsday scenarios to ever happen . . . again.

For example, fears of advanced technology (*Terminator 1* and 2) and nuclear miscalculations (*Fail Safe*, *China Syndrome*) seem to be pervasive themes in many of these movies. The "glass half-empty" approach would be to look at these fears as a harbinger of terrible tragedies that are about to occur. The "glass completely full" approach sees the fears, acknowledges them, and simply determines that, however complex the engine may appear, adding oil to the crankcase will keep the engine light off.

The China Syndrome and *Silkwood*

As we will see in other films in this chapter, we have had an obsessive fear of nuclear destruction ever since the Enola Gay dropped the atomic bombs on Hiroshima and Nagasaki to end World War Two. Once that genie was out of the bottle, we knew that we had invented (or rediscovered?) the ultimate power that could instantaneously annihilate the entire planet and everyone on it.

I put the word "rediscover" in there because it is my belief that most of us who are around in this period of time were also here at times of past cataclysmic destructions such as the devastation of Atlantis. It is not critical here that anyone accept the existence of Atlantis. The fear of nuclear destruction can certainly be justified by the mere existence of atomic power; however, I believe that a lot of us sense that we were around when Atlantis disappeared. I believe that most of us who do have that memory also feel that the destruction was self-inflicted; therefore, even though this is not the proper space for a detailed historic look at the potential causes of the destruction of Atlantis, it is important for me to at least note one of the predominant theories for the destruction of that ancient and advanced civilization.

As I previously noted briefly in chapter 3, Disney's animated *Atlantis*, released in the summer of 2001, is intended mostly as a children's adventure. As such, it posits that Atlantis still exists under the ocean and that it was destroyed by a tidal wave of unknown origin; however, it does contain one fascinating message about Atlantis that resonates with those of us who feel a strong affinity for the subject matter. According to the film, Atlantis was a highly advanced civilization that was powered by an enormous crystal. The generating source of the power of the crystal was the *collective consciousness of the citizens of Atlantis*. That's an amazingly evolved concept in a children's film and a powerful message for us all.

If one reads Edgar Cayce's work on Atlantis or any of dozens of other perceptions of that ancient world, it is very clear that Atlantis had indeed discovered some form of immense "crystal" power. Cayce's readings in particular point to something akin to a nuclear episode. That kind of cataclysm would certainly explain how an entire continent could disappear beneath the sea. If a lot of us were indeed around for that destruction, it would certainly bring up some pretty intense sense memories when nuclear power again rears its head in our world, wouldn't it?

Sense memory or not, we're going to look at several films in this chapter which project us out into the future *after* a major nuclear holocaust. That fear is at the root of the premise of *The China Syndrome*. What would indeed happen if we had a nuclear accident at one of the relatively new (in 1979, the year the film was released) nuclear plants that we were building? The title refers to one of the potentially frightening answers to that question: the resultant "burn" could go right through the Earth and come out the other side in China.

The plot of the film revolves around Jane Fonda and Michael Douglas (who also produced it) playing a television reporter and her cameraman who are doing a routine story on the plant when an accident occurs. They become embroiled not only in the incident but are firsthand witnesses to, and targets of, an attempted cover-up.

What makes the film so notable for us is not the plot itself so much as the amazing "coincidence" that occurred just *twelve days* after the film's release. A nuclear plant at Three Mile Island in Pennsylvania had an accident that very easily could have been cataclysmic. It uncannily and perfectly mirrored not only the plot of *The China Syndrome* but also the attempted cover-up of the incident itself. Only seven years later, our fears were realized in actuality when the nuclear facility at Chernobyl in Russia actually did have a nuclear incident.

This message reflecting the depth of our concern over the handling of nuclear power was so powerful that a movie was released just twelve days before an actual incident occurred. Coincidence? Sure, that's possible. I can't *prove* that such is not the case. It's an awfully odd "coincidence" though, isn't it? Michael Douglas had a very difficult time getting this movie produced (see chapter 14) and it didn't really garner a lot of attention until *after* Three Mile Island.

I believe that we sent a very intense message to ourselves and to the world through this movie that we are indeed playing with the ultimate "fire" and we better be awfully damn careful. The fear is not of having our hands burnt in the fire—it's of getting them blown off.

Five years before *The China Syndrome* was released, a worker at a nuclear plant in Oklahoma disappeared under very mysterious circumstances and was never heard from again.

Four years after the release of *The China Syndrome*, Mike Nichols directed Meryl Streep in *Silkwood*, the film version of Karen Silkwood's story, and I note it briefly here because it reflects again an underlying fear not only of the danger of nuclear power but the fear that individuals who try to alert the public to the real perils involved do so at the threat of losing their lives.

The China Syndrome, Three Mile Island, *Silkwood*, Chernobyl. The message in all these films and events is that we have a deeply engrained fear about the misuse of nuclear power and we are alerting ourselves to remember what's happened before when we failed in our attempts to safely harness it. We were reminding ourselves that the oil light is on—not that the engine was about to explode!

Fail Safe

Fail Safe, directed by Sidney Lumet, was released in 1964.

Fail Safe is a much more serious and extreme film about a different kind of "error" than that which is at the heart of both *The China Syndrome* and *Silkwood*. The error here is much more similar to other films like *Dr. Strangelove* (chapter 6): what happens when a "go code" is given to one of our bombers and, for whatever technological/human reason, it cannot be recalled?

The twist in *Fail Safe* is that the American president (Fredric March) knows that he can't recall the plane and realizes that he is facing the potential destruction of all mankind if the Russians retaliate (as he is certain, and they guarantee him, that they will.) He decides on a bold but agonizingly difficult course of action. He orders the American ambassador in Moscow (the plane's target) to stay on the phone while the bomber approaches. The President has been told by his advisors that he will hear a high-pitched whine when the bomb detonates as the phone in Moscow melts. This means he is ordering the death of the ambassador, and the ambassador knows it. Even more startling is the realization that the president has ordered one of our own bombers to drop a nuclear bomb in New York when the bomb detonates in Moscow (with the pilot being provided with a suicide injection). This is the promise that he has made to the premier in Russia that will prove that this was an accident for which we will exact revenge upon ourselves. The last piece of the macabre puzzle is the fact that the president's own wife is in New York and will perish when the bomb detonates.

The film ends with both bombs finding their targets.

This took our fears of nuclear war and made them very personal and that sense of "hitting close to home" is the message of the film. It's one thing to see bombs drop on cities where the people are unknown and quite another matter when the victims are Americans, and indeed our own family.

Terminator 1 and *2*

Released in 1984 (an "interesting" year for apocalyptic tales to be released—see *1984* in the next section), the *Terminator* films are seminal in several regards.

The storyline of *Terminator 1* took our *terror* of technology to spectacular new heights and then *Terminator 2* redefined the entire field of visual effects in 1992 by pioneering unparalleled *advances* in film technology in order to portray it.

T1 was the breakthrough film both for its star Arnold Schwarzenegger and for its director James Cameron (who went on to win the Academy Award for *Titanic*).

T2 was, at the time of its release, the most expensive film ever made, as a result of the new technology it pioneered.

As to the basic plot of *T1,* it is set mostly in the present into which a creature (Arnold) from the future is sent to kill a particular woman, played by Linda Hamilton. Another time traveler (Michael Biehn) is sent by opposing factions to protect the same woman. *T2* just builds on the same theme. The reason for her importance is that, in the future, she is going to father a son who leads the revolt against the machines, and the machines send one of their own back in time to try to kill her and thus prevent her son's birth. While the bulk of the action takes place in modern day, it is the films' vision of the future of humanity that is the core of its message and, as such, demands our attention in this section.

The premise of both films is that, in the future, man has lost to the "machines." Technology, in the form of massive killing machines, has developed its own independent consciousness, decided that humans are not only unnecessary but are actually threats, and, as a result, systematically hunts down and kills people with the intent of ultimately exterminating the human race.

To me, the message of both of these films (and *The Matrix*) is a distillation of our fears about the threat of technology ultimately destroying our humanity.

To accomplish the stunning visuals in *T2*, director Cameron spearheaded the most massive visual effects accomplishment in the history of film to that date, and, in so doing, also propelled the budget of *T2* to around $130 million, by far the most expensive film ever made. (Several years later, of course, Cameron would outdo even himself in that category by making *Titanic,* the most expensive film ever made—at a cost of around $250 million. This figure, by the way, exceeds the gross national product of several countries in the world. More on that in a moment.)

Cameron's team took computer technology to dizzying new heights in order to create a film about the ultimate dominance of technology. That's one reason why I quoted *Oh, God* at the beginning of chapter 16: "God is a comedian playing to an audience that's afraid to laugh." What an amazing and delicious irony.

Even more important, the genius of the technological accomplishments of *T2 deeply affected the course of the entire motion picture industry*; therefore, that phenomenon needs to be addressed here in some detail before we continue on with other visionary films.

T2 proved that digital effects could truly accomplish almost anything and the "almost" is probably superfluous. There is literally no location, landscape, or event that cannot now be created or dazzlingly enhanced in a computer—including, as we will discuss in chapter 7 regarding *Final Fantasy*, human beings ourselves.

Worlds that have been heretofore "off limits" to filmmakers can now be rethought because of computers. Just as a personal example, the afterlife of *What Dreams May Come* could never have been realized visually without the use of advanced digital effects. One of the challenges of that film throughout its torturous history (detailed later in chapter 15) was the fact that it is set almost entirely in the afterlife experience of its main character and, prior to the advent of digital effects, there was just no effective way to realistically accomplish that.

T2 also "raised the bar" to stunning new heights when it comes to audience expectations in films. The cliché of "how you gonna keep them down on the farm after they've seen Paree?" is totally applicable here. Audiences have now seen what can be accomplished in effects and, after *T2*, you could no longer try to do action or effects movies "on the cheap."

Remember the "afterlife" of *Heaven Can Wait*, for instance, in 1976? White clouds, an obvious set? It worked great then, but try to get away with that today and you distance your audience from your film immediately. Audiences now expect a certain level of technical accuracy and artistry, and we have to deliver.

One of the challenges of this "bar raising" is that it has produced a profound "sticker shock" effect on movie budgets where any kind of visual effects are involved. To continue to expand the art of visual effects, major films continually challenge their effects teams to create better and newer effects. The massive cost of visual effects comes mostly from their research and design phase, not from the challenge of actually manifesting them. Rendering the effects is expensive, but conceiving and designing the software is where massive costs can be accumulated. Once an effect is actually created and manifested, doing it the next time is vastly easier both because of the lack of further research costs and the explosive and rapid evolution of software and computers themselves.

Consider this. Virtually all of the effects that propelled *T2* to be the most expensive movie made at that time *can all now be rendered on a home computer!*

Again, a personal story can illustrate this point. (As much as I can, I want to use personal experience in this book because I can at least speak from firsthand knowledge about those events. When you have to talk to others about their experiences, you can never be quite sure how totally accurate the information is—not necessarily because of a lack of truthfulness, more because, as in *Rashomon*, everyone remembers things differently. Come to think of it, I'm sure that applies to me, too, but I'll do my best.) Those of you who have seen *What Dreams May Come* remember the dazzling nature of what we call "the painted world sequence" in the film, where Robin Williams first awakens in his afterlife experience. When our brilliant director Vincent Ward originally conceived of that world, no one knew how to accomplish it. And I mean no one. Vincent wanted the actors to interact in a painted world that was three-dimensional and looked like wet paint. The actors would have to be totally real and so would the effect. A great, inspired idea but how to do it? Every single visual effects company in the world was contacted, and everyone was fascinated by the challenge but, initially, no one knew how to accomplish the feat. The challenge and expense of actually designing and rendering that painted world effect ultimately caused each of the fifty-four visual effects shots in the sequence to cost approximately $250,000 per shot! The ingenuity and craftsmanship were remarkable and the team deservedly won the 1999 Academy Award for Visual Effects. The point that is relevant here, however, is that the technicians who were involved have told me to expect that very same technology to be put to use very soon in television commercials. . . . now that will be a real treat, won't it?

So *T2* opened the doors to a whole new way of visualizing movies and, contrary to the orders of any judge, no jury can truly disregard anything once it has been presented to them; consequently, whether we like it or not, we are now dealing as an industry with audience expectations that will only increase. The genie is not only out of the bottle—the bottle has been sent to the recycler never to be seen in the same form again.

These spiraling effects costs, traditionally referred to along with the other physical day-to-day costs of filming, as "below the line" costs, have also been matched by skyrocketing actor salaries, known as "above the line" costs. (The reasons for these descriptions is that film budgets list actor, writer, director, etc. costs first, then a line is drawn, and physical costs are listed below that line.) The combination of these factors, plus the explosion in marketing costs, has created an economic tsunami effect that has swept through the structure of the industry leaving dazed accountants and executives in its wake.

In 1975, the average cost of a studio film was $8 million and $4 million to market it, $12 million total.

In 2000, the average cost of a studio film was $54 million and $30 million to market it. $84 million total.

And those are the *average costs!* A bit more than mere inflation, right?

What's going on here?

As to marketing, the whole nature of movie marketing has been affected by a changing society in general, but most specifically (though not exclusively) by the precipitous decline of television network dominance, the invention of both video tape recorders (VCRs) and proliferation of the television remote control (now known as the "zapper"), and an increasingly competitive entertainment marketplace. The other major contributing factors are both the abdication by the major studios of their traditional role in the creative process and the corporate takeover of Hollywood.

The previous paragraph alone could be the basis of a whole book—or several books—but I will attempt to address the individual issues mentioned therein now in a few general paragraphs and then tie them back into our current discussion of visionary films because they do bear directly on the whole issue in front of us. To do so, I will have to summarize and generalize, so I want to state very clearly here that space restrictions require that these explanations be very simplistic. I do not delude myself, and do not want to mislead you, that these reasons are the whole story.

We've already detailed the technical cost explosion. As to the marketing costs, the major delivery system for movie advertising in the modern era has been network television. Thirty years ago, there were three networks (ABC, CBS, and NBC). At that time (according to a recent CNN study), ninety-two per cent of the people watching television in prime time were watching "The Big Three." Today, that number is forty per cent, a decrease of more than half. In addition, there are vastly more television sets, more people watching TV in general, and the costs of advertising have shot up. The "zapper," VCRs, and TiVo devices have made skipping around, through, and even eliminating commercials much easier so now there is really no way to know who is actually *watching* the commercial time that studios have purchased; therefore, a lot more of it is being bought and at much higher rates so that the potential audience can be reached, and reached more frequently.

In addition, there is a lot more competition for the entertainment dollar today than there was thirty years ago—videocassettes, video games, dozens of new cable networks, computers, the Internet, the explosion in the popularity of sports, both traditional and new ones—etc. So marketing has joined with technical costs in fueling the dizzying cost increases.

Now throw in the abdication of the studios' traditional role in the creative process and the total corporate takeover of Hollywood.

Until very recently (the last fifteen years), the overwhelming bulk of movie projects were initiated at, and developed by, the major studios. For various reasons too numerous and detailed to describe here, this situation has completely changed. Today, very few projects are being initially developed by the studios themselves; rather, a rapidly shrinking number of writers actually write scripts on their own (known as "specs," as in speculation) and then sell them to the highest bidders.

Studios also have become very enamored of paying major name actors and actresses huge salaries, often $10 million to even $25 million per picture. This explosion at the top end of the scale causes a bootstrap effect all the way through the salary structure of the entire industry. Again, many of the reasons for all this are beyond the scope of this book. In general, however, a lot of the underlying causes are rooted in the corporate takeover of Hollywood.

Over the past thirty years, every single existing studio and major production entity (such as Miramax) have been purchased by major multinational corporations. *This has changed both the personnel and the entire operating philosophy of the industry.* (The only current exception is Dreamworks, which was privately funded.)

Briefly put, the film business was founded and pioneered by entrepreneurs who saw the industry as both "show" and "business." The great names of Hollywood's formative years such as Louis B. Mayer, David O. Selznick, Harry Cohn, Jack Warner, Daryl Zanuck, and Irving Thalberg were men who were riverboat gamblers, mavericks, and visionaries. This is not to lionize them because, from all reports, they could be very difficult people, too. (There was a famous joke that circulated around after Harry Cohn's funeral drew almost three thousand people: give people what they want, and they'll show up.) The point is that they had a passion for what they were doing. They loved movies, and they took chances.

The film industry today is a very different business run by men and women who have entirely different outlooks from the founders of a few decades ago. The studios today are just a part of huge international corporate structures. In most instances, the purchase of these studios was accomplished on the basis of exorbitant price/earning ratios, thereby putting enormous pressures on studio management to produce bottom-line results and very quickly. As a result, the business is run today very much like a business. The entrepreneurial, wildcatting spirit of the 1930s and 1940s has been replaced by a corporate mentality.

Carl Sandburg has a wonderful phrase in "The People, Yes!": "Telling a frozen fish that it is a hot waffle does as much good as telling a hot waffle that it is a frozen fish." Simply put: studio management today has been primarily chosen for their right-brain business capacities, not their left-brain creative abilities. One cannot expect rampant creativity from managers who have been chosen for their administrative abilities any more than one can rightly expect creative people to become efficient administrators.

This is not to say that the people running the film business today do not care about the integrity of the product. In most instances, they do; moreover, there are studio heads today (such as Sherry Lansing at Paramount, Joe Roth at Revolution, and Bob and Harvey Weinstein at Miramax) who have a background in filmmaking and who love movies. In fact, contrary to popular opinion, the studios are mostly run by very decent people. The problem is that they have specific mandates from their parent companies to turn profits on a consistent basis and, as with most corporate structures, there is very little patience from the parent companies. In other words, studio heads operate in a very insecure environment that does not foster risk-taking and, indeed, regularly punishes those who dare to try to push the envelope unless they are immediately successful.

The "safest" way to protect oneself from second-guessing by corporate managers is to recycle ideas that have worked before. If you fail in doing that, you at least have the protection of historical precedent. If you take a risk on something new, and it doesn't work, the spotlight falls squarely on your own judgment. This kind of philosophy works well enough in a corporate structure but it is poisonous to creativity.

So, here is what studio heads face today:

☆ A corporate hierarchy that demands consistent bottom-line efficiency and huge box office returns and does not foster risk-taking.

☆ Ever-increasing competition for the entertainment dollar that puts more decisions on which films to make into the hands of marketing experts, not filmmakers.

☆ Film/marketing costs that have increased from $12 million to $84 million.

☆ A business where the creative process has been shifted outside the studio structure.

☆ A rapidly changing worldwide marketplace where foreign receipts now account for almost sixty per cent of all revenues, an increase from thirty per cent in less than twenty years. In the years ahead, this percentage may expand to seventy per cent.

☆ Almost one hundred years of filmmaking that now makes even finding original stories harder and harder.

You wonder why studio heads make such exorbitant salaries? If you can prosper in that kind of environment, your adaptive skills dwarf those of even the winners on television's "Survivor."

For all these reasons, *T2* both continued and accelerated the domino effect that had already been set in motion by the factors we have just discussed.

The result?

Titanic is a perfect metaphor for where the motion picture industry finds itself today.

Much like that fabled ship after it hit the iceberg, the industry may still look fine on the surface; however, beneath the waterline, there are deep and gaping wounds that are in the process of threatening its survival.

☆☆☆

What other terrifying futures can we imagine or remember—for ourselves?

Planet of the Apes (The Original)

In a fascinating "coincidence," the original Planet of the Apes was released in 1968, the same year which saw the release of *2001*. One classic film looking forward, one classic film looking backward . . . and forward?

Planet of the Apes is set "elsewhere." Astronaut Colonel George Taylor (Charlton Heston—personally, I never quite got past the notion that this was Moses in outer space) gets lost in space and time and winds up on a mysterious planet in the year 3978 A.D. where humans are a minor and reviled species in a society ruled by a hierarchy of apes and orangutans.

It's noteworthy to comment here for a moment not on the visionary content of the film but rather on its socially conscious nature. This was, after all, the sixties. Fierce wars were being raged on the frontier of race relations: civil rights marches, the 1964 Civil Rights Act and, in the same year of the film's release, the tragic assassinations of both Martin Luther King and one of his great supporters, Robert F. Kennedy. Crass racists often crudely referred to blacks as monkeys or apes, and then along comes this movie which completely flips the social order to apes being the ruling class! I have always looked upon this aspect of the film as being one of the delicious ironies of its existence and an eloquent statement about the ignorance and cruelty of racism. On this level alone, *Planet of the Apes* deserves a special place in film history.

Colonel Taylor is convinced (and so are we in the audience) that he has landed on some bizarre planet in the far reaches of the galaxy where "evolution" has been reversed. Humans are reviled and kept as slaves or just killed or banished. Discussions of humans are severely limited as well and are looked upon as a deficient, ugly species. He even meets a woman, whom the apes find to be as physically hideous as they find Heston, who, to us other humans, is quite stunningly beautiful. The eye of the beholder.

The most classic and memorable sequence in *Planet of the Apes* is certainly the ending. Heston and the girl Nova (Linda Harrison) that he befriends are allowed to ride out into the "forbidden zone" where no apes are allowed to venture. As they ride off, the leader of the ape society is asked what Taylor will find there and he enigmatically answers, "His destiny."

We follow Taylor and Nova on horseback along the coast of a bleak, barren shoreline until we see him dismount while looking at something he has found on the shore. Still not seeing what he sees, he falls to his knees in horror and anguish and screams, "My God! You idiots! You blew it, didn't you? You finally did it! You idiots!" Only then does the camera reveal the final shot of the film: Taylor has come upon the wreckage of the Statue of Liberty washed up on the shore of this desolate landscape. We know then that he is on Earth and that the society he knew has self-destructed. That's why the "lawgivers" of the ape society so reviled humans. They knew the real history of their planet and that humans had once ruled it and then allowed it to be destroyed.

That was quite a moment for moviegoers. What a shock!

Of course, that kind of shock was still possible in theaters. Today, I very much doubt that you could keep that kind of ending a secret. In the sixties, movies were just beginning to really be marketed on television and none of the obsession with all things Hollywood was existent at the time. No *Entertainment Hollywood*, no *Extra*, no *Premiere* or *Entertainment Weekly* magazines. Information on films and actors was not nearly as omnipresent as it is now, and you could still get away with that kind of ending in a major Hollywood movie and have it be a total surprise. Today, I'm sure that the secret would be out well before the film even opened, particularly on the Internet. It's safe to say that Internet movie gurus such as the ubiquitous Harry Knowles would have his spies in early test screenings. That is certainly one change brought about by the Internet. It used to be that companies could test-screen their movies outside of L.A. and be guaranteed of anonymity. Today, you just have to assume that several members of your test audience in every city will go right home after the screening, get on their computers, and spread the word. For instance, the word got out very quickly about the ending of *The Sixth Sense*. My daughters already knew the "surprise ending" long before the film even opened. Good, bad, or indifferent, there's really no such thing as an anonymous screening anymore. This puts a lot more pressure on directors than there used to be in that a really bad screening can destroy "the buzz" on a film very quickly. Unfortunately, this leads to fewer risks being taken and more homogenization of the product, but this aspect of the Internet is an unavoidable downside to what is, as I delineate in chapter 12, a huge boon for the future of entertainment.

Back to the *Planet of the Apes*.

The ending of the film was another classic distillation of the fears of a world in the grips of a cold war. What would happen if we didn't stop each other from escalating the arms race? How about "the end of the world as we know it" (a famous Barry Maguire song title and hit of the sixties). This was our greatest fear at the time and *Planet of the Apes* was a major message that, simply put, we need to be aware of our fears because the very act of facing them drains them of their power over us.

There were other films that also dealt with the same theme of nuclear war devastating the world such as Stanley Kramer's 1957 classic adaptation of the bestseller *On the Beach*—but I think we've covered the subject well enough to move on.

Armageddon and *Deep Impact*

How else could we destroy ourselves?

Or, perhaps more appropriate, how else have we perished before that still frightens us?

How about a meteor strike?

As with both Matrix and *13th* Floor, whenever two major films come out in the same year with the same basic premise, we know that we are working out something very major in our collective consciousness.

The core of each film is the same: a massive meteor is headed towards Earth. If it is not somehow destroyed before impact, all life on the planet will be destroyed. The significance of this one doesn't take a rocket scientist to figure out, on film or in life itself. We know that dinosaurs were made extinct by a meteor strike and we know that Earth has been devastated by other meteors as well.

In *Armageddon*, the real rocket scientists at NASA make the decision to send a team of deep core oil drillers (headed by Bruce Willis) into space to actually land on the asteroid and obliterate it by burying a nuclear bomb deep enough under the surface to shatter the asteroid.

In *Deep Impact*, NASA sends a team into space (headed by Robert Duvall) to attempt to basically shoot the asteroid out of the sky—or deflect it enough—so that it misses Earth.

The remaining plot points of the two films are really irrelevant to our purpose here (*Armageddon* is much more of an action/visual effects film and, except for its ending, *Deep Impact* is much more of a character drama).

Where the two films really diverge is at their climaxes.

In *Armageddon*, the good guys win the day by Willis volunteering to remain on the asteroid and detonate the bomb manually, which he does, saving Earth any impact while giving his own life.

In *Deep Impact*, the Duvall team also goes on a suicide mission and is only partially successful. The smaller of the threatening asteroid segments does strike the earth, destroying most of the coastal cities and killing thousands of people, including two main characters, played by Tea Leoni and Maximillian Schell, who wait on the beach for the tsunami that they know will destroy them. (This entire scene is eerily reminiscent of the last scene in *On the Beach* where the main character awaits the radioactive cloud that he knows is coming his way.) The main threat is, however, averted.

What is fascinating to me about both films is that they reflect not only our fears about these meteor strikes but also our paradoxical relationship with technology. *Only our advanced technical wizardry can save us in both films—and it does.*

This message reflects a real sea change in our apocalyptic thinking. These films actually reflect a newfound hope and conviction that we have evolved enough as a species to now be able to safely trust our advanced technology. We can have the com-

fort and security to accept that our technology could indeed prevent this kind of "global killer" where, in the past, we have not survived.

In essence then, the message in these movies reflects our decision that we need not fear tomorrow.

☆☆☆

The next two films, *1984* and *THX 1138* contain cautionary messages about the loss of personal freedoms in a world where we at least seem to have temporarily lost a sense of connection to our very humanity.

1984 and *THX 1138*

Obviously, the core classic in this particular arena is George Orwell's prophetic and best-selling novel *1984* which was released as a film in 1956.

1984 projected a future world where individual freedoms had been abolished and the government, personified constantly on omnipresent video screens everywhere by the visage of the leader known as "big brother," decided everything. (Today, it might be Joe Isuzu.) Those who refused to obey the strict code of conduct were "re-educated" by being forced to encounter their darkest fears which, in the case of the main character played by Edmond O'Brien, was rats. Anyone who saw the chilling scene in which O'Brien is thrown into a roomful of rats will never forget it.

☆☆☆

THX 1138, directed by George Lucas and released in 1971, is very similar to *1984* in that its grim future involved not only government oppression and overpopulation but also took the pollution concept to the extreme. The air had supposedly become so toxic that no human could live or even dare set foot on the surface of the earth. The population lived underground in tiny capsules where their occupants are only identified by numbers and letters (hence, the title) and are not even allowed to have sex or even to love, and are prevented from doing so by having to consent to being constantly drugged. Again, video screens watch every movement. (By this time, "big brother" from *1984* had become synonymous with government oppression and the phrase itself became a part of the everyday American lexicon.)

The main character, played by Robert Duvall, stops taking his medication and, along with his girlfriend and others, seeks to break free from the oppression. In the climactic scene, he actually succeeds in fighting his way to the supposedly poisonous surface of the Earth where the air actually looks as peaceful and serene as does the spectacular sunset that he encounters. The fascinating question left unanswered at the end of *THX 1138* is whether the air is as clean as it looks, meaning that the government is perpetrating a giant hoax just to subjugate the population, or is the seemingly clean air really polluted, meaning that the Duvall character will truly die as a result of his escape.

What binds *1984* and *THX 1138* together for our purposes here is they both project societies where love is actually outlawed. That fear runs deeper, I think, than the threat of destruction. We are the only species on this planet with the ability—the gift!—of *consciously* being able to choose to love. If we lost that ability, what would be left of our humanity?

The message of both films is not a frightening look at what may be coming. It is simply a reminder not to lose sight of either our unique ability to love or our cherished individuality.

Soylent Green

Released in 1972, *Soylent Green* starred Charlton Heston, who has come back from his shock at the foot of the Statue of Liberty to become a hardened and devoted policeman in a futuristic American world where the overcrowding and pollution is so oppressive that there literally are no free spaces in which to move, food is at a premium, and police regularly wear gas masks when patrolling the streets. The government police are everywhere, particularly when the public food supply—a green cracker-like item called soylent green—is distributed to a hungry populace.

Heston becomes suspicious of the government's methods and secretly begins his own investigation into what soylent green really is and how it is manufactured. The climactic scene shows Heston sneaking his way into a massive industrial complex where he learns the secret of soylent green. The "crackers" are the end result of a manufacturing process that has as its source the bodies of dead human beings. The population has been turned into a race of unknowing cannibals.

Again, the message of this film is a cautionary one about a nightmare world into which we might be headed if we don't address issues such as overpopulation and pollution. When one looks at the world today, it is obvious that we are indeed closely examining the issues of pollution and population. *While these challenges will not be solved overnight, we are subjecting them to the kind of intense scrutiny that results most often in resolution, not failure.*

In our next film, it could be said that some of the population have become intentional cannibals, at least in a certain sense.

A Clockwork Orange

Released in 1977, *A Clockwork Orange* was a deeply controversial and disturbing look at a world in the near future in which violence has become a way of life for much of the younger people in it.

Alex (Malcolm McDowell) and his band of "droogs" roam the night looking for violence and having fun with it—beating up derelicts, participating in gang fights and rapes, and terrorizing random citizens, including a man and his wife. The woman is raped and terrorized so savagely (to the disquieting music of "Singing in the Rain") that she dies, and the man is left a cripple. Ultimately, Alex is arrested. He is then "re-educated" by the government—brainwashed and tortured so completely that he becomes a human version of Robby the Robot in *Forbidden Planet* (chapter 7) in that he basically shuts down at any mention of violence.

Directed by Stanley Kubrick, the film represents our escalating fears of the violent society that had become America by the late 1970s. *Orange* has the benefit of both Kubrick's wicked sense of humor and also his visionary genius. The fact that the film was so deeply disturbing to so many people is yet another testament to Kubrick's singular artistry.

The message of the film is again a caution to look at the violence within our society and realize the depth of its threat to our well-being. All we need do is look at the passionate debate that is currently raging about violence in media and in society in general to know that we are indeed examining what we might be able to do to address this threat to our safety and security.

Waterworld and *The Postman*

Floods are an archetypical motif in all cultures.

One of the many fascinating points made in Graham Hancock's extraordinary book *Fingerprints of the Gods* is that every single culture in the world has a cultural "myth" about a great flood destroying all life on the planet (except, in some cultures, for a Noah and his ark full of creatures). It seems that we have deeply embedded memories of times when the waters of the Earth have risen above our heads and drowned us all.

In *Waterworld*, distinguished more for its whopping cost overruns ($150 million) than for anything else memorable in the film itself, the polar ice caps have melted and what's left of humanity sails the infinite seas of the world looking for safety that is nowhere to be found. Kevin Costner plays a mysterious character known as the Mariner who winds up befriending a woman and her child, and they all come into conflict with

"The Deacon," who gives Dennis Hopper the best scene-swallowing over-the-top villain to play outside of the Batman films.

As we debate the effects of global warming, we are reminded of the consequences of not addressing the issue so that we can adopt corrective measures to prevent it, and that is the underlying message of the film.

All of these films illuminate doomsday fears and challenges; however, their real purpose is to create an awareness that will lead to the resolution of the threats, not their realization.

And, just to end this chapter on a clearly positive note and to illustrate again that all disaster films are not necessarily linked to negative events, we end this chapter with: *The Postman.*

Kevin Costner must have been in an apocalyptic frame of mind because he followed *Waterworld* with *The Postman,* which takes place in 2013 after a nuclear holocaust. That's the good news. The bad news is that there is no more mail service. Say again?

This is one disaster film that projects a future that has almost certainly already occurred.

The enormous success of FedEx and other overnight couriers has combined with the widespread use of Internet email to guarantee that the days of the U.S. Postal Service are very definitely numbered.

There probably won't be too many mourners at the funeral except for our courageous mail carriers.

"I see dead people. All the time."

—*The Sixth Sense*

CHAPTER FIVE

Life after Life

Death.

Just mention the word to a lot of people and the conversation ends immediately. Do you think that religion is a "taboo" subject for conversation? It pales in comparison with death. You can actually see a physical revulsion on some people's faces at the mere mention of the word.

Death has always fascinated me. When my father died right before my fourth birthday, I got firsthand experience at a very young age with the sadness of death. Realizing that the person who died is just not going to be around anymore—in physical form—was one of the very first life lessons that I had to learn.

As I got older, the whole experience of death began to fascinate me, not from a morbid/obsessive standpoint but from a philosophical one. Death just didn't make sense to me in the way it was presented by most people and literature. The supposed finality of death has always seemed inappropriate to me. I didn't know why, but I just knew that some of my life was going to be directed at the issue of what death may and may not mean.

In the 1980s, I became aware of Elisabeth Kübler Ross's work on death and dying, and I started to read as much as I could find on the subject. When I would hear songs like the

Kansas hit, "Dust in the Wind" ("all we are is dust in the wind"), I would think, "Wait a minute. That just doesn't feel right." It never made sense to me, even before I came to a consciously spiritual awakening, that we are just born, live, and die. Dust in the wind? No way. Carl Sandburg's take on it always seemed so much more reasonable to me: "When death comes, it is an ocean that looks easy to wade in."

Looking back, I'm sure that I was just preparing myself for the moment when I would read "Bid Time Return" (later retitled *Somewhere in Time*) and discover the true path of my life. When I read that book, it all just clicked in for me. Even though the two lovers do not actually get together after life in the book, I knew that was the way the story had to end and I knew that dealing with this life/death challenge in the realm of movies was one of my life's purposes.

It is, then, no "accident" that I produced both *Somewhere in Time* and (with Barnet Bain) *What Dreams May Come.* I believe with all my heart that our traditional attitudes about death are no longer viable if, indeed, they ever were.

This is not the appropriate forum for a lengthy argument about what is to me the irrefutable proof that death is only a transition into a new form; moreover, this is another one of those situations where one can only authoritatively speak from one's own belief. The continuum of life, death, and rebirth can neither be proved nor disproved. Passionate arguments can be made on both sides, and every individual must make up his own mind. I only want to make one "point" here about all of these beliefs. Life-after-life researchers have actually indeed "scientifically proven" at least one thing: People who are declared clinically dead and are then revived (or just return) have for centuries related a universal experience. A comforting white light, seeing a tunnel, relatives and friends who have died, and a sense of peace. These stories are told in every culture and every society in the world, even primitive ones where there is no contact with outside culture of any kind. Even skeptics acknowledge the phenomenon but call it a mass hallucination. Funny. That's how some of us look at this experience we call "life."

Interestingly enough, there is one group of people who

relate a very different afterlife experience from what we have just described. In Richard Matheson's research for *What Dreams May Come*, he discovered that those people who have tried to commit suicide and are subsequently revived tell a very different and frightening story. This discrepancy is what motivated him to write *Dreams*.

For me, there is no doubt that I have been here for thousands of years. I have done various versions of past-life regressions, and I know that those experiences were real. I feel them on a cellular level. I also know that I have lived several lifetimes with my daughters, my friends, my parents, and other intimates in my life. In fact, it is part of my belief system that we do travel through the ages in soul groups. We have karmic bonds to one another, and we help each other grow and learn through a myriad of lifetimes. We change roles and relationships to each other but always help each other learn and incorporate whatever lessons we have chosen to experience in a specific incarnation.

When we meet someone with whom we have one of those pacts, we resonate immediately to them, often for reasons we either don't understand or even misinterpret at times, but we just know.

One of the most wonderful examples of this kind of encounter was related to me a few years ago by a friend of mine from Northern California. She was driving in New Mexico, a state in which she had not previously ever been. As she was driving through a small town, she stopped at a traffic light just as a young man was crossing the road in front of her. She had never seen him before, but she knew him and he knew her. He walked up to her car, smiled at her, and simply said "We're only supposed to say hello this time." He then smiled and walked off. She knew that he was someone within what James Redfield defines as her "soul group," with whom she was not going to have any other contact in this incarnation other than that single moment of saying hello. That was their deal. Just check in with each other once and say hello.

Going even further, I believe that we actually choose who our parents are going to be, too, for both the lessons that we can learn from them and for the lessons that they can learn from us. Those roles can switch from lifetime to lifetime. My father now could have been my daughter before, etc. It's like there's a big "boardroom" meeting in the afterlife. All of us who are between lives and who have soul group relationships sit around a big table (well, at least a virtual one) and discuss what we need to learn and how best we can help each other learn whatever those lessons might be. Then we're born. Part of the experience is that we lose all conscious connection with those bargains that we made, so we have to discover them as we go along in our lives, and sometimes that's very aggravating, right? Another friend analogized this process in a wonderful way: it's like we go out to a running track in the morning (between lives) and set up some hurdles to jump. Then we go out to lunch (we're born). We then come back to the track in the afternoon (after we're born) and, as we start to run the hurdles, we get really angry at whoever set the hurdles up (forgetting it was us) because they're so high and too close together.

If you follow this kind of philosophy, you eventually understand that everything that happens to you in life is your own responsibility and that acceptance, in turn, erases the concept of "blame." Neale Donald Walsch wrote a wonderful book called *Little Soul and the Sun,* which takes this concept a step further: even the people who cause you heartache in life are seen differently because you come to accept that they are only playing roles that you both agreed to before you were born.

Anyway, it is issues like those contained in this bit of a digression that I've allowed myself here that have convinced me and millions and millions of others that death is but a passage into another existence. Skeptics often say that such a conviction is based solely in wish fulfillment; that is, because we fear death, we create the illusion that death is only transitory, so as to allay our own fears. Okay. Fair point. I can't "prove" that those skeptics are wrong. On the other hand, they can't "prove" that they're right either.

To me, there are very hopeful and transformational messages in these films. If we all believed that there is an existence beyond death in which we examine our lives and see what we still need to learn in our next one, wouldn't that have an interesting effect on *how* we actually live our lives now? What if, for example, the universally related experience of having your life flash before your eyes is real? What if we do actually examine the life we have just lived with totally objective eyes? Wouldn't our actions during life be very different if we actually knew that we would be experiencing this objective self-examination without the ability to rationalize? (My favorite line about that actually comes from a wonderful film that we are not going to be otherwise looking at in these pages. In *The Big Chill*, one of the characters claims that our need to rationalize is more important than our need for sex. When challenged, he says, "Okay. I can prove it. Have you ever gone a day without a rationalization?")

Even if we can't "prove" any of this, the world seems a kinder, gentler place with this philosophy than without it. I was once asked by a friend to give her a copy of the book of *What Dreams May Come* for her mother, who was dying of cancer. My friend didn't believe in the whole notion of life after life but thought it might help allay some of her mother's fears. Her mother read it, literally on her deathbed, and passed away in peace.

The notion of life after life is a bridge of belief that some choose to cross, and others don't. If you don't see death as a transitory phase, there are thousands of movies out there where death is final. You live, you die. That's it. Over and out. I couldn't possibly begin to list them.

The movies we discuss in this chapter see death in another way. The message we glean from all these movies is not only that life extends beyond death but that great beauty and love await us there, just around the corner. Anything that can provide that kind of comfort comes from some place much more beautiful than here.

The Sixth Sense

This brilliantly conceived and executed movie is as close to being a perfect commercial vehicle for the message about the continuum of life as I can imagine.

Making the character of Cole (played by Haley Joel Osment)

a child was nothing less than inspired genius by the writer/director M. Night Shyamalan. The experience of a child who is terrified of his own visions is not only something to which we can relate from our own childhoods, it also allows us, the audience, to be more concerned for Cole than we might even be for ourselves. That conceit forges a brilliantly conceived path over that bridge of belief that confronts every filmmaker as we venture into these realms. *How do you make it believable and relatable?* Seeing it through the eyes of a child makes it frightening, yes, but so amazingly believable and relatable, just as it was in *The Exorcist* and *E. T.*

Cole sees "dead people walking around," and we never doubt him. We just want to help him. Why is that? Why do we automatically trust the responses of a child even more than we often trust ourselves?

I share with others the belief that, as babies and young children, we all have a very strong connection to who we really are and the worlds between lives. Children seem to still be connected to a sense of their divinity that fades, as one moves past the early stages of childhood. Ever see babies looking at each other? Doesn't it seem that they are conducting a very special non-verbal conversation? I also think that is one of the reasons that *The Sixth Sense* was such a huge hit: we understand that children know something very special. In the film, it is Cole who is so connected that he actually sees the spirits of dead people, and we find it very easy to believe him.

There's another message in *The Sixth Sense* that also resonates deeply within us. As would any child, Cole begins by being terrified by the people he sees. It is only when the psychiatrist who is trying to help him (Bruce Willis) tells Cole that maybe these people are just asking for his help that Cole's fears ease.

The notion of spirits lingering on the Earth plane because of unfinished business has been used in movies for almost as long as film has existed. Sixth Sense *is a moving reminder that these beings need not frighten us; rather, our love and understanding can help them transcend this plane and rejoin the loved ones who await them, and eventually us, on the other side.*

This concept has also generated hundreds of horror films, of course, where the lingering spirits have a malevolent intent.

How much less frightening does contact with these kinds of spirits become when we accept that perhaps they only need some help, rather than fear that they need to eat our brains or commit some other such groundless terror?

Another aspect of the beauty of *The Sixth Sense* is that it just takes the continued existence of these people after death as a "given." You don't see any elaborate justifications for the events that are transpiring. There are no "Moishe the explainer" scenes. This is a kind of industry shorthand for scenes where one character just stops the movie in a way, so that certain things can be explained to the audience. It is very hard to set up the rules of a film without one of these scenes, so the trick is to try to do it in a very compelling visual and dramatic manner. One of the best scenes ever of this type was in the original *Raiders of the Lost Ark*—chapter 3—where Harrison Ford explains the Ark of the Covenant to government agents. (Ford may just be the winner emeritus in perpetuity of the Moishe the Explainer award for that scene.) *The Sixth Sense* accomplishes its task without one of those scenes or characters and is exceedingly unique in that regard.

Of course, *The Sixth Sense* also benefits from a brilliant plot device that tracks from beginning to end when you watch it again. The fact that the Willis character is also dead—even though neither he nor we as the audience are aware of it until the end—says a lot about the nature of what we ordinarily refer to as reality, doesn't it?

If Willis doesn't know the demarcation point between life and death, isn't it reasonable that we ourselves are testing those so-called boundaries as well? This wonderful film contains yet another message to remind us all that "we're not in Kansas anymore."

Our next film also deals with the idea of spirits who linger in their old realities because they have unfinished business.

Ghost

Released in 1990, *Ghost* was a huge box-office success, mostly as a result of its clever blend of romance, comedy, and mystery.

As with many films in this genre, *Ghost* was around a long time as a script—almost ten years—before it was finally made. The unlikely impetus for finally getting a green light (production approval) for the film was that Jerry Zucker went to Paramount and begged to direct it. Zucker was one of the directors of *Airplane,* a gigantic hit for Paramount but about as odd a calling card for directing a romantic film like *Ghost* as one could imagine. Zucker had made a lot of money for Paramount, however, and had a great concept for making the psychic character Oda Mae (eventually played by Whoopi Goldberg) more comedic. The idea was brilliant because it eased the dramatic tension of the rest of the movie by giving the audience a character with whom they could relate, particularly if they had their own doubts about the idea of being able to contact the dead. Oda Mae thinks she's a fake until Sam (Patrick Swayze) actually does communicate with her.

Zucker got the job, and the film got made. Movies get made at studios for myriad interesting, and often bizarre, reasons. Directors who have made a lot of money for studios in the past are among the least bizarre catalysts for green lights.

Sam is murdered at the opening of *Ghost* and does not move on because of his love for his wife Molly (Demi Moore) and because of the danger his ex-partner Carl (Tony Goldwyn) poses to her. The spirits in *The Sixth Sense* lingered and appealed to Cole because they needed his help. Swayze stays because he wants to help and comfort his wife, and I think that connection strikes a deep nerve with people. How many stories have we all heard about individuals losing loved ones and then feeling the presence of those loved ones after their death?

The presence is almost always comforting, particularly if the one left behind is open to the contact. We reversed that in *What Dreams May Come* because the Ann character had always believed that "when you're dead, you're dead." As I have mentioned earlier, my father died when I was four. For years, I had the sense that there was "a man in my wall" in my bedroom at night. It was not until much later that I came to realize that this presence was my father checking in on me to make sure I was okay.

We all want some kind of comforting sense that our loved one has passed through and is at peace; moreover, I believe that we would like to send and receive the message that those loved ones are there protecting us from harm wherever possible. This is one of the enduring messages and comforts in Ghost.

The other notable aspect of *Ghost* is how it differentiates between the afterlife experience of what we might call here the just and the unjust. When Sam actually "moves on" at the end of *Ghost*, he does so in a beautiful white light in total peace and happy expectation. When Sam's actual killer and his partner die in the film, frightening shadow figures emerge from beneath the streets to claim their souls. You see the terror in the faces of those so claimed, and it is obvious that they are not exactly seeing white lights and happy relatives. To some, this can certainly be interpreted that they are going to Hell. I guess it depends on how you define Hell. As the Cuba Gooding character says in *What Dreams May Come*:

"Hell is not always fire and brimstone. The real Hell is your life gone wrong."

Could self-examination without the ability to rationalize be the worst Hell? Imagine a soul who has come to life to learn certain lessons but goes way far off that track. What worse pain could a soul imagine than knowing it has actually devolved rather than evolved?

To paraphrase a wonderful line in Neil Simon's *Chapter Two:* what if you had gotten all the way to *m* and realized that you had to go back and start at *a* again? What if you don't have either the crutch of blame or the manipulation of self-pity at your disposal? You just have to trudge back to the start of the line and begin again.

That is a very powerful and important message as we try to negotiate the narrows of the challenges of life at the beginning of this new millennium.

What Dreams May Come

The entire saga of *Dreams* is detailed in chapter 15 at the end of this book, but I'm going to discuss one aspect of the story here because I believe it is one of the most relevant movies in this chapter.

The story of *Dreams* revolves around Chris (Robin Williams) and Annie (Annabella Sciorra) Nielsen. Their children die at the beginning of the film. Annie almost doesn't survive the loss, and it is only her love for Chris that gets her through the trauma and allows her eventually to go back to her life as a painter and art museum curator. Chris dies three years later. In grief over his death, and left completely alone, Annie takes her own life.

Not exactly a Mack Sennett comedy, right?

This all happens in the first third of the film. The rest of the film takes place in Chris and Annie's afterlife, as Chris first experiences his continued existence through Annie's paintings and then goes on a journey to find Annie and rescue her from a personal Hell to which she has sentenced *herself*.

Not *the* afterlife. *His* afterlife.

Not *the* Hell. *Her* Hell.

The distinctions are crucial.

The core message of Dreams *is that we create our own reality, in life and death.* Everyone has his or her own concept of what afterlife is like. We do not presume to ever say that we are depicting *the* afterlife as though that experience is universally dictated. Yes, this is where we separate ourselves from some traditional religions and, for that, I make no apologies.

I do not believe that there can ever be a universal truth when it comes to matters of faith. For me, everyone is entitled to believe as he/she chooses, and I respect *all* those views as long as they are honoring of the essential sanctity and integrity of each human life. (This obviously rejects concepts such as Nazism and other beliefs that depend on degrading others.) I respect Catholics, Buddhists, Moslems, Jews, etc., and I do not in any way believe that my beliefs are more valid or more "true" than the tenets of those religions.

Where I have a major problem is when I am told that I am wrong and that my beliefs are in violation of any "true" faith. It is *precisely* that kind of bigotry that has started most of the major conflagrations of history. Once any group thinks they are the only true believers, people usually die for holding other beliefs.

When the Catholic Church first came to England several hundred years ago, the Druids actually welcomed them and offered to work side by side with the church as a separate but equal faith. Eventually, the Church had enough of a foothold in England that it felt safe and it went after the Druids, who were believers in all things metaphysical and magical. The Druids were hounded and eliminated until they receded into *The Mists of Avalon* (Marion Bradley's magnificent book, which was unfortunately adapted into a television miniseries that, in my opinion, missed the whole point of the book and the time period).

Our premise in *Dreams* was that we each create our own realities in life and death.

Chris is operating in a world of his wife's paintings because that's what's comforting and familiar to him. I have always joked that it would have been an entirely different afterlife if Woody Allen had been our star—an endless New York City street full of bookstores, theaters, and coffee houses.

Annie is living in a nightmare version of her life with Chris because this is the karma that she has chosen in order to work out her issues over having taken her own life.

It is fascinating how so many people created different realities for themselves over what we very carefully laid out on screen. I want to relate one experience here that illuminates the very different manner in which people can perceive a seemingly singular event.

A few weeks after the film opened, I attended a birthday party in Santa Barbara for my dear friend Gay Hendricks at his home. Gay and his wife Katie are world-renowned relationship experts who have written several best-selling books, including *Conscious Loving*. They are also cherished friends. Gay is also infamous among his friends for loving to see us squirm whenever he can devise an appropriate moment to cause that to happen. At the beginning of the party, Gay quieted the sixty or seventy people in attendance and thanked us all for being there. He also went on to announce that he knew most of them had seen *Dreams* (this was a very metaphysical group), that one of the producers of the film was in the room, and that Gay was "sure Stephen Simon would love to hear all of your comments about the film. He's right over there." With that, he pointed me out with a totally mischievous grin that basically said, "Let the games begin." Thanks, buddy!

I'm only going to describe the first four of a few dozen conversations that then occurred. These particular four discussions took place in less than ten minutes. Total.

First, a very nice man came up, introduced himself, and told me that he had seen the film with a close friend of his who had asked him to deliver a message for her if he ever met anyone involved in the film. He then very politely asked permission to do so, and I immediately encouraged him to tell me.

"She wants you to know that you are an inhuman monster."

I am not often struck speechless, but I was sure at a loss for a response to that, even though I immediately sensed what had prompted her reaction. He confirmed my suspicion when he told me that his friend's father had committed suicide years before and that she read the message of the movie as being that all suicides go directly to Hell. I completely understood and sympathized. Even though we went to great pains in the film to explain that there were no rules or judges and that Annie chose her existence out of her own free will, this woman had experienced a very different reality. The man then walked away and said, "I hope that wasn't too personal." No, of course not. Nothing personal about being called an inhuman monster, is there? Seriously, though, I had heard this kind of response before, and I respected the pain that she must have felt.

Next, and I mean just as this man left, a woman walked up with tears in her eyes and embraced me while she thanked me for "making such a beautiful message about suicide." She worked for a suicide prevention hotline in Santa Barbara and told me that she knew that the film had already prevented some would-be attempts. She said she was sure that the message of the film was that we control what happens after we die and that Annie chose to live in her nightmare existence so that she could evolve and learn.

Next, a very angry and agitated man walked up to me to upbraid me for "finally having the opportunity to do a spiritual movie about the afterlife and destroying it by the use of *traditional Christian images* (my emphasis added) throughout the film." He then abruptly turned and walked away.

Literally right behind him was a young man in his twenties

who told me how much he loved the film and that the one thing that had impressed him the most was that we "had not used a single *traditional Christian image* in the whole film."

These people had all sat in a theater and watched a singular version of *Dreams,* but they each perceived it in a totally different manner. As Cuba said in the film, "We see what we want to see."

Heaven Can Wait

This film is based on an earlier version of the same story entitled *Here Comes Mr. Jordan.* In *Heaven Can Wait*, released in 1976, professional football quarterback Joe Pendleton (Warren Beatty) is prematurely brought to an afterlife way station because one of his guides (Buck Henry) mistakenly claimed his soul and, by the time the mistake was discovered, his body has been cremated. As delightfully explained by the erudite Way Station Executive, Mr. Jordan (James Mason), Beatty's soul is not yet due for departure from earth. As a result, Beatty can find a new body so that he can still achieve his goal of winning the Super Bowl.

He finally agrees to temporarily inhabit the body of a wealthy tycoon and, in that body, buys his team (the Rams) and trains for the Super Bowl. Mr. Jordan continuously assures him that, if it is his fate to play in the Super Bowl, then indeed he will. As he says: "There's always a plan, Joe." (Although I'm not a total believer in fate, I do believe that we have specific intents as we come to life and that we will do just about anything to accomplish them.)

As an audience, we see Warren Beatty but, as is explained by Mr. Jordan, everyone else sees Leo Farnsworth, the body that he has inhabited. What a wonderful and ingenious metaphor for the soul's separate identity from the body!

For most of the film, however, there is a distinction in that Beatty is *consciously* aware that he is inhabiting another body. As we near the climax, the Farnsworth character is killed by his wife and her lover, and Joe loses his chance, at least temporarily. Tragically, we see his replacement quarterback killed on the field (a bit of a stretch, yes, as no one has ever actually died *in* a game, but perfectly acceptable poetic license nevertheless). At that point, Beatty's soul steps in and carries the team to victory; however, this time, it's for real and not temporary. As such, he loses all memory of what brought him through the challenges along the way.

Sounds complex, I know, but it's more difficult to explain than it is to see.

The message here is that Joe had set up a life for himself wherein he was going to win the Super Bowl. That was part of the very fabric of his being. *Somehow, his soul found its way to its destiny even under the most difficult circumstances. If we find our true path, we need not worry about how we are going to traverse it. Our soul will light the way.*

After Life

From one kind of afterlife way station to a very different one.

After Life is a Japanese film that was released in America in 2000, and it is pure and simple genius.

The premise is simple. After you die, you must choose one memory from your life and then spend eternity in that memory.

The film takes place at a way station in the afterlife where people are given a week to choose that one memory, and then they supervise the recreation of the memory so that they can live within it.

The choices are all poignant.

- ☆ a man chooses the moment in which he enjoyed his first taste of salted rice after almost starving to death in World War Two.
- ☆ a woman chooses the moment of birthing her child.
- ☆ a woman chooses the moment she is reunited with her fiancé after the war.

By the way, no one chooses a work-related memory. As the old saying goes, no one ever says at the end of life that they wish they had spent more time at the office.

They are told that they *must* choose a memory; however, it is revealed late in the film that all the people working in the way station are there so that they can help others remember because they themselves either couldn't or wouldn't choose a memory themselves.

The most moving story in the film involves an elderly businessman who led such a "so-so" life that he can't choose. Finally, he chooses a moment with his wife where they were sitting on a park bench and decided to see a movie together. His was an arranged marriage, and they were never passionate with each other. She had a fiancé who was killed in the war and who was the love of her life. We discover that the man who is helping this gentleman choose a memory was indeed that fiancé who was killed. He realizes that the woman herself chose a memory when she died of the moment she sat on a bench with him before he went off to the war. This then allows the young man who has worked at this way station for forty-five years to finally choose the same memory that his fiancé had chosen. He makes this choice not because that memory was so happy for him but because "it was a part of someone else's happiness."

If we knew that we would have but one memory to keep with us for eternity, that awareness would make each moment of life much more precious.

Which memory would you choose?

Field of Dreams

Even if this weren't a wonderful movie on many different levels, its core message would deserve its place in the pantheon of spiritual movies simply for its phrase:

"If you build it, they (or he) will come."

Kevin Costner plays Ray Kinsella, an Iowa farmer who begins to hear a voice telling him to build a baseball field right in the middle of his farm. Despite the fact that the building of the field seems nonsensical to both Ray and his wife Anni (Amy Madigan), he feels compelled to build the field. When he builds it, Ray gets the delight of watching famous ball players emerge from the cornfields to play on the field. These are men he has idolized and idealized through the years, and he gets to watch them play the game he so dearly loves. He provides a space for them to live out their dreams and, in so doing, Ray vicariously gets to play out his fantasy life as a player. Despite all the obstacles he faces from his wife and other factors such as the financial burden of putting his meager resources into the unlikely enterprise of building a ball field in the cornfields of Iowa, he follows that "voice."

Why? Who or what is that voice?

Is it the voice of God? The voice of a guardian angel? The voice of his father?

I don't think so.

It is his voice. His internal voice. That voice we all have in the depths of our souls that speaks truth to us in our most important moments. That voice that is our connection to the divine, however we might individually interpret that word. The voice that often we confuse with all those other little voices we hear, like that of our ego or our inner child.

This connection to that divine voice within us is to me the crux of the power of *Field of Dreams.*

Field of Dreams was released in 1989, just as we entered the decade of the nineties when so much of the literature pertaining to our evolving awareness of spirituality was focused on connecting with the divine within us. My dear friend and mentor Neale Donald Walsch got to a place of such pain and desperation in his life that only his awakening to that voice held him back from toppling into the abyss. His visionary *Conversations with God* books all pertain in some way to connecting to that unique voice within each one of us, which is our individual connection to the divine.

Ray listens to the most sacred place within himself and that's why, without any so-called rational reason, he sets in motion the actions of the building of the field. He can't really explain it. He just knows. One of the hallmarks of wisdom is the ability and courage to look beyond logic and reason without losing sight of it. Costner's character succeeds in doing just that. Even more importantly, he trusts that inner voice, even in the face of mounting opposition and the fact that he himself cannot justify his actions in any rational way. He is in fact following his heart and his destiny. (It's interesting that two of the seminal films in this arena—this one and *Heaven Can Wait*— are both built around sports metaphors, one, football, and one, baseball.)

A note here for those of you who might ask about the wisdom and integrity of people like Timothy McVeigh, who also could claim he was following a voice within him. My response would be to quote a line in a song entitled "Cross of Changes," that was written and performed by Enigma who, for me, so accurately echoed the spiritual feelings of the nineties in their music: "There is no God who would act in this way." One of the great challenges of life is to be able to differentiate those various voices we hear inside of us on a daily basis. Whatever voice McVeigh may have heard and acted upon was not his connection to the divine.

Movies that connect on such a deep level as *Field of Dreams* have powerful messages inside of them or we would not resonate so deeply to them. This film not only illuminates our connection to that voice within us, it also parts the veil between life and death with love and forgiveness at its core. In discovering what transpires at the end of the film, we understand the real reason that Ray's inner voice has compelled him to build the field: reconnection and forgiveness with his own deceased father. This theme resonates for us, I believe, on the obvious level of our desire for resolution with our parents, but it also connects to the deeper issue of forgiveness.

The power of forgiveness is at once an immense power and also a formidable weapon.

When we choose to forgive, we release both ourselves and the person that we are forgiving. Once the power to forgive is exercised, the energy shifts. When we withhold forgiveness, we keep ourselves and the one seeking forgiveness in the places we have maintained as victim and perpetrator. We can, of course, hold grudges forever and keep ourselves in that place of the wronged party or we can forgive and move on. Choosing to forgive and being forgiven is at the core of the climax of *Field of Dreams*. Ray forgives his father and thus allows them both to heal. For everyone, that is a powerful and resonant message.

For many more, it is a critical life lesson that we have chosen to play out in this lifetime.

As previously noted, a surprisingly large number of people who are on a conscious spiritual journey in this lifetime have experienced severe childhood trauma and struggle in their backgrounds. It is as though so many of us chose very challenging and "high hurdles" to overcome in childhood—from every manner of abuse to abandonment, and more. Ultimately, the pathway to resolution of these issues runs through the garden of forgiveness.

For those who have dealt with and are dealing with these issues, *Field of Dreams* contains then a particularly powerful message about forgiveness.

Jacob's Ladder

Jacob's Ladder (1990) was written by Bruce Joel Rubin who also wrote *Ghost*. Bruce is one of the very few prestigious writers in the mainstream film industry who really understands and embraces this kind of material.

The film was a critical and commercial disappointment because it was just too difficult for audiences to distinguish what was real and what was not in the film. And that was precisely the audacious and daring message of the film.

As I mentioned in our discussion of *Mulholland Drive* in chapter 2, my interpretation of the intent of the film was to show what we might experience at the moment of death. The ending of the movie made it very clear that the entire story of the film was what the main character (Tim Robbins) experienced at his moment of death.

Remember, all the stories that are related by those who have survived near-death experiences are that a certain version of our life flashing before us does occur. It does not, however, occur in linear time as it does during life. We jump back and forth between real and even imagined events that relate to the experiences we have had during our lifetime.

The problem of this film is that the experience of disjointed time and space provides the exact same response in a viewer in a theater as it does with the one who is living it: disorientation.

We went through this on *What Dreams May Come* as well. The original concept for the first act of the film was for Chris to have a totally disjointed experience of the events of his life right up until he let go and allowed himself to move on. We edited the first cut of the film exactly that way. Unfortunately, the audience we showed it to had absolutely no idea what they were seeing and, instead of intriguing them, it annoyed and distanced them from the film. When we experience that disconnect after life, there's nothing we can do about it. In a film, you go back to the editing room and, if you can, make the film more accessible. In *Jacob's Ladder*, the disorientation is weaved within the fabric of the story itself. The whole point was that the experience was a mystical afterlife journey and, as such, it is a very brave and unique experience.

Flatliners

Released in 1990, *Flatliners* took our fascination with the afterlife experience to another level. Medical students decide that the only real way to determine whether or not the tunnel/light/loved one experience is real or not is to actually die and find out! They develop a scheme where they will experiment with dying and then have their gathered colleagues revive them, so that they can report on what they actually experienced.

The frightening consequences for the students who artificially try to create the death experience comprises a very brief and simple message that prematurely causing our own death carries grave consequences. Pun very much intended.

"There is no Hell, although I hear Los Angeles is getting close."

—*Defending Your Life*

CHAPTER SIX

Comedy

"Dying is easy . . . comedy is hard."

So spoke famous comedian W. C. Fields in his last days, and the quote is just so appropriate that this chapter has to follow the last one.

There is actually a lot of truth in the great comedian's observation.

Comedy is probably the most difficult genre in which to work (not counting the spirituality genre that *would* certainly win that dubious accolade today because the genre itself has not yet been recognized. I hope this book will help change that status so we can soon be saying that "spirituality is easy . . . comedy is hard.").

If you do a stunt in a movie that isn't quite right, nobody really cares that much. If a dramatic speech isn't quite right, you can usually rally elsewhere in the script. In comedy, a joke that isn't funny just sits there like an ugly rotten tomato that no one wants to clean up. There's nothing quite so lame or embarrassing as a joke or a sight gag that doesn't work.

Very, *very* few writers and directors can turn out comedies that really make us laugh on a consistent basis. Usually, they make a few good movies (or sometimes only one) and then their stuff isn't funny anymore. "One hit wonders" are not the exclusive province of the music business and, in the film business, they are more plentiful in the comedy arena than elsewhere. Actors seem to have a very short shelf life in this arena too and that's what makes the great masters at this art so special. Charlie Chaplin, Abbot and Costello, Laurel and Hardy, Jerry Lewis, Danny Kaye, and Jim Carrey (although his longevity is still to be determined) come to mind as comic actors who have been able to consistently turn out funny movies. Very few women, right? I'm not comfortable with the political correctness of that observation but only the legendary Lucille Ball comes to mind and her great success was basically in television. Mae West and Judy Holliday perhaps? So many of the women of film who have done great comedy, however, did not really immerse themselves mostly in the genre. Shirley Maclaine, Carol Lombard, Barbra Streisand, Katherine Hepburn, Meg Ryan, etc., all had wonderful turns in comedies but also did a lot of notable work in dramas as well (likewise for great comedic actors like Tom Hanks).

Another problem with comedy is understanding how to time out jokes and laugh lines in films. Stand-up comics get immediate feedback from an audience and can time their deliveries accordingly. Timing out a joke on screen is a much more treacherous business, and extensive previews are actually very helpful in the editing process.

Still another challenge is the timeliness of the joke or sight gag itself. Jay Leno and David Letterman get a lot of mileage out of events that have happened that very day and are still fresh in the audience's mind. Movie writers and actors work on a twelve- to eighteen-month window, so timely references can be just deadly if the subject matter has become stale in the interim.

As it relates to our subject matter, I learned a fascinating lesson (one of hundreds) from my mentor Ray Stark very early on in my career. When I started working for Ray, he had been trying for some time to develop a script with Warren Beatty that would be a remake of a film from the 1940s called *Mr. Peabody and the Mermaid.* That film was a drama in which a man found and fell in love with a mermaid and kept her in a pond behind his house. Ray and Warren had been trying to figure out how to do the film in a modern-day environment and then *Splash* was released in 1984. Ray and I saw the film together. When it was over, he said to me "Well, Stephen, that's the end of our Beatty mermaid project and there's a great lesson here for both of us: there is some material that audiences will buy in a comedy that they just won't accept in drama." Wise words from a wise man.

As audience members, we are usually willing to suspend our disbelief in films and give the filmmakers the benefit of the doubt, certainly at least in the setup of the film. As long as "the rules" are explained to us, we tend to accept them as long as those rules are in some way relatable and understandable; however, some subject matter, like falling in love with a mermaid, is just a lot easier to accept when we are laughing *with* the movie as opposed to doing our best not to laugh *at* it. That's a huge distinction for us to make as filmmakers, particularly in the spirituality genre. This concept extends to having comedy *within* dramatic films as well. For example, I've already mentioned the comedic change that Jerry Zucker made in the Oda Mae/Whoopi Goldberg character in *Ghost*. The premise of the film was dramatic enough that the audience really needed and appreciated the comedic relief of a character who thought she was a fraudulent psychic until she actually began to hear Patrick Swayze's messages.

Comedy is a great refresher in these films; however, we also face the challenge of not throwing in comedic lines and bits simply for their own sake. An audience can smell that kind of manipulation all the way out at the popcorn stand, and we can just as easily alienate them as we can amuse them. For instance, we tried very hard to put more humor into *What Dreams May Come* because we realized how challenging both the premise and the journey were. The problem was that most of the comedic breaks we tried to accomplish just were not organic to the film, the characters, or the tone. Could be our failure. Could be the aforementioned impossibility of telling a hot waffle that it's a frozen fish. I don't know.

Comedy can also be used satirically to illustrate the absurdity of certain situations in life and the first film in this chapter not only fits squarely in that category, it actually defines it.

Dr. Strangelove (or How I Learned to Stop Worrying and Love the Bomb)

It is only fitting that we start this section with another film from the master Stanley Kubrick. (Contrary to popular opinion, this was not the strangest movie title of that amazing decade of the sixties which was characterized by excess in every imaginable arena. That dubious distinction should, I believe, be held by a whimsical Anthony Newley farce entitled *Can Hieronymous Bosch Ever Forget Mercy Humpe and Find True Happiness?*)

Let's note here that, just by another "odd" coincidence, *Strangelove* opened in 1964, about 18 months after the Cuban Missile Crisis of October, 1962. The world had been brought to the brink of nuclear war and, I believe, visions of past self-destructive ends to other civilizations were thrust onto the center stage of our awareness.

Enter Mr. Kubrick's wicked satire on all things nuclear. *Strangelove* takes every possible doomsday message and stereotype and raises them to the most extreme and darkest ends imaginable:

☆ Afraid that a rogue military officer could start World War III? Meet the oh-so-subtly-named General Jack D. Ripper (Sterling Hayden) who is obsessed with the sense that the "the Russkies" are secretly tampering with our "personal bodily fluids."

☆ Afraid that our technology advances will get us to a place where neither they nor our overzealous military can be overcome by our humanity? Meet General Buck Turgidson (George C. Scott), who is so enraptured in his explanation to the president of our military's prowess in avoiding radar detection that he just conveniently forgets that it means the end of the world.

☆ Afraid that this same technology is too smart for its own good? Meet U.S. bombers with such sophisticated equipment and technology that they can't be recalled in certain scenarios no matter what.

☆ And, by the way, that "no matter what" scenario? Afraid that we can get into World War III because of a mistake in communications? Meet Captain "King" Kong (Slim Pickens), the pilot of the bomber in question who doesn't believe anyone or anything once he's given the go-ahead to drop the bomb.

☆ Afraid that some foreign head of state could start a war because he's just having a bad day? Meet the Russian premier, who is drunk during the hot line calls with American President Muffley.

☆ Afraid that rogue scientists—particularly those "not-to-be-trusted-former-Nazis-who-have-emigrated-to-America"—will actually cause World War III just to test their doomsday scenarios? Meet Dr. Strangelove (Peter Sellers, who actually plays three roles in the film), a repatriated German scientist with a prosthetic arm which alternately snaps into a Nazi salute and . . . well, as to its other function, see the movie . . . this is a "family book."

☆ Afraid that some in the military love war enough to start another one? Well, reacquaint yourself with Captain Kong (Slim Pickens), who, with his cowboy hat thrust in the air, actually rides the nuclear bomb he has just dropped down to the ground as if it were a bucking bronco.

And that's not all of it!

Strangelove is one of those movies where you just sit there shaking your head, thinking lines like "He didn't just do that, did he?" or "He's not going to do that, is he?" and then you find that the film itself immediately exceeds even your wildest guesses.

Kubrick and brilliant screenwriter/satirist Terry Sothern took everyone's deepest fears and projected them onto the screen. As mentioned before, we were very afraid of technology at that point. We had created nuclear weapons that could literally destroy the world. Without going into too much detail again here, it is my belief that the fear of misusing technology and inadvertently causing the end of the world is rooted for many of us in Atlantean lifetimes. Reading any of the stories of Atlantis leads to the conclusion that the Atlanteans also misused and misunderstood advanced technology, ultimately leading to the devastating consequences that followed.

Taking our fears of technology to their most extreme end, Kubrick created another brilliant, eerie, cautionary final shot.

After we see Slim Pickens astride the nuclear bomb whooping and hollering like the rodeo cowboy he also was, we see various shots of nuclear bombs exploding all over the world, our deepest, darkest fear at that time. Over the otherwise silent footage of these explosions, Kubrick plays the old, classic song:

> *"We'll meet again.*
> *"Don't know where. Don't know when.*
> *"Just know we'll meet again . . . some sunny day."*

☆☆☆

Sitting in the audience, I just remember my jaw dropping open at that ending.

Strangelove *succeeded in making the arms race look completely insane and that was indeed the point of the message. We recognized the absurdity of the escalation of our mutual threats to destroy each other and were reminding ourselves that we had decided to avoid the consequences of that hostility this time.*

Forty years ago, Russian Premier Nikita Khrushchev vowed to the United States that Russia "will bury you." Today, the Cold War is over, the Berlin Wall is gone, and Russia looks to the United States as its model for democracy.

We first heeded the message of Dr. Strangelove *and then transcended it.*

Dogma

Released in 1999, *Dogma* looks at religion with the same caustic irreverence that *Strangelove* looked at nuclear war.

Dogma starts with a printed disclaimer that calls the film a work of comedic fantasy and asks the audience to consider that "before you think of hurting someone over this, just remember that God has a sense of humor. Just look at the platypus."

Why such a disclaimer?

☆ Instead of a loving, kind, gentle God, as in the guise of George Burns in *Oh, God,* the film presents an angry, defiant God in the guise of rock singer Alanis Morrisette who will go to almost any lengths not to be proven wrong. She is also a skee-ball fanatic who gets trapped in human form on one of her secret excursions to Earth to play her favorite game.

☆ Angels have no genitalia because they couldn't be so trusted, and they're none too pleased about that; moreover, they can't "imbibe" alcohol, so they taste and spit it out.

☆ The Muse Serendipity (Salma Hayek) is working as a stripper in a low-rent bar, so she can inspire men in a new way.

☆ The Catholic Church through "modern" Cardinal Glick (George Carlin) is undergoing a "Catholicism Wow!" campaign to update its image. Among other "minor adjustments" is that the crucified image of Christ is out, replaced by a smiling Christ pointing at us with one hand and giving us a thumbs up (Roger Ebert, rejoice!) with the other hand. (Maybe Gene Siskel was on the other side and had a "hand" in helping inspire this idea. Gene was, by the way, an acquaintance of mine. We knew each other since college and we always joked that he never liked a movie that I produced. He joked. I winced because it was true until *What Dreams May Come,* which Gene truly loved. It was one of the last films he reviewed before his death, and I have always wondered how much his own impending death affected the way he perceived the film. He was, by the way, a terrific man.)

Dogma came very close to not getting made at all. Even with superstar talent and a well-respected young director, *Dogma* was a very hot potato that no one wanted to pick up until Lion's Gate stepped into the fray and took a chance that ultimately paid off well for them.

As you can already surmise, *Dogma* is as black as black comedies can ever get. Talk about doing this as a drama—no way! Basically, the plot involves two fallen angels, Bartleby (Ben Affleck) and Loki (Matt Damon), who have been banished from heaven by God because Bartleby convinced Loki, who was the angel of death, to stop doing God's violent dirty work for Him (Her, actually). They have been stuck on Earth since but they think they have found a loophole that will sneak them back into heaven. God sends all kinds of messengers to prevent them from doing so. One of them, Metatron (Alan Rickman), explains to a young woman, Bethany (Linda Fiorentino), who has been recruited to help (and turns out to be grand niece of Jesus) that all reality is based on the acceptance of God's perfection and if these angels sneak back in, God will have been proven fallible and all reality will cease. God does show up, stops the last angel from crossing over, and does handstands while the humans work out their issues.

The significance of *Dogma* is simply that it exists at all. Yes, it is outrageous and outrageously funny but that is way beside the point. The fact that the film came into being speaks volumes about where we are today as a humanity.

Organized religion (translation: the Catholic Church) has traditionally been considered one of the sacred cows in film. Don't touch it, don't discuss it, and certainly don't lampoon it. We can joke about death, race relations, and even the Holocaust. Mel Brooks' Broadway version of his earlier film *The Producers* won a record twelve 2001 Tony Awards (outdoing *Hello Dolly* by two awards) and its centerpiece sequence is "Springtime for Hitler"! If a Jew can make fun of the Holocaust, it's way past time that we can also have some fun with the Catholic Church, isn't it?

The fact that we have reached a point of openness on some of these questions is a sign that we are indeed questioning whom we are, wondering why we are here, and looking deeper into some of the answers to those questions that have heretofore been off limits.

This is not to say that we are rejecting religion. We are simply looking at it with new eyes. In fact, Bethany asks in the film what she is supposed to do about these new answers to old questions. Is she just supposed to forget who she was and all that she knew?

The answer and the message of the film is very simple: "Continue to be who you have always been. Just be this as well."

As God leaves at the end of the film, Bethany asks her why we are here—and God just smiles and tweaks her nose, winking as if to say that the asking of the question is the answer to it. Dogma, indeed.

Oh, God!

From one end of the "God" spectrum to the other.

George Burns playing God. Who else possibly could have played that part in this film? Actually, there may not have been another person in the world who could have played this part at that time other than George Burns because *Oh, God* is a textbook example of delivering a message in a comedic vehicle that just would not be digestible in a drama. If you're going to actually personify God in a film, it better be with humor and be played by someone who has such a deep well of good will as a personality with the audience that they will suspend their disbelief and enjoy the journey (unless you're going for the outrage of the casting itself, like Alanis Morrisette in *Dogma*). Try that in a drama and see how it works. (Actually Metafilmics is taking on that subject matter in a dramatic filmed version of Neale Donald Walsch's *Conversations with God* series of books. Our films, however, do not try to personify God in a separate being. The God in Neale's books is within all of us and personified by each of us.)

In *Oh God*, God appears to Jerry, a grocery clerk (John Denver) and then personifies himself so he can speak to him about the way humans are handling their lives. The film does have a plot about Jerry being convinced to be God's messenger and being doubted (by his wife, played by Teri Garr), his boss (David Ogden Stiers), and the world (including a skeptical talk-show host in Dinah Shore). Jerry is also confronted by religious leaders and actually sued for slander by one of them, an evangelist (played wonderfully by Paul Sorvino), whom Jerry confronts as a fraud.

The film winds up in a courtroom where God actually does appear and then vanishes into thin air. Jerry wins the libel suit but fails to "prove" God's existence.

This movie is not, however, about plot. It is about George Burns playing God and delivering messages about God's observations of humanity in his inimitable and gentle manner. Much of the dialogue reads like a new age manifesto in the seventies (the film was released in 1977). They might have called the film *Oh, God,* but this God doesn't talk like any traditional deity. He talks with humor and wisdom in a way that would be totally off-putting to most traditionalists if it weren't for the gentle manner in which Burns works and the simple clarity of the dialogue.

For the fun of it, I'm going to quote some of the dialogue here because *there are messages in this movie from twenty-five years ago that form the basis for some of the spiritual awareness of the current age.*

All the lines are from George Burns:

☆ "Even non-believers want what you have here to work. I set the world up so it can work."

☆ "Religion is easy. I'm talking about faith."

☆ "Men and women's existence means what you think it means. Nothing more, nothing less."

☆ "I'm God only for the big picture. I don't get into details. I gave you a world and everything in it. It's all up to you."

☆ "You have free will. All the choices are yours. You can love or kill each other."

☆ "Young people can't fall from my Grace. They're my best things."

☆ (For environmentalists) "You want a miracle? You make a fish from scratch. You can't. And when the last one's gone, eighty-six on the fishes, goodbye sky, so long world, over and out."

☆ "Sure, I make mistakes. Tobacco. Ostriches, silly looking things. Avocadoes, made the pit too big. But, hey, you try."

Just as he disappears from the courtroom, his last line is:

"If you find it hard to believe in me, know that I believe in you."

Defending Your Life

Another movie that would be very, very difficult to pull off as a drama.

Albert Brooks (whose real last name is Einstein, by the way) plays Daniel Miller, an ad executive who gets hit by a bus and wakes up in Judgment City, yet another afterlife way station where all humans go to examine their just-ended lives. Each person is assigned a defender, a prosecutor, and two judges who look into various days during each just-concluded life that are deemed pivotal. The decision is then made as to whether or not we "move on" (without defining to where) or go back to Earth and try it again in another incarnation. The number of days that are examined says something about how vigorously you might have to defend your life. Daniel has nine days to look at while Julia (Meryl Streep), a woman he meets and falls in love with, has only four.

Underlying all the funny sight gags and comic riffs, there is a very poignant message about fear.

There is a cliché about a coward dying a thousand deaths, a brave person only one. Facing our fears is not only the key as to whether we move on or not in the film, it also is the underlying message of the movie. We spend too much of our lives avoiding our fears, rather than unplugging their power over us by simply facing them. Defending Your Life *uses comedy to "coat" the message but it comes through very clearly: Winston Churchill was right when he said that "the only thing we have to fear is fear itself."*

Groundhog Day

Released in 1993, *Groundhog Day* is a wonderful human comedy about being given the rare opportunity to live several lifetimes all in the same day. Of course, that's not how the film was marketed but, for our purposes, I believe that concept is at the soul of the story.

Bill Murray plays cynical weatherman Phil Conner who gets sent to Punxatawney, Pennsylvania, for what has become his annual covering of Groundhog Day, an event he dreads and loathes. Phil is an equal opportunity punisher of all around him, most particularly Rita (Andie McDowell), the segment producer on the shoot. After the event, the crew is stranded by a snowstorm and forced to stay another day. Waking up the next morning (to the sounds of Sonny and Cher singing "I Got You Babe" on the radio), he discovers that it's Groundhog Day all over again. Everyone and everything is the same except for him. And it keeps happening. Day after day after day.

At first, he sees it as the perfect way to hone his seductive designs on Rita. Every day he learns more about her and then uses it the next day to try to impress her. For her, everything is new each day. Ultimately, he realizes that nothing is going to get her into bed in just one day. He gets depressed, so much so that he actually tries to commit suicide. Several times. Several ways. The problem is that he still wakes up the next morning at 6:00 A.M. to Sonny and Cher.

At first, he goes through, in precise order, the five stages of dealing with death: denial, anger, bargaining, depression, and acceptance. After a while, he decides that he should probably do something better in his life, and he actually starts to help people. By now, he knows absolutely everything that is going to happen in that town on that day so he can, for instance, always be under the right tree to catch a boy who falls out of it—or perform the Heimlich maneuver on a choking diner, etc.

Finally, he has really changed, and Rita does fall in love with him, for who he actually is on that particular day. That night, she does fall asleep with him and, when he awakes the next day, Groundhog Day is finally over and he can move on with Rita, a changed man.

The film is very funny in the beginning but, as it progresses, you see that there is more at work here than just a wonderful premise. It is obvious that this experience is happening over hundreds of days to Phil, maybe even thousands, and we see him evolve. Each day, he learns something new about himself and the world around him, and he uses it the next day.

In the beginning of his experience, Phil uses these new insights for ego-centered reasons *but he gradually begins to realize that he has a greater purpose for being alive and begins to utilize those insights to grow and interact more positively with the people around him.* Groundhog Day *thus provides a perfect metaphor for the lessons we seek from lifetime to lifetime. We learn and grow in each one as we evolve.*

If time has no meaning (and for Phil, it doesn't), then who is to say what one day signifies? In *Inherit the Wind,* Henry Drummond, the character based on Clarence Darrow, asks Matthew Brady, the character based on William Jennings Bryan, about the definition of a "day" in the Bible. Confirming that even the Bible did not determine how long "a day" is, Drummond presents a theory that, without the measures we have now for a day (the sun), that it could be of indeterminate length. "Could be 24 hours, could be a week, could be a month, could be a year, could be ten thousand years!"

Groundhog Day is a metaphor for that growth process and has become a common term now in modern life for a day that seems to go on forever. When a phrase from a movie takes on that kind of life ("Trust the force, Luke"), there is something going on in our hearts and minds that extends well outside the confines of a strip of film.

Bill and Ted's Excellent Adventure

Okay. I have to at least make reference to it at the end of this chapter because it is a very funny comedy, with which I was very involved, and I have been told by my friends that it belongs in this book.

While I'm not sure about the film itself, the story behind the film does pertain to how subjective and ephemeral the perception of what is or is not funny can be and to how relationships can be the crucial key to getting films made.

Bill and Ted was written by Richard Matheson's son Chris and his writing partner Ed Solomon. Richard called me one day in 1985 to ask me if I would talk to Chris, who was very depressed because his agents had rejected a script that he and Ed had written. When I spoke to Chris, he told me that they had written a script that he thought was very funny and original but his agents had rejected it out of hand. They told Chris and Ed that the script should never be shown to anyone because it would not only never sell but it was "so stupid and inane" that it might ruin their careers before they started them. I felt so bad for Chris that I offered to read the script and give them another opinion. Chris was completely against it because he was now embarrassed and didn't want to humiliate himself or Ed. After much cajoling, he finally agreed to let me read it.

That first draft of *Bill and Ted* is still the absolutely funniest script I have ever read in my life. I was howling all the way through it. Sure, it was stupid, but it was brilliant in its stupidity! Funny is funny, no matter what the guise, and that script was just hilarious. Chris was shocked but thoroughly pleased to hear that I loved it, and I told him that I had an idea about how to sell it.

I was about to leave my deal at Fox and take an executive position at a new company called New Century Productions with my old friend and mentor Norman Levy who was also leaving Fox. Put simply, Norman had been fired as executive vice chairman by a new regime and my producing deal was being terminated. I was about to take an executive position, so I knew I could not produce *Bill and Ted.* I needed to find a partner who would actually do the producing.

When I was working with Ray Stark, we made a film called *Casey's Shadow,* with Walter Matthau, that was a real marketing challenge. We went into a marketing meeting, and a young marketing executive named Robert Cort made a presentation to Ray that so enraged Ray that he literally threw poor Robert up against a wall! I had never met Robert, but I tried to defend him, and we became friends.

Five years later, I was at Fox about to start prepping *All the Right Moves,* and I did not like the production executive who had been assigned to the picture by Sherry Lansing, who was the first woman to head production at a major studio. (Since then, she has become one of the most successful executives in the industry and is still enjoying a long and successful run at Paramount.) I had known Sherry from our mutual Columbia days and I went to her to ask a favor. Robert Cort had also come over to Fox as a production executive but he as yet did not have any movies to supervise. I asked Sherry to put Bob on *All the Right Moves* instead of the guy she had originally assigned. After warning me that I was about to make a major enemy of the first guy, she agreed, and Bob took over. (While making the film, I got in all kinds of trouble, and Bob was a stalwart defender, so he definitely repaid me in spades.)

Back to 1985 now and *Bill and Ted.* Robert Cort was also leaving Fox. (Executive changes are like periodic purgings in our industry. A whole new team comes in and everyone who was there before gets thrown out and very unceremoniously so. Many an executive has come to the studio during one of these purges to find that their coveted parking spot has already been repainted with someone else's name. That is one of the more humbling indignities in our industry.) Bob was going off with Ted Field to Ted's new company Interscope and I knew they were looking for material. I gave Bob *Bill and Ted,* and he loved it as much as I did, as did Ted when he read it. So they committed to producing the film and I went off to be an executive, having agreed to be an executive producer on *Bill and Ted.*

I helped Bob, and he helped me. I helped Bob and Ted. Later, Ted would be the key player in *What Dreams May Come*, and so goes the relationship game in our town.

All the producing credit for the success of *Bill and Ted* belongs to Bob Cort, Ted Field, and Scott Kroopf, who actually produced the film. My only real involvement was saving the script from the scrap heap and getting it to the right people. And that's another way to get a "producer" credit and a fee in Hollywood.

Now as to the film itself, I was recently in a serious business meeting where someone brought up the "underlying societal significance" of *Bill and Ted.* Honestly, I had no idea what he was talking about. The "message" here is simple. Sometimes a cigar is just a cigar.

"We will not go quietly into the night."

—*Independence Day*

CHAPTER SEVEN

Aliens

Since the beginning of movies, our relationship with aliens has been a major source of movie storylines. Hundreds, if not thousands, of movies have been made about our love/hate relationship with aliens. The films either reflect our terror of aliens as threats to our very existence or as friends who can help us reach our full potential. Whatever their characterization, we obviously have a very deep and primal fascination with humanity's relationship with extraterrestrials.

Why? What deep spiritual significance do aliens represent to us?

Some of the fascination can certainly be explained in very simple terms. We have always looked up at the stars and wondered whether or not we were alone in the universe. Although, in our primitive past, we did not know exactly how many worlds there really are out in space, we in the modern era now know that there are millions of other worlds in the universe. How could anyone reasonably believe that we are the only consciousness in all that space? Think about that for a second. Isn't that just the height of earth-based human arrogance? This small planet—as significant in scale to the universe as a speck of sand is on any beach—as the only repository of human consciousness anywhere? Forget the scientific, mathematical certainty that there are other conscious beings in the universe. Just look at it from a standpoint of pure common sense. This one has always just amazed me. It seems to me such a foregone conclusion that the only arguments against it can be either the quasi-scientific ("prove it to me in a lab and I'll believe it or show me an alien body!") or religious ("it's not in the Bible!"—although even that can be argued). I have great respect for both science and religion but I do not personally believe that either philosophy (and I see them both as fitting in that category) can justify a fair conclusion that we are alone in the universe.

I do, however, accept and respect that others do not share this view and that those people actually believe that we are in fact alone. I also recognize that this arena potentially contains a very hot "religious button" as well. In *2001*, the discovery of the monolith on the moon had been classified as top secret because of the threat of destabilizing the population, particularly when religious beliefs are brought to bear. This theme runs not only through dozens of films but also through the constant public fascination with "Area 51" in Nevada (as shown in *Independence Day*, for example, as we will discuss shortly) and with all the famous UFO sightings throughout history. The entire Fox Television network was built on the foundation of the smashing success of *The X Files,* which is also based on the premise that our government knows and regularly interacts with aliens but thinks that such information would be too destabilizing for the general public.

In addition to this fascination with "contact," there is also the question in so many aspects of world cultures over whether or not aliens either "seeded" the Earth originally with humans or played a major role in our evolution by stepping in at some time in our distant past to do some "genetic engineering." Again, hundreds of books (such as *Chariots of the Gods*) have been written on these various theories. Briefly put, the theories hold that the Earth was visited in our distant past and literally seeded as an experiment. Other theories contend that the reason that scientists have never found the "human" missing link that accurately ties primitive man into modern man is that no such creature ever existed because aliens bio-engineered that genetic quantum leap.

Adherence to any of these theories is, of course, anathema to traditional religious beliefs so the movie convention that such information would be destabilizing is indeed based in some fact. Without taking sides here, the heated nature of the debate has, to me, always seemed somewhat unnecessary. If we did find irrefutable evidence that aliens are here—have been here—whatever, why couldn't organized religion simply acknowledge it and—with fair reasoning—just conclude that God created the aliens too and take the viewpoint of . . . "so, what else is new?" Or, as Billy Joel so succinctly put it: "She never gives in, she just changes her mind." Really, it seems to me that the potential existence of aliens does not in any way refute the existence of God, but I do admit that such a conflict creates great drama.

Whether one believes in aliens or not, movies have an extensive and intensive love affair with the subject matter. We seem to know they're out there, whether we question their motives or not. They fascinate us and compel us to regularly remind ourselves through movies that we are not alone. I believe that this sense of connection is one key ingredient in our spiritual fascination with aliens. In this increasingly challenging world in which we live, disaffection and fear are unfortunately constant companions to hundreds of millions of us.

The messages in films about aliens have a two-fold purpose and both messages are ultimately positive.

One message is clearly comforting and reassuring. If we see aliens as benevolent friends, we can experience them as fellow travelers from whom we have nothing to fear and much to learn.

The other message is that, even if we see aliens as threats to our very survival, such a viewpoint can be the catalyst to resolving our culture clashes in the face of an external enemy.

Either way, it is a "heads, we win—tails, we succeed" scenario.

If, then, this chapter were a multiple choice quiz, it would look something like this:

A. Aliens with unfriendly intent.
B. Aliens with friendly intent.
C. Both of the above.

There is no box for "none of the above." That omission is purely intentional.

So let's begin with:

A. Unfriendly Intent

Independence Day

Although we could look at any number of classic unfriendly alien films, *Independence Day,* released in 1995, embodies that energy as well or better than any other film because of the direct way it approaches its aliens' intent.

The aliens of *Independence Day* have no interest in negotiations or warnings. They send their massive ships into strategic places in the major countries of the world and then, with a coordinated signal, they start to wipe out every city and every human on the planet. When the president of the United States (played by Bill Pullman) actually confronts one of the aliens with the question "What do you expect us to do?" the answer is a very simple and chilling: "Die."

This represents our essential fear about unfriendly aliens. They simply want to annihilate us. Period. Over and Out.

Why would such a message exist?

These types of films provide a common enemy for the world to unite against and I believe that desire is the critical component of these films' appeal. People look at the world around them and often see it as frightening and on the brink of extinction. Nuclear war, terrorism, pollution, overpopulation, crime, etc., all serve to often present a truly threatening vision of the hopes for our survival; however, if the world could unite against a hostile invasion from aliens, then perhaps we can come together in unity. At least, that's how this particular theory plays itself out in films.

I truly believe that part of the appeal inherent in these kinds of "nasty alien" films is that they send a message that we need to find a way to come together as a species and, if it takes an alien invasion, so be it.

In *Independence Day*, for example, we see Arab and Israeli pilots bonding together in the desert to jointly attack the alien spaceships. That's a quintessential and powerful subliminal image: if Arabs and Israelis can unite, then surely anyone can. Sure, the action and effects of *Independence Day* are fantastic and fun just on that level, but films that become the kind of blockbuster that it did also have things going on below the waterline, so to speak, underneath the radar. Not to belabor the point (or stretch it beyond credulity), it should nevertheless be noted here that the two people selected to actually infiltrate and destroy the alien mother ship are an African-American (Will Smith) and a Jew (Jeff Goldblum). Accidents of casting? Perhaps, but equally possible is the fact that audiences responded on a deep cellular level to what they might perceive as the unlikely brotherhood of that duo.

Independence Day is also notable in its representation of the storied Area 51 in the Nevadan desert. Rumor has always held that the facility not only houses the remains of aliens killed in the Roswell incident but also is so top secret that not even presidents of the United States are informed of its existence (talk about stretching credulity: do we really believe that there are *any* secrets that tightly held in this day of instant and constant investigative reporting? Wouldn't Geraldo Rivera have already sneaked in?). *Independence Day* actually uses Area 51 as the staging area for the alien counterattack, the President is shocked at its existence, and the facility not only houses three alien bodies but an alien spaceship as well.

Independence Day plays every single note in the "unfriendly alien" opera and does so with considerable style, wit, and adventure. It also contains, however, a quintessential moment of illumination on why these kinds of films often stir our hearts.

Just as the final battle with the aliens is about to begin, the president addresses the pilots who are about to engage the aliens.

"We can't be consumed by our petty differences anymore. We will be united in our common interest. We will not go quietly into the night. We're going to live. We're going to survive."

This message is simple. We recognize our deep yearning to

come together as one humanity but some of us are still not sure how to do it without an external threat to our very survival. The hope in these films is that the existence of an external threat to our existence would then remind us of our similarities and focus us in on them, rather than our differences.

B. Friendly Aliens

For me, these aliens are more interesting.

Look, if aliens are actually bloodthirsty killers bent on our destruction, what's stopping them? I mean, really, if they have the technology to warp time and engage in interstellar travel, don't they kind of have to be able to destroy us rather handily if they so desire? So why haven't they eliminated us already?

What if they are simply observers here? Isn't that more interesting—for us and them?

If they're here just to observe us, what exactly makes us so fascinating to them? So fascinating that they've been around for thousands of years and seem to be particularly sensitive about not interfering in our progress (unless our own flirtation with self-destruction threatens them—the premise of the 1952 classic, *The Day the Earth Stood Still*).

Civilizations have destroyed themselves so many times that such an occurrence is certainly back page news in the universe by now. I would find it hard to believe that any self-respecting alien would traverse the galaxies just to watch yet another species go extinct. They could simply stay home and watch their own versions of old *Star Trek* reruns. Yet, they seem to be around us in ever greater numbers so their interest in us must derive from a far different curiosity.

I think that the answer lies in the extraordinary and perhaps even unparalleled evolution of consciousness that is occurring on our planet at this time. If we are indeed consciously committed to, and in the process of manifesting, a whole new paradigm of human achievement, it would certainly make us the "E-ticket" and hottest destination of the universe, wouldn't it?

E. T. and *Close Encounters of the Third Kind*

Taken together, these two films are, to me, the best reflection of our fondest hopes about the true positive intentions of aliens. It is no surprise that they were both directed by Steven Spielberg, who deserves to be acknowledged as the most commercial filmmaker in the history of cinema. That's a big statement, I know, but look at the record. Not only these two films but the *Raiders* series and *Jurassic Park* as well. Spielberg really understands the awe and innocence of hopes and dreams and these two landmark films exhibit his extraordinary ability to put that optimism on screen.

Spielberg's first foray into this arena came with the 1976 release of *Close Encounters of the Third Kind,* in which aliens begin planting visions in the minds of ordinary people, personified by Richard Dreyfuss, fresh off his success as Spielberg's everyman alter ego in *Jaws*. As a telephone lineman, Dreyfuss has a close encounter of the second kind when he experiences an alien craft. From that point forward, he is obsessed with the image of a mountain that he knows is important but can't identify. Even as his marriage begins to collapse around him, he feels compelled to leave home and travel to Devil's Mountain in Utah, which he recognizes on television as the mountain of his obsessions. Once there, he joins with other people who have been drawn there and is interviewed by the lead government scientist, played beautifully by legendary French director Francois Truffaut. Truffaut realizes that Dreyfuss and his fellow interlopers have been consciously and purposely drawn there by the aliens themselves; hence, his memorable line to the military types who want to prevent Dreyfuss from climbing the mountain: "These people are guests. They were *invited!*"

One of the most ingenious moments in thc film is entirely shot on the face of an adorable child who comes into a room in his house that is being visited by the aliens. We never see anything but the looks on the child's face as they progress from surprise to intrigue to amusement to sheer delight. No fear at all.

I can't think of a better way to transmit a message about "friendly" aliens than to see that they provoke absolute delight in a young child. If that's the case, one must wonder, what is there for any of us to possibly be afraid of?

The climax of the film sees the landing of the colossal alien mother ship and the realization that an agreement has been made with the aliens that several Americans are going to board the ship to go "home" with the aliens, and Dreyfuss gets to join them. As part of the deal, the aliens release a lot of other people who seem to have disappeared over the years (I personally was looking for people who resemble Amelia Earhart, Judge Crater, and Jimmy Hoffa), including the little child with whom we have become acquainted earlier in the film, and who actually seems sad to leave his alien playmates.

Perhaps the most memorable moment of the film is when the Truffaut character engages in a sign language greeting with the leader of the obviously benevolent aliens. Truffaut smiles at the alien and we see the alien try to be accommodating and smile back even though it is quite obvious that such an expression is not de rigeur for this particular breed of aliens. The resultant goofy smile is one of the most endearing images ever put on screen.

The whole message here is that these aliens have been around the Earth for a long time, benevolently studying us, and now they have reached the point of feeling secure enough to consciously interact with us. The whole mood of that message is both comforting and exhilarating.

Released in 1982, *E. T.* became the largest grossing film in the history of the movies (and retained that crown until it was surpassed by *Titanic*). Building on the themes of *Close Encounters,* Spielberg took all the frightening alien stories and stood them upside down.

What, the premise asks, would happen if an innocent young boy found an innocent young alien who gets lost and trapped here on Earth while his alien family is here on an observation trip? (In a way, *E. T.* is like an earlier alien version of *Home Alone,* except for here it is more like *Away Alone.*) The entire film is seen through the eyes of a young boy named Elliot and his E. T. friend. E. T. is just as afraid of Elliot as Elliot is of E. T. E. T. just wants to go home, and it is Elliot who needs to help him.

What a simple and beautiful message about the fallacy of the assumption that all aliens must be bad. To me, it is just as absurd to say that all humans are uni-dimensional as it is to assume that all aliens are as simply categorized. Doesn't it stand to reason that there is just as much diversity in alien cultures as there is in human societies? Look at it this way. If an alien ship landed in the middle of a barbaric cannibal tribe (or some place even more horrifying, like Hollywood), couldn't they rightfully look upon all humans as vicious creatures, if that was their only experience of us? It certainly would not be appropriate for all humans to be generalized in that fashion, and I'm sure that the same applies to alien cultures. (Kind of like the differences between the Vulcans and the Klingons in *Star Trek,* right?)

The end of *E. T.* takes the emotion of the finale of *Close Encounters* and personalizes it. (If your eyes didn't at least well up with tears, you're a tougher audience than I. Then again, my kids have a running joke in our family that I'm so emotional that I cry at card tricks.)

Anyway, Elliot and E. T. have to say goodbye and it saddens them both. They have become friends and have shared a great adventure together and now they have to part. *The message here is clear and comforting: aliens exist and at least some of them are different from us only in form, not in substance. As such, they are not to be feared. In fact, they can become trusted friends.*

Starman

The theme of benevolent lost aliens was given an adult face in *Starman*, released in 1984 (*that* year again).

In *Starman*, Jeff Bridges plays an alien who is stranded on Earth and, through DNA cloning of a single hair, takes on the persona of the deceased husband of a lonely young widow played by Karen Allen (three years after her role in the first *Raiders* film). At first terrified, she begins to realize that the alien wants nothing more than to go home and, as he is literally a replica of her deceased husband, it is not hard for her to fall in love with him.

Throughout their adventure together, we see the alien's kindness, both to her and to a deer that the alien actually resurrects after it has been slaughtered by a hunter. The coup de grace is that, as the alien leaves, he gently informs her that, in making love to her, he has placed her husband's DNA within her and that she is pregnant with the child she never had before.

Again, *the message here is that we can indeed trust that at least some aliens have the same moral structure as we do. If we help them, they can help us.*

Contact

Released in 1997, *Contact* also has a very optimistic attitude regarding aliens.

These aliens not only make contact but they also send along a design for a space/time travel device that we then build to specifications. Ellie Arroway (Jodie Foster) is a space nut because her Dad was. She also blames herself for her father's death because she believes that she could have gotten him his medication when he collapsed if she had been quick enough. Although she was only a child at the time, she has carried that blame with her along with her doubting attitude about the existence of God. She feels certain that aliens are real and "out there" . . . but not God.

Though she is not originally chosen to be the one who gets to try out the machine when it is ready, she defaults into the opportunity when her original mentor/tormentor (Tom Skerrit) is killed as the originally designed device is destroyed by a terrorist. A wealthy eccentric (John Hurt) has built a duplicate machine in Japan with the understanding that he gets to go into space to arrest the growth of his cancer (Dennis Tito must have seen this film). This time, Ellie gets to go.

When she actually "arrives" (after going through a sequence very reminiscent of the light show in *2001*), she finds herself speaking to someone who appears to be her dead father on a very strange "beach" on a distant star named Vega. Ever the scientist, Ellie knows it is not really her father, a fact that the alien admits, gently saying "we thought it would be easier this way."

The meeting is actually very brief because these aliens know that contact must happen "in small steps." Their only desire was indeed to make contact because *"the only thing we have found that makes the emptiness bearable is one another."*

For that one message alone, the film is important. On one level, the film certainly illustrates the power of Ellie's belief and commitment, but the first major message in Contact *seems to be the word itself—not only as it pertains to contacting aliens as in communications but also as in our commitment to keeping contact with each other.*

There is another powerful message that emerges from *Contact.* Ellie begins the movie believing in aliens, although she cannot prove their existence and, paradoxically, does not believe in God because she can't prove that God exists. After her encounter on Vega, she is put in the position of having to prove that her experience actually occurred and, scientifically, she does not have the requisite "proof" to convince a skeptical world.

The lesson she learns in the film comprises its other powerful message: if you only believe what you can "scientifically" prove, you'll never believe in God.

Cocoon

Released in 1985, *Cocoon* centers on the discovery of an alien "nesting site" in a Florida pool by a group of senior citizens. When they actually come in contact with the water where the pods are being incubated, the effect is like diving into the fountain of youth.

(I mean, really, doesn't it make sense for that ancient "fountain" to be discovered in the same state where it was originally supposedly sought by Ponce de Leon? Talk about a visionary. If anyone had paid close enough attention to the real significance of Senor de Leon's placement of the site in Florida, one could have become the Donald Trump of retirement homes and communities. Florida. Isn't that just perfect?)

This film deserves particular note for the more than kind intent of its aliens. In fact, it probably deserves a special place in alien lore. In one of the most memorable scenes in the film, an alien takes the shape of a beautiful young female human (Tawnee Welch, Raquel's daughter). Swimming in the pool with Steve Guttenberg, she is kind enough to cause him to experience what an alien orgasm is like. Now, *that* is friendly intent.

To see great old actors like Wilford Brimley, Hume Cronyn, and Don Ameche literally strutting home to share their newly-rediscovered "manhood" with their shocked and delighted wives is reason enough to not only see the movie but for the movie to have been created in the first place.

The whole message of this movie could easily have been projected out of the wish fulfillment of just the senior citizens in Florida. Simply put, the message seems to be that *we're never too old in years to be both young at heart and in spirit.*

C. All of The Above

Forbidden Planet

Okay. Right up front. This is one of my favorite five films of all time. It touches on so many different themes that I've included it here at the end of the Aliens' chapter because it seems to reflect not only the whole spectrum of our connection with other worlds but also fascinating insights into our attitudes about violence, both in the world and within ourselves. In my opinion, *Forbidden Planet* was way, way ahead of its time (1955) in the complexity of the themes it explored.

The basic story is standard sci-fi. A rescue mission lands on Planet Altair 4, where a scientific team disappeared years before to find that only one man, named Morbius (Walter Pidgeon), and his daughter, Altaira (Anne Francis), have survived.

It's what else they discover that makes *Forbidden Planet* such a seminal film.

Professor Morbius has built a robot named Robby to do the physical chores necessary on the planet. Robby the Robot was a physical marvel. He could do anything—lift impossible weights, manufacture liquor (to the delight of the rescue team), and actually sense danger when it approached. Robby could not combat danger, however, because Morbius had programmed Robby to actually short circuit and shut down rather than engage in any violent act. In essence, Robby had been programmed with a hypersensitive human conscience that could not perpetrate an act of violence.

Full disclosure requires me to acknowledge here a very personal connection that I have to this film that extends beyond my adult fascination with it. When I was eight years old, one of my best friends was the son of the man (Nicholas Nayfack) who produced *Forbidden Planet* so Nicky Jr. and I actually got to visit the set of the film in 1954 (when it was shot) and interact with Robby the Robot. Robby became a huge action toy as a result of the film and I was just dazzled to be around him. (The best analogy in recent years for an eight-year-old boy would, I think, to be welcomed to a Pokemon factory or a taping of Mighty Morphin Power Rangers.) Robby was the very definition of 1950s "cool" and I never forgot the experience. Obviously, it wasn't until many years later that I began to make a very different kind of connection to the film.

The underlying reason for Morbius' abhorrence of violence lies within the film's most fascinating theme—the Krell, a highly advanced alien civilization that had lived on the planet and disappeared long before humans set foot there. Morbius had uncovered their laboratory and many of their advanced devices without actually being able to understand the purpose of many of them; however, he did find that they had tapped into the actual power of the mind. Unfortunately, that had become their undoing, in that they unleashed forces within themselves and on their planet that ultimately destroyed them and "this all-but-divine race disappeared in a single night." (Echoes of Atlantis?)

Some members of the crew are attacked and killed by an invisible and vicious killer. Ultimately, we find that the killer is actually "a monster from the id;" that is, a creation of the subconscious mind of the professor who has sublimated his own violent tendencies so completely that they can only be expressed by the actions of this invisible murderer, which he creates.

The climax of the film revolves around the creature from his own subconscious coming to attack him and his daughter. He has denied his own rage to the extent that it has now taken form—and independence—and comes after him and his daughter. Desperate—and still in denial—he turns to Robby and commands him to kill this creature but, as Robby is not programmed for violence in any way, he just shuts down. Morbius was so afraid of his dark side that he created a literal physical monster from his subconscious that would do the violence in the world that he didn't have the will to execute in his conscious state. That is some kind of advanced spiritual content for a 1955 sci-fi movie. Ultimately, the professor himself realizes what's happened, and it is only his death that actually stops the creature.

Robby is a metaphor for our increasing distaste for the notion of resolving conflicts by violent means. The film stands as a reminder to us that we have committed ourselves to acknowledging and then transcending that tendency.

Final Fantasy—The Spirits Within

Released in the summer of 2001, this is the first film in which all the human characters were digitally created. The astounding technological and human consequences of this breakthrough are so extraordinary that I believe this film will ultimately have as profound an impact as *The Jazz Singer,* the first film to utilize sound; furthermore; the story itself is a deeply spiritual odyssey.

The digital creation of human beings on film presents a powerful stimulus to our misgivings about technology and actually mirrors the current sociological debate about human cloning; that is, *should* we be doing something simply because we are ABLE to do so? As to the film world, the answer is a resounding yes! Digital human beings are not going to replace actors any more than animation could ever replace live action films. There are certain worlds that can best be rendered in animation and there are audiences (families) for whom animation works extremely well. Movies that feature digital actors will provide opportunities for imaginative storytellers to create certain films that might not be otherwise feasible, both financially and visually. For example, portraying the lost civilization of Atlantis in a realistic manner would involve the creation of an entire world on film that might have no significant relationship to any location that could actually be filmed in live action. Digital technology could make such a film feasible and breathtaking to behold.

Films that are focused on characters in more relatable and familiar surroundings have no need of utilizing digital actors and would not be accepted by audiences if they did. We still, and always will, want films in which we can relate to the actual human being we are watching on screen. Again, there is no reason to fear these new inventions. We do not need to make a choice between human and digital actors. We can have both.

The digital actors in *Final Fantasy* are not yet realistic enough for us to lose sight of their digital nature; however, the technology is breathtaking in its bold originality and we must remember that this was the first such attempt. Just look at the advancement in standard visual effects over the last thirty years and you can get a sense of where this technology is heading. It will raise some interesting questions in the future, such as being able to digitally create a younger version of certain actors. In fact, there is a project currently in development in Hollywood that is considering just that. The idea is to use film clips from earlier Mel Gibson films and utilize digital technology to create a young version of Mel chasing the current version of Mel. To use one of my daughter Heather's expressions—that is way cool.

As to the story of *Final Fantasy*, I want to address the stunning spiritual message at the end of the film. On its surface, the film is a faithful adaptation of an extremely popular video game; however, as its subtitle *The Spirits Within* indicates, the story itself is a dazzling spiritual quest.

The film takes place on Earth in the year 2065 after a huge meteor has struck the Earth and unleashed millions of alien creatures that ultimately take over the planet. Sounds as if it belongs in the "Unfriendly Aliens" section of this chapter, doesn't it? Sure, it could, but there's a much bigger agenda here.

The heroine is Dr. Aki Ross, who has been infected by the aliens but has had a protective shield implanted in her chest so that she can survive while she searches for the solution to the puzzle of the aliens' powers. These aliens actually seem to absorb the etheric bodies of their human targets. Aki is convinced that the answer to the life or death challenge facing humanity is to *channel and collect the eight spirit waves of the Earth (these are the "spirits within" of the title), so as to save Gaia, the soul of the planet!*

Through her dreams, Aki realizes that the alien creatures are from a planet that was so violent in nature that it literally exploded, sending the meteor to earth. The aliens themselves were killed in the destruction of their planet and the creatures on Earth are actually the ghosts of those who were killed in the fiery end to the alien civilization. They are not marauding invaders but are rather lost souls who are seeking respite from their torments. Aki comes to realize that they have brought the Gaia of their planet to Earth and that a communion with the Earth Gaia will provide a peaceful resolution to both humans and aliens. At the climax of the film, the souls of the two cultures are indeed commingled and peace comes to all concerned.

Just the recognition that the Earth has its own spirit is a quantum leap for movies. Add to that the concept that alien cultures and planets also have their own spirits and you have a connection between the souls of the two species. The resolution of combining the Gaia of human and alien races to create peace and safety in the universe is a simple and unifying message of hope, no matter which perspective one might have about aliens.

"If you know my IQ is so high, why would you even ask if I understand how amazing that is?"

–Powder

CHAPTER EIGHT

Enhanced Powers and Sensibilities

It has been said that most humans only utilize about three to five per cent of our brain capacity. Supposedly, Einstein utilized six to eight per cent, although how that actually got estimated is a bit murky to me. Anyway, we are always fascinated with people who seem to have senses that are enhanced beyond those of most of us, be it ESP, psychic abilities, etc. (Superhuman powers have always been a fascination, as in *Superman* and other sci/fi titles, but they are outside the scope of this book.)

As mentioned earlier in our discussion of the dark shadow of our nature, there is a light side to the shadow as well.

This light shadow holds both our most precious dreams and the most beautiful aspects of our real self. Our talents, our love, our abilities to inspire, encourage, and heal ourselves and others—all are held within the light shadow part of our being. What makes the light shadow even more interesting is that it appears to frighten us much more than the dark shadow. Most of us are willing enough (sometimes too willing) to look inside to see our darkness, even if we don't admit it to others; however, how reticent we are to look at our beauty and strength. Really look at it. Not through our ego eyes, but through the eyes of our soul. Our whole experience as humans seems to have weighed us down with a penchant for the negative. The hunter-gatherer-survival impulses that powered us through our primitive stages still survive today. These are well-honed habits that have far outlived their usefulness, but they persist within us and are expressed in the world as our obsession with struggle and overcoming obstacles.

A good analogy for this process can be found in the persistent nature of the childhood defenses we create to cope with trauma. As children, we build those defenses so that we can actually survive. When we reach adulthood, we no longer have the need for those defenses but that doesn't mean that they automatically disappear. To the contrary, they often stubbornly persist and cause serious problems in our adulthood.

Even language itself seems weighted to the negative. Think back to the last time you had a really awful day where everything went wrong. You talk to your wife/husband/friend about it, and the two of you can go on for hours, dissecting your childhood, your relationships, your karma, whatever. Millions of words. Fine. Now think back to a day where everything just went perfectly and you go to share that day with someone. Once you get out a few words, most of which are synonyms for "wonderful," that's it. Your friend says, "That's great. Wonderful. I'm happy for you." And then you kind of stare at each other, right? We don't seem to want to process our great moments with the same enthusiasm that we devote to our sad or aggravating ones.

How often have we in Western society glorified struggle? Just as another simple example, how many times have we said and been told by others "how hard we're working"? That mantra seems to have become a badge of honor in life, hasn't it? How do we view someone who says, "Oh no, I don't struggle at all anymore. Whatever I want, I create through my willingness, and it just happens." Huh? What did he say? Is transcendence really "worth it," if it comes with ease and grace rather than turmoil and struggle?

The light shadow beckons us to that grace within us. How odd that such ease is so threatening.

Part of the promise of this "new age" is that we are beginning to embrace the light shadow component of our psyche and are thus daring to become the extraordinary beings that we know we were born to be.

This chapter is going to look at the manner in which movies portray the way in which humans respond when their ordinary senses are enhanced to the point of making them extraordinary.

Phenomenon

This movie is, for me, both a fascinating reflection of our own fears of tapping into our innate powers and also a cautionary tale of how Hollywood too often winks at these kinds of films without really believing in them.

The premise of the film is that George Malley (John Travolta) encounters a mysterious light and immediately becomes both psychic and possessed of telekinetic abilities (being able to move objects with the power of his mind). Before he is so changed, he is an amiable, well-liked, small town mechanic. Once he changes, the town gets very suspicious and increasingly hostile towards him.

So far, no problem. The fear of people being different is deeply engrained in much of consensus society. Conformity is expected and rewarded. When an individual dares to stand out, he/she is often ridiculed and ostracized. I think this is a fear that lies deep within the hearts of a lot of people. I know so many people who have deep feelings of spirituality and even more extraordinary experiences with profound powers within themselves that have materialized in amazing ways. So many, however, are afraid to "come out of the closet," so to speak, for fear of being laughed at and branded crazy or delusional. I know *this* one very well myself. I lost several friends and acquaintances that I had before I became an outspoken member of the spiritual community.

One of the great services that have been performed by the courageous authors in the field of visionary books and novels is that they have helped these kinds of experiences become more mainstream occurrences. When Larry King devotes whole hours to this kind of subject matter, you know a shift has occurred.

Those of us who are on this conscious path owe a deep debt of gratitude to those who have blazed the path and, in the film industry, the key person who deserves a special place in our hearts is Shirley MacLaine. When she wrote *Out on a Limb* in 1983 and went on talk shows to bravely state who she is and what she believes in, she was absolutely crucified in mainstream media. Undaunted, she stayed the course and really opened the way for all of us who have followed her lead, and, for that, she deserves a very special heroic status. Thank you, Ms. MacLaine for your courage and dignity.

Our perception is often that stepping out there into the light and stating the truth of our perceptions can be very hazardous so you need to be committed to staying the course if you do. That's one of the messages in *Phenomenon* and a very timely and powerful one.

It's the other message with which I have some real trouble.

George contracts a brain tumor and ultimately dies. For me, that's where we blow the whistle and throw the flag.

Come on! Great message here, right? Sure, we say to each other, you can become enlightened and tap into your powers. Just be prepared to be ostracized and then, just for good measure, be prepared to get sick and die!

There's a powerfully empowering message. Not. This one really got to me. How can filmmakers do this to us, if they actually believe in what they're doing? Could anyone with a belief in the real powers of our minds and hearts and souls really consciously want to deliver such a dreadful message, or was all of this just another Magellan ship for those involved? I don't know. I do know that we have been greatly criticized for the idealistic endings of both *What Dreams May Come* and *Somewhere in Time,* and I couldn't care less. When you make a film that shows people the potential depth of how beautiful we *can* be, I think we have a responsibility to embrace that potential. I have often been told that I am very corny and sentimental in this manner. My usual response is to say thanks for the compliment.

The writer of *Phenomenon*, Gerald diPego, is a wonderful writer and I want to acknowledge that and him; however, I know that there was such a better and more appropriate ending to *Phenomenon.* In fact, a talented writer friend of mine named Nick Thiel came up with it within ten minutes of leaving the theater. (I also know that Nick and Gerald play poker together—don't fight, guys!) Anyway, the idea is this: let George recover. He comes back to town, and he has lost his powers so the townspeople welcome him back. He's the same, good ol' George again. We see in the last scene that he has married Lace (Kyra Sedgwick) and is sitting at the breakfast table with her and her two boys. Everyone else is arguing over something, and they ignore him when he asks for the syrup to be passed to him. We see that the syrup container is one of those old-fashioned ones with a metal top that you pull back with your thumb. (Some of you other "first-tier" baby boomers will remember those.) Anyway, he just smiles as he opens his hand and the container slides across the table into his palm. End movie. So, we see that George has not lost his powers at all. He has just realized that people aren't quite ready to deal with them yet, so he's going to bide his time until a more appropriate moment occurs.

Wouldn't you have felt a whole lot better about this when you left the theater? That's a much more optimistic spiritual approach. I really believe that those of us making these films need to be conscious of the effects they have on people who are seekers in this world.

(Another recent case in point: *Pay It Forward.* This one got to me, too. They put Haley Joel Osment in this at a time when he is a real hero to kids everywhere as a result of *Sixth Sense.* Here, he plays a kid who gets involved with a plan that rages quickly around the world based on doing nice things for other people, if someone does something nice for you. Great idea, right? Terrific message—except he dies at the end of the film as a result of trying to be nice. Wonderful message for kids there: sure, be good to everyone, but be prepared to die!)

It is not the aspect of death that is the problem here. Obviously, I have a viewpoint on death (chapter 5) that does not hold it in such fear. My problem here is that death is used as a punishment for becoming too evolved.

How could it have turned out this way?

The writer may indeed have been ordered into this by the

director or the studio, that was, in this case, Disney. It's also intriguingly possible that the filmmakers chose to do this because they are reflecting a fear of martyrdom that is still so deeply engrained in our collective consciousness that it needed to be personified here.

As humans, we have a long history of martyrdom. Suffering and dying for the cause, right? We have exalted that act of sacrifice throughout human history. It is a very treacherous terrain to approach, because we also have a long list of real heroes who have been willing to give their lives for a just cause, and I have no desire or intention to try to sully memories of them. I do believe, however, that we have suffered enough for our causes. Died enough for them. For a long time, that type of commitment may not only have been honorable but also necessary; however, times change and people evolve. We're now at the dew line of a new reality where we prosper and live the dreams rather than die for them. As we have mentioned before, we have thousands of years of sense memories of times when we did die for our beliefs, sometimes in fact because of them.

It seems to me that this new Age of Aquarius into which we have just entered is about new ways. This is the time of creative feminine energy that thrives on the resonance of empowerment. The old Age of Pisces was about male, impact-driven energy. We fought wars. Killed people. Died. Often. We're now on a new plateau.

We are remembering powers we had forgotten about:

In *The Sixth Sense,* Cole is terrified of his abilities to see the dead, and he winds up isolated and alone until he is ultimately encouraged to accept his gift and use it for people's good. The scene in the car with his mother where he helps her overcome her grief at her own mother's death is beautiful and a powerful reflection of what we can accomplish when we come to peace with these awakening senses.

In *Stir of Echoes*, Kevin Bacon is dragged kicking and screaming into his new awareness, but winds up solving the murder of a young child.

In *Resurrection*, Ellen Burstyn becomes aware of the fact that she is a healer, but is so vilified and doubted that she escapes to a small gas station in the middle of nowhere, where she still works her healings in a very quiet and private manner.

Are we still afraid of coming into that new power? If so, that may indeed be the message we sent to ourselves through *Phenomenon.* As more and more of us step into the public arena with our beliefs, are we still afraid that we will martyr ourselves because that is the only energy we remember?

This is a good place for us to make mention of actors and actresses in addition to Shirley MacLaine who have faced those fears and the potential scrutiny that comes with the public acknowledgement of their interest in spiritual subject matter.

Stars and star directors have a great deal of power in Hollywood and can be the major, if not sole, determinant in whether a film gets made or not. When stars or directors believe in certain issues, their participation in a film can make the difference in whether or not the film gets made.

Hollywood history is rich in this tradition with stars and directors. All one need do is look at the collected works of such giants as Frank Capra and Stanley Kramer, for example, as directors who courageously pursued their interests in socially significant subject matter in their films.

In the 1970s, Jane Fonda's participation got both *Coming Home* and *The China Syndrome* before the cameras. One can think what he wants of Fonda's politics but no one can challenge her courage in putting her films where her heart is.

Recently, some stars have put their considerable power behind films in the subject matter of this book and willed those films into existence. John Travolta is at the absolute head of that class. *Phenomenon*, *Michael*, and *Battlefield Earth* do not get made without Travolta. Whatever we might think of those films, Travolta showed the courage of his convictions in getting them made.

Meg Ryan got behind *City of Angels* and (with Tom Hanks) *Sleepless in Seattle.*

As stars and directors are emboldened by the public acceptance of these ideas, more and more films in this genre will see the light of day.

Powder

Powder is another movie in this genre released by Disney in 1995 that actually did possess the courage of its convictions.

Powder has an awful lot on its mind about being different and suffering the ostracizing that goes along with it. Just as in *Phenomenon*, the main character here is rejected and made an outcast because of his ability to tap into certain powers that frighten people.

The film stars Sean Patrick Flannery as an albino young man who is abandoned by his father after his mother dies during childbirth (having been struck by lightning). He is brought up in the basement of his grandparents' home and never sees the sun; hence, the name Powder.

After his grandparents die, he is discovered and brought to a boys' home where he becomes the target of terrible derision and bullying for being so different.

Watching the film in 2002, the feeling one gets in those scenes is much more eerie than when the film was released seven years ago. Since 1995, a lot of innocent kids and adults have died at the hands of kids who felt they had no choice other than to retaliate for the bullying they received. (That is not to excuse it, only to explain it. Watching *Powder*, one can actually feel the shame that the victims of bullying and taunting feel. It is unsettling and powerful. It's a powerful message come too late for some and right on time for many more. It would be great to have this film shown in Life Skill classes in high schools. I think it could actually save lives.)

Powder is befriended by two sympathetic adults (Mary Steenburgen and Jeff Goldblum) who make an attempt to reach out to him. Goldblum plays a teacher who comes to understand that Powder is almost pure energy. His IQ tests are off the charts and he exhibits powers and abilities way beyond what we experience as normal. (In one of the most powerful scenes in the movie, he is outraged when he sees a deputy sheriff shoot a deer. He touches the deer and grabs the deputy's wrist and literally transfers the deer's pain and terror into the deputy.)

Goldblum explains to Powder (and us) that Einstein theorized that if we used the full capacity of our brains, we would become pure energy and not need physical bodies anymore. It is obvious that Powder is a harbinger of what we may become and that fact frightens people around him.

When he actually helps the sheriff communicate with his comatose wife, Powder tells him that she "didn't go away, just out," when she died; that is, that she became a form of energy. That comment presages Powder's own destiny. Unable to find peace anywhere and seen by most as a freak to be feared and shunned, he eventually runs literally into a lightning storm and becomes pure energy.

When I first saw this movie, I thought that the ending was a copout. They didn't know what to do with him, so they got rid of him, as in *Phenomenon*. Watching it again from the perspective of this book, I have changed my mind. George did not want to die in *Phenomenon*. Here, Powder decides for himself, and he doesn't actually die. He voluntarily changes form. He just came to the conclusion that he had no choice. The people around him could not deal with who he was. It reminds me of "Vincent (Starry, Starry Night)," the Don McLean song of many years ago whose refrain was "the world was never made for one as beautiful as you."(A line that Goldblum actually speaks to Powder in the film.)

I would amend that slightly to say that I think the message of the film is that we're not quite ready for that beauty, but we're getting awfully close.

When we embrace our differences rather than kill or go to war over them, we'll take that next step.

Powder was also surrounded by an awkward controversy. Just as the film was about to be released, it was revealed that its writer/director Victor Salva had been a convicted child molester. On a Disney film. You can imagine how that went over in the Magic Kingdom. The film's marketing suffered and the whole patina of the film had an awkward edge. Talk about expectations determining result. There are a few very tastefully handled scenes of potential homosexual attraction in the film. Without the controversy, no one would have noticed, and if they did, they would have to say that the scenes are handled quite beautifully. Knowing what we as an audience knew put those scenes in a different framework for many people.

So both Powder and Mr. Salva were pretty much banished from their respective societies. Without even commenting on the propriety of that response, it must be said that Mr. Salva did a beautiful job on this film, and it is a film to be treasured by those of us who look for beauty and spiritual messages in films.

The lasting message of both *Phenomenon* and *Powder* is that any and all of us can tap into the source of our extraordinary human powers.

The Shadow

The concept of this book actually first occurred to me on July 1, 1994 when this film opened less than three weeks after O. J. Simpson allegedly murdered his wife Nicole and a young waiter named Ron Goldman.

I knew O. J. Not well, but I knew him. I was a student at UCLA in the sixties when O. J. was becoming a legend at USC. Both O. J. and my friend Michael Dellar were marketing majors. I used to hang out with Michael around the campus so I met O. J. He was truly dazzling to be around. So charismatic, so charming, so attractive, so funny, and so unbelievably talented. Even though he was a hated rival, you just had to love and admire him.

O. J. went on to become one of the greatest running backs in the history of professional football and just about invented the modern concept of athletic charisma. He was unquestionably one of the most beloved people in all of American culture.

Then came the night he allegedly murdered his wife and young Mr. Goldman. Yes, in my reality, he murdered those people. As a metaphysician, I know we all create our own realities, so I readily acknowledge that there are realities in which O. J. did not commit those crimes. That's a wicked paradox for a lot of people, I know, but I believe it and respect it.

By the night of the murders, I had gone through a total spiritual awakening and transformation so I was looking at life through very different lenses. When O. J. was actually arrested, I sensed right away that this was a watershed event in our society, but I didn't immediately know why. Here was this charismatic, beloved figure who obviously had a dark side so full of rage that it erupted in a double murder. What a staggering contradiction for a consensus reality that has a hard time reconciling paradox. People are heroes *or* villains, right? Certainly not both. Black hat/white hat. Simple. What happens when that image is blown away in such a public spectacle? Can someone who is so talented and likable also be a cold-blooded murderer and, if so, what does that mean to all of us?

As I pondered that question, *The Shadow* opened.

Alec Baldwin stars as Lamont Cranston, the famous "Shadow" of radio serial days. As a kid, I remembered being spooked by the eerie motto of the character: "Who knows what evil lurks in the hearts of men? The Shadow does!" And then came this evil, scary, demented laughter. The main character that Baldwin plays in the film is a split personality. One persona is totally dedicated to truth, integrity, and justice, while the other persona is violent, ruthless, and capable of anything. The character's background is the cause of this duality. Originally, he was a bloodthirsty, murdering tyrant who gets turned to the light by a religious figure who knows that darkness can be transformed into a power for justice.

I was just thunderstruck by the "coincidence" and then thrilled by the awareness that the opening of *The Shadow* just nineteen days after the Simpson murders was no accident.

Developing, financing, producing, marketing, and distributing a movie takes a minimum of eighteen months, and often much longer. *The Shadow* had been "in the works" for a couple of years, and it had been set for release on July 1, long before the Simpson murders. It was not bumped and pushed into distribution to take advantage of the similarities with "real life." If one had in fact even suggested that to the marketing people involved in the film, they probably would have told you that you were crazy in seeing any connection.

As to the movie itself, it seems apparent that some aspect

of our denied self was being powerfully personified by O. J., so much so that we would create a powerful and unmistakable message for ourselves.

For me, this message is as simple as the powerful and horrifying message that we received less than a year later with the Oklahoma City tragedy: the enemy is within.

The shock of O. J. was that he seemed to be so contradictory. As reflected also in the Lamont Cranston character, he could be charming and warm and charismatic and then become cruel and violent. This message is about ourselves and that's why I connect it to Oklahoma City because it's a perfect metaphor. We always thought that terrorism represented an external threat. Sadly, we found out that the real danger was the terrorist in and from the heartland; that is, the terrorist within.

Put another way, our greatest challenge is to look within ourselves for the troubles and violence that we see in the world because those dangers are reflections only of our own denied selves. Once we accept our entire being, those dangers disappear because we no longer have to project them into the world to stimulate our own awareness of them. All this is a textbook distillation of shadow theory. Once we accept that we personify all these aspects of self, we can then look at the "really scary" stuff: our beauty and power. As mentioned previously, it seems that our integrated selves present much more of a challenge to our consciousness than our disintegrated selves. We seem more comfortable looking at our faults than our strengths; however, I believe that we are rapidly moving in the direction of the resolution of our fears. We are seeking solutions, hope, and empowerment, and that is why there is so much interest in spiritual growth and products that reflect the yearning for such transformative information.

Simply stated, the message here is that we need to look within ourselves and accept the totality of who we are. Once we do that, we eliminate the need to project our disintegrated selves into the world and we can begin to focus on the even more deeply denied beauty and power of our unique humanity. When we can harness and direct that power, nothing can defeat or even harm us.

Altered States

Released in 1980, I think this is one of the most underrated movies in the entire genre and is also one that has constantly inspired me throughout the years since its release.

Dr. Edward Jessup (William Hurt in the role that launched his career) has no problem staying true to his convictions. In fact, even he considers himself an "unmitigated madman." Doing research in an isolation tank, he begins to have visions of his father's death and to experience other unexplained phenomena. He also meets a fellow researcher, Emily (Blair Brown in the role that also launched her career), who falls totally in love with him and convinces him that they should get married. In that memorable scene, she says to him:

"You're a Faust freak, Eddie. You'd literally sell your soul to discover some great truth but there are no great truths, Eddie. We're born in doubt and live our lives in doubt. One of the ways we get through that is by loving each other. Like I love you."

The irresistible force of the seeker meets the immovable object of the lover. About as archetypical a love story as you can create.

Unfortunately, Eddie can't deal with the marriage. They agree to separate, and he decides to go to Mexico to find an Indian tribe that purportedly uses a sacred mushroom that propels the users into an experience with their immortal souls. Eddie's fix on this:

"There is a pathway to our real selves, our true selves, our original selves. It is a real, commensurate, quantifiable thing, and I'm going to find the fucker!"

At any cost, right? Faustian yes, but also the reflection of a man who is so committed to finding the true meaning of life and his place in it that he will brave anything to find the answer. He knows the dangers and plunges ahead despite them. It has been said that courage is not rushing forward into battle without thinking of your own safety when you see a friend injured. Real courage is being terrified that you will be hurt or even killed and still rushing to help your friend. Again, that same refrain: face your fears, run not away, but towards them, so that you can embrace the fear and thus end its power over you.

Eddie goes to Mexico, tries the mushroom, and descends into a terrifying journey within his experience of his original soul.

Bringing the mixture back to Boston, he takes it and enters an isolation tank where he actually experiences his original self as he kills and eats a goat in primitive times (with no Kubrickian monolith in sight). When he is brought out of the tank, he can't speak, and has blood all over his face. X-rays reveal that he has a laryngeal sac in his throat, which is "strictly simian," as he relates to his friend, a very frightened and suspicious traditional doctor who shrugs off the experience as a seizure. When Eddie persists after "reconstituting" back into his human body, his doctor refuses to believe that he could "de-differentiate his entire genetic structure." Pretty heady dialogue for a mainstream film.

Unfortunately, the film veers off pretty wildly here into a long section when Eddie actually reverts all the way back to his simian existence and brings it to the present where he races around Boston a bit as a monkey (Well, as Joe E. Brown said to Jack Lemmon at the end of *Some Like It Hot:* "Nobody's perfect").

At the end of the film, Eddie goes so deeply into the experience that he is truly doomed until the love of his wife saves him. For that reason I debated long and hard with myself about the chapter in which to discuss the film. It belongs here because of its core message of the hidden powers that we can resource, but its denouement demands that we pay particular attention as well to its overpowering message about the primacy of love.

Eddie gets so immersed in his quest for finding answers to the ultimate questions that he totally loses sight of everything else, including the obvious adoring love of his wife. As his friend Arthur (Bob Balaban) says to him, "You're married to one of the great women of the world, who adores you." Eddie totally ignores this fact as being somewhat superfluous to his life and actually seeks a separation from his wife, so he can pursue his quest.

At the end of the film, he is about to disappear into what

could be best be described as the molecular equivalent of a black hole in space. Risking her own life, Emily literally reaches into the abyss to retrieve him. Later that night, he finally acknowledges that she has saved him from himself, and he professes his love for her, even though he feels he is disappearing into the abyss again—and he's right. He begins to disintegrate and she reaches out for him only to be electrified into the experience herself. Seeing her in this terror is what finally gives him the strength to pull himself out of it and to wrap his arms around her to bring her back. That's how the film ends.

Okay, I am an incurable—even untreatable!—romantic. I admit that. But still—what a romantic ending and a beautiful message.

Remember, this was the seventies. The dawning of the "me" years.

This film is a wonderful reminder about both the primacy of love and also about being loved. So many of us are much better at giving than receiving. When you are loving, *you feel in control, but when you allow yourself to* be loved, *you are also exposing your vulnerability and, for a lot of us, that is much scarier than disappearing into the abyss.*

Brainstorm

Going from the expansion of one person's mind to the ability to inhabit the senses of anyone.

Brainstorm was released in 1983 with that exact premise. Notable otherwise in a sad way for featuring Natalie Wood's last performance (she actually died during production), the film centers around the development of a technology that allows the user to actually inhabit the recorded senses of another person. Of course, our favorite bogeyman "the government" (Cliff Robertson) wants to take it away from its creators (Louise Fletcher and Christopher Walken), so they can put it to military use.

I only mention the film briefly in passing here because it was the precursor to virtual reality—before anyone knew what virtual reality was. The user could actually experience fully an entirely separate reality. Remember the scene we discussed in *Cocoon* about alien orgasms? Well, there is a scene in *Brainstorm* where one of the assistants on the project gets a sex scene on a virtual endless loop . . . and almost dies.

Maybe the real threat to our evolution is not actually the government. Maybe it's the porn industry.

I hope not.

I say that only somewhat facetiously because it does raise another issue that I think is worth noting. Where is it mandated in the rules of spirituality that people on a conscious spiritual path are expected to forego the enjoyment of sex and, for that matter, wealth? If there was some great afterlife convention that addressed these issues, I guarantee you that most of us didn't get to vote.

There has indeed been a sense throughout history that truly spiritual people must be abstinent and penniless, and I'm sure that's why the notion is seemingly so deeply engrained in our society. I respect fully that some formal religions actually adhere to that belief; however, many of us have confused this religious tenet with a spiritual requirement. There is a difference.

Other than the core concept of everyone creating their own reality, metaphysics is actually all about the lack of systemic beliefs. One can be deeply spiritual and not religious; however, in mainstream journalism, the words are often held to be necessarily synonymous. They are not different words that automatically connote the same beliefs, but they have been so defined for so long that they are very often confused with each other.

One of the paradigm shifts that we are experiencing now is that we are foregoing our martyred existences. The notion of not making money as a more spiritual lifestyle choice is changing and I, for one, think that's progress. I'm not talking here about people who unscrupulously manipulate others in the name of spirituality and get wealthy because of it. Certainly that's as hypocritical a practice as any other "con." I'm talking about people who both "talk the talk" *and* "walk the walk."

Enjoying the good things in life is actually a more spiritual practice than denying them. After all, who says that the Universe doesn't want us to have fun? If not, why are there roller coasters, sunsets, and chocolate?

And why give us the bodies we have and then make the healthy enjoyment of them and each other something only for "sinners"? If that was the case, wouldn't we be doomed to suffer the fate of the angels in *Dogma* who are denied their sexuality because God thinks it's fine for humans but not angels? Fine. Okay with me. When I become an angel, I'll reconsider, but for now, it seems we should be sending ourselves the message that we can enjoy ourselves in both of those arenas while we're here.

I looked for movies that deliver precisely that message but couldn't find exactly the right one.

Coming soon, I hope?

"I'm mad as hell and I'm not going to take it anymore."

—*Network*

CHAPTER NINE

Tube Fear

The invention and explosive impact of television just may be perceived by historians to be the most significant societal occurrence of the twentieth century. Sure, I see some eyebrows raised, but just think it through. Television has changed the way we look at ourselves, the world, and each other in such a radical manner that everything else seems like an isolated incident.

Television has connected everyone in the world on an instantaneous basis. Before television, we depended on newspaper reporting and occasional newsreels to inform us of events happening in the world. Today, we have instantaneous electronic images from any news event happening almost anywhere. And a picture is worth millions, not thousands, of words.

As we have already commented, the observer affects the outcome of the experiment through expectation. Immediate reporting is changing the way news is reported and indeed made. Vietnam was the first televised war, and a lot of what happened to affect that war happened as a result of what we saw on TV. Seeing our boys getting killed was no longer a distant experience related only by veterans after the fact. It was in our living rooms every night. In fact, there was even a very black joke that circulated during the sixties. ABC was by far the lowest rated network at that time and the joke was that "we should put the Vietnam War on ABC as a series so it could be cancelled quickly."

The Gulf War made international figures of Peter Arnett, Bernard Shaw, and all the CNN personnel who were broadcasting the war *live*. We actually heard and saw the bombs as they exploded in Baghdad.

World leaders no longer have the protection of anonymity, and on the other hand, terrorists such as Osama Bin Laden have found a frightening communications medium for their images of horror. Timothy McVeigh talked very openly of his idea that the single most important result of his cowardly massacre was to have Americans see the horrific images of the Oklahoma City bombing on television.

The universe certainly doesn't always need movies to deliver a powerful message.

We watched the *Challenger* explode; the triumphs of the U.S. womens' soccer and men's hockey teams win against impossible odds; Robert Kennedy, Lee Oswald, and Jack Ruby shot; Neal Armstrong walk on the moon; Chinese protesters murdered; the 1968 riots in Chicago; Kennedy debate Nixon; and of course the tragedy of 9/11. All *live*.

Instant villains and heroes are created before our very eyes. Joe McCarthy, Tiger Woods, Sirhan Sirhan, Oprah, the Palestinian terrorists in Munich, O. J., Michael Jordan, Brandi Chastain, Gary Condit, and infinite numbers of others.

Politics has become a whole different business under the searing eye of the tube. Could Ronald Reagan have been elected president *without* television? Could Franklin Roosevelt have been elected *with* television?

Perhaps most crucially, the entire family structure of our lives has been changed by television. The average American teenager watches at least four hours of television per day, much more time than any interaction in their lives other than school.

Simply put, almost *everything* in modern day life has been either changed or at least seriously affected by television. Some for the better, some for the worse. But changed nevertheless.

Anything that pervasive has the threat of controlling our lives and, in fact, that very observation has often been advanced about television—that it has indeed become the tail that wags the dog. As such, it is not surprising that films have looked at the phenomenon of television with a very wary and sometimes even frightened eye.

This whole book could be devoted to looking at the phenomenon of television and the personalities it creates (*A Face in the Crowd, Quiz Show,* etc.); however, I have chosen three films that I think are the most illustrative of our love/hate relationship with television and the messages we receive both through it and about it.

As Marshall McLuhan so prophetically observed: "The medium is the message."

Network

Brilliant, funny, and prophetic, *Network* has something very chilling in common with *1984,* in that subsequent reality made the actual message of both films pale in comparison.

The ad line for the film was, "Television will never be the same."

The most famous line is "I'm mad as hell and I'm not going to take it anymore!"

The basic story of *Network* (which was released in 1976) was of an aging television anchorman named Howard Beale (Peter Finch), who gets so disgusted with the world around him as he is being fired for his plummeting ratings that he actually announces that he will be committing suicide on the air in a week.

He then begs to go back on the air and apologize, and the network allows him to do so, only to watch him tell the audience that he "just ran out of bullshit." He works himself into a frenzy, and he then passes out. The ratings for his newscast actually go way up. Knowing that they can't get rid of a ratings winner, Beale is actually encouraged to spill his bile every night, which he does and then, on cue, passes out.

He adopts the motto of "I'm mad as hell and I'm not going to take it anymore!" and the sentiment sweeps the country. He encourages people to shout the sentiment "from the rooftops" which they do in huge numbers.

The show becomes a huge ratings success and Beale

becomes a media star even though he has become as mad as the proverbial march hare. The situation spins out of control as the former "news" show is glamorized—much to the horror of the actual news department that was supposed to produce it, but has now been supplanted by the entertainment department. The show begins to introduce features such as "Sybil the Soothsayer." Beale rails against the "shocking notion" that people are actually looking at television news as both being more real than the world outside (imagine that!), and also as entertainment rather than straight news.

To put this latter prophetic observation in historical context, it is important to note here that *Network* was released four years *before* the debut of CNN. In the seventies, news at the network and local level still at least looked like news most of the time. CNN changed all that. As a former newscaster once told me, CNN took all the viewers who really cared about legitimate news, leaving local stations to create exploitative stories to attract viewers.

Ultimately, matters get out of hand and Beale's rants turn so depressing about the state of humanity that his audience begins to tune him out; moreover, he torpedoes a huge deal that the network is planning with Arabian interests. The network figures out that the only way to ever get control again is to assassinate Beale *on the air,* which they do, employing assassins from a new show they are developing called the *Mao Tse Tung Hour*.

The voiceover at the end of the movie simply intones that the story of Howard Beale was "the first known instance of a man who was killed because he had lousy ratings."

You're asking yourself, "Yeah, so? What's so outrageous about that?" And that is precisely the point. It is no longer outrageous at all. Howard Beale had nothing on Jerry Springer, that's for sure.

Remember the Fox show, *Who Wants to Marry a Millionaire*, with the now infamous Darva Conger and Rick Rockwell? They would have been perfect for Howard Beale, and a lot of the absurd elements of *Network* actually pale in comparison to shows like *Temptation Island* and the aforementioned Fox *Millionaire*. If you had told Howard that a registered nurse was going to go on television to try to lure a millionaire to marry her, win, then get the marriage annulled and appear nude in *Playboy* magazine, even ol' Howard might have been hesitant to believe it.

One message in *Network* was to "Watch out, because here's where you're going." We went way past that warning some time ago.

The other message of Network *that was so prophetic was the "I'm mad as hell and I'm not going to take it anymore" litany of Howard Beale. Most films have a key moment that crystallizes the message of the movie, such as the barn-building sequence in* Witness. *In* Network, *it is Beale's litany. What made Beale's rallying cry so relatable was that he was actually ranting about things that made perfect sense to all of us in the audience. We had begun to reach the point where we simply couldn't "take the bullshit" anymore, as Beale put it, and the film crystallized that sense of a turning point for many of us.*

Being There

Another prophetic and very funny movie that both accurately reflected our growing obsession with television and also foresaw the current political age of image being dominant over substance, *Being There* was released three years after *Network*.

Based on a novel by Jerzy Kosinski, *Being There* is a whimsical but biting commentary on our American obsession with image. Even more important, its spiritual message is succinctly conveyed in both the ad copy for, and the last line, of the film:

"Life is a state of mind."

Everything that Chance (Peter Sellers) does comes from a pure naiveté of spirit and, with absolutely no conscious intention except his love of gardening and television, he becomes a famous and important man.

Peter Sellers gives one of his best, and certainly calmest, performances in the film. He plays a gentle gardener who has lived his entire life caring for the garden of a very rich benefactor, who has allowed Chance to completely retreat from any sense of contact from the outside world except for his television. Chance either gardens or watches television. That's all.

When his benefactor dies, Chance is forced out into a world for which he is completely unprepared (to an amusing jazz version of "Thus Sprake Zarathtustra," the *2001* theme music, a nod of the head to Kubrick from director Hal Ashby).

Chance is so separated from any sense of the "real" world that, in a classic scene, he actually tries to prevent himself from being assaulted by pointing his television remote control at his potential attackers, believing that he can just switch the channel. If ever there was a searing image of the potential power of television to alter our perceptions of reality, that was it.

Mere "chance"(a very intentional pun) finds him being slightly hurt by the car of a wealthy woman named Eve (Shirley MacLaine) who takes Chance home to her palatial estate so that the doctor who is caring for her critically ill husband Ben (Melvyn Douglas) can look at Chance's injured leg. On the way, she gives Chance a drink and at the same time asks his name. Sputtering over his first-ever drink of liquor (in his first-ever car ride), Chance coughs out that he is Chance the gardener, but Eve hears Chauncey Gardner and the name sticks.

Once at this new home, Chance only wants a place to stay and work in the garden but everyone around him takes his gardening comments as metaphors, not pure intent. Ben is a powerful man, who is close to the president of the United States (Jack Warden). Chance's comments to the president on the seasons of planting ("as long as the roots are not severed, all is well in the garden") are construed again as metaphors on the economy and Chance is thrust into the limelight, even finally appearing on his beloved television.

Chance spends every waking moment watching television, if he can manage to do so. Even when Eve tries to seduce him, he can only relate by saying his favorite line, "I like to watch," She mistakes this for his desire to watch her and she obliges by "pleasuring" herself while Chance serenely watches an exercise show on television.

Chance is soon chosen by a dying Ben to watch out over both his business and Eve. At Ben's funeral, the president gives the eulogy while members of his own party are talking about Chance being a potential candidate for president, as they act as pallbearers.

While the president is speaking, Chance wanders off into what I believe is one of the most memorable final shots ever in a movie. He is walking toward the estate, and there is a pond before him. Having no concept of walking around it, he walks out into the pond. Instead of sinking, he seems to be walking *on* the water. He even puts his umbrella down in the water to test its depth. Right next to him, the water is very deep but he continues walking as we hear the last line of the president's eulogy: "Life is a state of mind."

There has always been a lot of controversy about that final sequence because, I believe, the walking-on-water aspect was misunderstood to be a reference to Jesus. I never saw it that way. "Life is a state of mind" is the way Chance lives. He literally lives in a separate reality from all those around him. His life has always been stress-free. Someone and something has always protected him from adversity, so much so that he has a pure and complete *expectation* that he will be protected no matter what. There is nothing in his experience that would cause him to think otherwise. He is serenely unaffected by anything around him that could connote danger to anyone else. He just expects things to be "fine."

When Chance walks out into the water, he just wants to get to the other side and his instincts tell him that he can go through the water. It is apparent that he is actually walking in shallow water, not on *the water. His intuitive sense tells him there is a safe way across the pond and he finds it. Period. If the water had been deep all the way through, he would have known to go around. Expectation creates reality. After all, "life is a state of mind."*

Now *that* is an amazing and exhilarating message in a movie made in 1979.

Richard Matheson gave me a beautiful framed line etched in calligraphy from the novel of *What Dreams May Come* (which he wrote in the same year that *Being There* was released) that says *That which you think becomes your world.*

If you haven't seen *Being There* for a while (or if you've never seen it), look at it again in that context, and I believe you will see the breathtaking beauty of its message in perhaps a new light.

The Truman Show

Released in 1998, *The Truman Show* was an impossible-to-describe-easily movie that was around for a long time before it got made. Only when Jim Carrey agreed to star for a fraction of his "comedy rate" and visionary director Peter Weir agreed to direct, did the film get its green light.

Peter Weir is one of those few directors who really know how to create a world or a mood in a film and sustain it. Both *Last Wave* and *Picnic at Hanging Rock* are extraordinary mystical movies and Weir was the perfect choice for *Truman.*

Insurance salesman Truman Burbank (Jim Carrey) lives on idyllic Seahaven Island, where he is married to a lovely nurse (Laura Linney) and seemingly lives in a world where he is king. And he is. Actually, he's the star of a 24/7 television show which, through the use of five thousand cameras and countless cast members, has chronicled every moment of his life since his birth thirty years before. The only one who doesn't know it's television is Truman himself.

Every thing and every one in his life is manipulated by the needs of television. When the show's obsessive Machiavellian creator/director Christof (Ed Harris) became concerned with Truman wanting to leave the island, a staged drowning was created to "kill" his "father" and terrify Truman about boats and water. Interestingly, as a child, Truman wanted to be an adventurer much like the George Bailey character in *It's a Wonderful Life* (chapter 11). Both give up the dream, but Truman is manipulated into it. One of the problems with some of the believability in the film is that this little boy was so dramatically and publicly traumatized. Great ratings seemingly allowed the practice of child abuse on a grand scale.

From time to time, people infiltrate the show from the outside to try to reach Truman, but they always fail. It is only when little glitches occur (a lighting lamp falling at his feet, a "rainstorm" that temporarily only soaks him, a false backing on an elevator door, etc), that Truman starts to get very suspicious.

Ultimately, he figures it out and sets sail on a boat to face his fears. Enraged that Truman might actually find a way to the truth, Christof tries to drown him with waves and wind until he finally relents. Truman's boat hits a set "wall" that looks like the horizon and a confrontation occurs with Christof whose voice booms from the clouds above (no symbolism there). He actually identifies himself to Truman as "the creator . . . of a television show." He tries to dissuade Truman from actually leaving "the set" and walking into "real life," but ultimately Truman walks through the door backstage and the show is over, along with the movie.

Early on in the film, Christof is asked in an interview why Truman has never caught on and his answer summarizes the entire power of the message of the film: "We accept the reality of the world that we're presented. Simple as that."

Simple as that, indeed. Until movies like *Matrix* come along and challenge the very structure of the belief.

Truman does accept the world in which he lives because he is never given any reason not to. When he does begin to look deeper, the façade actually falls apart very quickly. As Christof also says, he "couldn't keep the truth from Truman if he really, really wanted to know it"(Neo in *Matrix*). Truman does want to know the truth and he discovers it pretty quickly.

I find this to be a delightful and beautiful message about our own growth. We all can, and often do, live in the so-called reality of the world as it is presented to us. To Chance in *Being There*, the world of television has absolutely no distinction from the world around him. He just accepts it at face value. This is also one of the most controversial aspects of the long-term effects of television. Where does life begin and "TV life" end and vice-versa? How many people today confuse the two?

How deeply does television's version of "reality" seep into our consciousness? One simple and poignant example: Eating disorders in young women were absolutely non-existent in the Philippine Islands until the advent of American television.

Now, they have the same problems as we do with young women actually dying of starvation/malnutrition trying to live up to images created by and for television.

Truman accepts the world around him until he sees that there is something wrong. He then looks behind the façade and finds a whole new version of "reality." When one is on a spiritual journey in life, that is exactly what meditation and self-examination are all about. You look deeper. You question reality.

Once the veil is lifted, you can never pretend again that it is still in place. I have always found it amusing when judges tell juries to "disregard a statement." How does a human being just wipe that kind of information out of one's mind? *Once you hear, you never forget. Once you ask, you never stop asking. And so it is with Truman. He represents the innocent seeker in all of us who wakes up one day to discover that the reality he thought he knew is changed, and he finds himself desperately wanting to know what is just beyond the horizon.*

The other major message in the film centers around the obsessive identification issues we have with television personalities.

Truman is a worldwide phenomenon. People watch him sleep at night when they have trouble sleeping. Every move is scrutinized. In short, it is very easy to lose oneself in *The Truman Show* and that is certainly one of the major criticisms of television—that people lose their own identities in it and through it.

Truman transcends all this eventually and, to the cheers of some and tears of others, walks away.

The lasting meaning of what he did? The last shot of the film has two security guards who have been devoted viewers of the show watch Truman end the show and then immediately ask each other, "What else is on?"

"This is a difficult case, giving a man back his heart."

—Michael

CHAPTER TEN

Angels

"We are not alone" does not only apply to our attitude about aliens.

Angels and spirits have been aspects of our consciousness since we first began our evolutionary journey as human beings. Going all the way back to our most primitive ancestors, cave dwelling paintings of angels comforted and fascinated us.

Certainly, evil spirits such as the one who inhabited Regan in *The Exorcist* or invaded the home in *Poltergeist* are also the source of fascination in hundreds of films and form the core of a successful genre of their own—that of the horror film. This chapter, however, focuses on other spirits; namely, those that seem to be around when we most need them in our dark nights of the soul to comfort and encourage us. (That's why *Dogma* is in chapter 6 rather than here.)

Throughout our history as humans, there have been stories about beings that just seem to appear at the most critical times in our lives. Sometimes they are physical, in the guise of a person whom we meet for a short period of time and then never see again. Sometimes it's just a sense, a feeling of a presence around us. Another one of those experiences that you can't "prove," you just know.

I found something very eerie, and yet very beautiful, as I

looked again at the movies about angels that have always affected me, and I realized that they all have something very interesting in common. The films that we might remember as being about angels really never are about the angels at all. These movies are always about the subject of the angel's focus, rather than about the angel itself. It's kind of a heavenly version of the old vampire legend of not showing up as a reflection in a mirror. Angels seem to be like invisible ink on celluloid. Now you see them, now you don't.

Even the television series *Touched by an Angel* focuses on the week's human challenges, rather than on either Roma Downey or Della Reese, and that's not easy to do when they're the only continuing characters, week in and week out.

It really feels as though we have an unspoken arrangement with each other about this subject matter. Angels are all around us. They're here to comfort and guide us, preferring to stay out of the spotlight of conscious awareness as much as possible. Out of respect for that, I almost decided not to include this chapter at all, but ultimately decided that I would be remiss in just skipping it altogether. So, it's a quiet moment, distinct from the chapters before and after this one in both form and length.

Movies have always embraced the notion of angels.

Clarence (Henry Travers) in *It's a Wonderful Life* (chapter 11) is perhaps the best known and beloved angel in our cinematic history. For the last fifty-six years since that film's release in 1946, people have been watching Clarence earn his wings by showing George Bailey what an amazing gift human life truly is.

In the 1947 film, *The Ghost and Mrs. Muir* (made later into a television series), a grieving widow is taught again the beauty of love by a spirit who appears to her in the guise of a sea captain.

In 1948, the classic *Portrait of Jennie* was released in which a painter is inspired by the spirit of a beautiful young woman.

That's three movies in the three years immediately following the end of World War II in 1945 that all deal with the concept of comforting and inspirational beings.

The closest that any film I can find comes to focusing on an angel itself is 1998's *City of Angels*, which is an Americanized version of Wim Wenders' film, *Wings of Desire*. *City of Angels* stars Nicolas Cage as an angel (Seth) who falls in love with a doctor named Maggie (Meg Ryan). What's interesting about Seth, however, is that he decides to "fall to earth," so that he can become human and actually feel Maggie's touch as a human being. He learns that angels can actually become human from another fallen angel, the appropriately named Nathan Messenger (Dennis Franz), who also fell in love—with his wife and food! Even with that decision, the focus of the film is on Maggie and her life, not Seth. We know everything about Maggie's life as a doctor, her relationships, her childhood, etc., but all we know about Seth is that he is an angel. As in many films about angels, Maggie has no belief in anything spiritual until she encounters Seth.

Even in *Michael*, which features a major star (John Travolta) in the title role, the focus of the film is on Michael's efforts to get Frank (Bill Hurt) and Dorothy (Andie McDowell) together as a couple. It is Michael's twenty-sixth and supposedly last trip to Earth and, even though he is unique (a sugar freak and a womanizer), the focus is still on his human friends.

In Bob Fosse's brilliant autobiographical *All That Jazz*, Jessica Lange is the angel who appears to Joe Gideon (Roy Scheider), a self-destructive, alcoholic womanizer who also is a brilliant choreographer and film director. Joe knows he is rushing headlong to his death and Lange's unnamed angel does her best to get him ready for it, knowing full well that he has chosen his own destiny and all that she can do is be there to comfort him.

The message of all films which feature angels seems to be that we have "unseen friends" around us when we need them the most—not necessarily always when we want them, but when we need them. This message comes through in every film that features angels; moreover, we never seem to go too long without an "angel" film appearing in theaters. I perceive this as another quiet and gentle reminder that we are never truly alone.

It really seems that our filmic experiences with angels is intended to be quiet and almost beyond the veil of our perception. And so, like the "fog" in Carl Sandburg's famous poem, both angels and our brief moments with them here . . . "come in on little cat feet and quietly slip away."

"I'm not a smart man, but I know what love is."

—*Forrest Gump*

CHAPTER ELEVEN

The Power of Love

In director Baz Luhrman's brilliant, dizzyingly romantic *Moulin Rouge,* the main character's lesson is that *"the most important thing you will ever learn is simply to love and be loved in return."* The entire film is a dazzling visual and musical tour de force and a tribute to love itself. For our purposes here, however, it is that beautiful message about the primacy of love that begins this last subject chapter. "The most important thing," indeed.

Even immortality can be a curse without love. In *Highlander*, the main character becomes immortal only to have to watch the women he loves die (to the music of a great Freddie Mercury/Queen song called "Who Wants to Live Forever If Love Must Die"). In *Pandora and the Flying Dutchman,* the accursed Dutchman must sail the seas of the world forever until he finds a woman who loves him so much that she is willing to die for him.

The power of love transcends everything else. For a while, I thought this should perhaps be chapter 1 until I realized that the book would then have a very long chapter 1, and almost no others. At least half the films in the preceding chapters could also have been included under the heading of "The Power of Love."

We are left then with a handful of films that I have saved for last because of their particularly powerful messages of love.

Love is all there is, and love is not enough.

My favorite paradox.

Humans are the only species on this planet with the ability to *consciously love*. Why is that? What is the special relationship that we have with the concept of conscious loving? Animals instinctively love. We do, too. Loving our children is an instinctive response. We, however, can choose to love or reject the notion as well and at least be potentially aware of all of the consequences of those choices. Why?

When we address that question, we strive to touch the God within us.

Material success and fame have their rightful places in our lives. They are valuable and desirable. When we engage those energies as separate desires and not substitutes for love, we can approach them for their intrinsic value. Often, however, we all know that we use those energies as a substitute for love. We often even confuse them with the very act of loving. We excuse ourselves from loving and being loved because we feel we have to pursue other things in order to earn love or deserve love or even justify love. Workaholics, for example, can use all kinds of rationales for so burying themselves but, more often than not, a crisis will completely change that attitude, lift a veil from their eyes and allow, even force, them to see life anew. How many times have we heard those driven by stress to heart attacks and other ailments talk about "waking up" to "what's important" in life?

Love is there for all of us, whether we embrace it or not. Love is the all-inclusive binding energy in human life, whether we acknowledge it as such or not.

That's why we have such a love affair with love itself in movies. Love stories are the backbone of movies. They have been around since the early nickelodeon days, and they will be around until "the twelfth of never." Other genres wax and wane. Teenage comedies are in, and then they're out. Westerns, musicals, sci-fi films, even comedies—have their cycles as magnets for filmgoers. A great love story is *always* in fashion. That does not mean, of course, that every love story always makes money at the box office; however, as I can attest, their audiences do eventually find them.

You'll soon note here that three of the five films we detail in this chapter star Tom Hanks and one stars Jimmy Stewart. In *Cast Away,* Tom Hanks plays a man who has his whole life figured out, and it certainly seems like art is imitating life in that. Tom Hanks is one of a handful of actors who just seem to have unerring instincts for the right material. How long has it been since he starred in a "clunker"? You probably have to go all the way back to *Bonfire of the Vanities* in 1990, and the main reason that movie didn't work was because audiences couldn't then accept Hanks as a bad guy.

Just look at the films he's made: *Splash*, *Big, Philadelphia, Sleepless in Seattle*, *Forrest Gump*, *Saving Private Ryan,* etc. He truly is a deserving successor to Jimmy Stewart as the quintessential American hero. If Hanks had been around a few decades ago couldn't you have seen him in *It's a Wonderful Life* or *Harvey* or *Mr. Smith Goes to Washington?* And couldn't you just imagine Jimmy Stewart in *Gump* or *Cast Away,* or really any of Hanks' films?

These two actors personify the quintessential American hero. They are strong, idealistic, kind, and sensitive. The ultimate "alpha" males on screen. As such, they personify for us who we can be when we resource that innate goodness and strength in all of us. It is no surprise, therefore, that they star in the films that, for me, best represent the energy of the power of love.

Cast Away

For many, if not most of the people I know, the last couple of years have been a time of great turmoil. Things we thought we knew for sure have been brought into question. We seem to spend more and more of our time "unlearning" the precepts that we thought were bedrock reality. I was recently sent an email called "Message from the Hopi Elders" that I believe is an eloquent recital of this turmoil:

"To my fellow swimmers:
"There is a river flowing now very fast
"It is so great and swift, that there are those who will be afraid.
"They will try to hold onto the shore.
"They are being torn apart and will suffer greatly.
"Know that the river has its destination.
"We must let go of the shore, push off into the river, keep our heads above water.
"At this time in our history, we are to take nothing personally, least of all ourselves,
"For the moment that we do, our spiritual growth and journey come to a halt.
"The time of the lone wolf is over.
"Gather yourselves. Banish the word struggle from your attitude and vocabulary.
"All that we do now must be done in a sacred manner and in celebration.
"We are the ones we have been waiting for."

Nowhere could this philosophy be more eloquently represented than in *Cast Away* which stands as the most eloquent possible message to ourselves that the time has come to leap into the unknown and trust that both the power of our love and the love of the universe will guide us.

In *Cast Away*, Hanks plays globe-trotting FedEx employee Chuck Noland who is in love with Kelly Frears (Helen Hunt) and knows he is going to marry her—until the plane he is taking crashes and he winds up alone on a tropical island for four years.

He is so lonely and depressed that he contemplates suicide but somehow accepts that he must go on.

Finally, a plastic shell from some kind of container washes up on the island and he realizes that he can use it as a sail to get beyond the huge onshore waves that have kept him there for so long. He then escapes. Near death, he is rescued and soon returns to America, where he seeks out his former fiancée, who has actually married someone else (Chris Noth, who finally seems to have moved on from his relationship with "Carrie" in *Sex and the City*). The reunion scene between Kelly and Chuck is handled as beautifully as any such scene I can remember. Even though Kelly acknowledges that Chuck really is the love of her life, she has made a new commitment and has a young child. How can she just walk away from those commitments? They both know that she cannot go with Chuck. What is he going to do?

This is where the real spiritual message of the movie and the power of love kick in. To explain, we have to go back to the beginning of the movie.

In the opening, we see a FedEx truck making a pickup at an isolated ranch-style home in Kansas. We are also told by the sculptor Bettina (Lari White, an interesting masculine name for such a beautiful woman), whom we hear but don't see until the end of the film, that there will be another pickup in a few days. We follow the original package to Moscow where it is delivered to the sculptor's husband who is obviously living with another woman. Chuck is also in Moscow at that time training a new FedEx crew. Neither Chuck nor Bettina could have any idea at this time where their lives were headed.

When Hanks' plane crashes, he is washed up on his island with a lot of FedEx packages from the plane. After a while, he opens all but one of them to see if he can salvage anything useful, but the most useful is actually a Wilson volleyball which becomes his only companion. We see that the one package he doesn't open has the distinct wing-like logo of the sculptor from the first scene. He keeps that one package, so that he can someday deliver it when he gets off the island and, when he does leave, he not only takes it with him but he paints the wing-like logo on his sail.

After he realizes that his relationship with Kelly is over, he heads to Kansas to deliver the package. Arriving at the home, he finds no one there, so he just leaves the package with a note that simply says, "This package saved my life."

Out on the highway again, he stops to decide where he is going to go, and a pickup truck with a beautiful woman driver stops to help him. There is an obvious chemistry between them and, as she drives off, we see the wing-like logo on the back of her truck. It's Bettina, the sculptor. Hanks' eyes show that he is going to follow her home.

He spent four years on that island and the power of his love kept him alive. He *thought* that love would be shared with Kelly. He wound up somewhere entirely different; however, it was still the power of his love that got him through the ordeal. On the island, he had come to the understanding that "he had to get up every morning because you never know what the tide is going to bring in." It was that very acceptance and understanding that created the opportunity for the plastic container to be washed ashore. He may have used the physical sail to move beyond the wave barrier around the island, but it was the emotional acceptance of trusting that he just needed to go on that brought the sail to him in the first place.

So the universe had a plan all along, even though he couldn't see it until the very end of the film. The power of love is sometimes disguised in experiences we don't know how to interpret until we have lived them. Surrendering to our faith that the universe will indeed embrace us, if we trust in that power, is a beautiful and indelible message.

Sleepless in Seattle

I have always found this to be one of the most uplifting and beautiful love stories I have ever seen. For everyone who has loved and lost, the powerful message of this movie is a great comfort and inspiration.

Without saying it specifically, it raises a fascinating issue about soul mates. What if we don't have just one?

I know that will raise some hackles with other incurable romantics such as myself, but it's a question worth asking, particularly in light of the enormous popularity of both *Cast Away* and this film.

Sam Baldwin (Mr. Hanks of course) and his eight-year-old son Jonah are shown in the very first shot of the film at the funeral for Maggie (Carey Lowell) their wife/mother. Heartbroken, Sam moves to Seattle to get a new start, and it is very clear from the beginning that he is absolutely sure that the kind of love he shared with his wife "doesn't happen twice." (It's interesting that Tom Hanks plays this character and the one in *Cast Away* where second soul mates are the central theme of the love stories. Hanks's marriage to wife Rita Wilson is his second and acknowledged to be one of the most solid in Hollywood.)

After eighteen months, Jonah tricks Sam into speaking to a late-night talk show host about his grieving process. As he speaks about how he knew at first touch with his wife that "it was magic" and that "he had it perfect once," Annie (Meg Ryan) "just happens" to hear the show on her car radio. She is engaged to a very nice but cautious man Walter (Bill Pullman). Regardless of her engagement to Walter, she becomes obsessed with Sam; however, so do thousands of other women who send letters of proposal to Sam. Jonah reads and rejects all of them. He knows his Dad "needs a new wife" and when he reads Annie's letter (sent without her knowledge by her friend/boss Becky, played by Rosie O'Donnell), Jonah knows he has found his new Mom. He even tells Sam that he is sure that Sam and Annie were together in another life! Sam pays no attention and continues to date another woman whom Jonah loathes.

Jonah's attitude here is worth mentioning. Single parents realize very early on that our kids know us much better than anyone else. Children in single-family homes have an enormous influence on the chances of success of subsequent relationships. Those of us who have been down that road know how wise our kids can really be in that situation and it's a wonderful auxiliary message in *Sleepless in Seattle*. Trust your kids.

Annie actually tracks Sam to Seattle, and he sees her without her knowledge as she exits the plane. He is totally drawn to her but loses her in the crowd. Later, she sees him with his sister (Tom's real-life wife Rita Wilson) and mistakes her for a girlfriend; however, before she leaves, their eyes do meet.

Annie's letter has suggested that they all meet on Valentine's Day at the top of the Empire State Building (à la Annie's favorite "chick flick," *An Affair to Remember*). When Sam refuses, Jonah takes off for New York himself, forcing Sam to follow. At the same time, Annie is in New York with Walter, telling him that she just can't go through with the engagement. When she sees a large heart illuminated on the Empire State Building, she takes off running.

All three do meet eventually at the top of the building, and Sam realizes that he has seen her before. As he takes her hand, Jonah is finally at peace, and we know they will all be together.

Sam loved his wife, had it perfect, and she died. He was

sure that he could never "grow a new heart." He was wrong. How is that? Are we not saying to ourselves here that the concept of just having one soul mate may indeed be true for some but not for others? It seems that the only way that Sam could be connected to Annie was for Jonah to coax Sam to get on the phone. Sam wanted no part of another woman and Annie was engaged to another man. In the end, all that mattered was that they find a way to be together.

Sam talked about his first moment with Maggie "being magic," and the same magic occurs when he finally meets Annie on top of the Empire State Building. True love, like lightning, can strike more than once. That's a beautiful and encouraging message for anyone who has loved and lost.

Forrest Gump

I don't think I've ever walked out after a movie feeling better about being human than I did when I left *Forrest Gump* for the first time back in 1994.

When a movie puts even one of its lines of dialogue into the public consciousness, it's quite a feat. Most movies never even come close and the ones that do usually have that one famous line for which we remember them ("Frankly, my dear, I don't give a damn"; "This is the start of a beautiful friendship"; "Winters must be cold for those with no warm memories"; etc.).

Forrest Gump has *five* of those lines:

- ☆ "Life is like a box of chocolates. You never know what you're going to get."
- ☆ "That's all I have to say about that."
- ☆ "Stupid is as stupid does."
- ☆ "I'm not a smart man but I know what love is."
- ☆ And, of course, "Run, Forrest, RUN!"

When a film penetrates our consciousness, is a huge box office smash, and wins armloads of Academy Awards like *Gump,* something very powerful is at work.

On one level, *Gump* is also grounded in the same theme as *Being There:* life is a state of mind. Forrest has the most amazing experiences and simply cruises through them as the same simple but extraordinary man. He meets three presidents (Kennedy, Johnson, and Nixon); inspires the style of Elvis Presley and the song "Imagine" for John Lennon; and just "happens" to play a major role in Vietnam, the Washington Peace March, desegregation in the South, and Watergate! He also starts a shrimping business out of loyalty to a dead comrade, and it is the only boat to survive a hurricane, so he becomes wealthy and then has all his money invested early in Apple computers!

Chauncey Gardner had nothing on Forrest.

The key to Forrest is his unconditional love. He received it from his mother (Sally Field) and he shares it with everyone with whom he comes in close contact, but most particularly for Jenny (Robin Wright before she added Penn), the love of his life. He meets Jenny on the bus on his first day of school, and that's it for the rest of his life. No matter what Jenny does, Forrest loves her and never wavers. As peace loving and gentle as he is, he attacks three different men whom he sees hurting Jenny (he's right twice—once, it was just heavy necking) and he continues to love her unconditionally.

The key moment in the film happens after he sees Jenny at the Washington Peace March. She has already abandoned him several times—sometimes for other men—and she is about to take off again with someone who Forrest punched to defend Jenny. As she is about to leave him, she asks him why he is so good to her and he answers: "Because you're my girl."

She gives him absolutely no evidence to support this assumption; in fact, she constantly abandons him for someone or something else. It doesn't matter to Forrest. To him, Jenny is his girl, and nothing can ever change that. Talk about the power of a belief system. He just knows that she is his girl and that they will be together. Ultimately, she does come to him, gets pregnant with his child (a very, very young Haley Joel Osment) and leaves again, only to return after being one of the first women to contract AIDS (never specified but strongly hinted). She dies, and he has a "smart" son to raise.

The clear message of Gump *is the power of love and Forrest's unwavering, unquestioning belief in it. No matter what, Forrest loves purely and unconditionally. Love motivates him and everything around him ultimately conforms to the power of his love.*

Family Man

The messages of the first three films of this chapter relate to our maintaining our belief in love regardless of the obstacles that might get in the way.

What if we just lose sight of love altogether?

The world of the second millennium is a fast-paced demanding one for most of us. In our constant striving for fame or money—or both—it is often difficult to maintain perspective. Very often, we feel as if we have to choose between our careers and our families. As a single parent with four daughters, I have often faced those difficult choices. How important is that business meeting, if you have to miss open house at school? Can you balance love, family, and career so that no one, including you, feels cheated?

Many people have made choices in the last ten or twenty years to forego having families in order to focus on their careers. This is a very recent phenomenon. Until the sexual revolution of the sixties and seventies, men didn't have to forego anything. They just pursued their careers and basically left the raising of children to their wives. The revolution changed all that. Women quite rightfully said, "Hey, we deserve and demand our own identities, too." So DINKS were created (double income—no kids), and those couples with children try valiantly to find the right balance. Even more extreme are the individuals who forego relationships altogether because they want to focus on their work.

Single family households also now represent almost half of all American homes and single parents find that taking care of their children and working leaves little time—or energy—for other relationships. This challenge also exists for traditional two-parent families as well, because both partners now work, and they have to find equitable ways to share responsibilities. As a result, children live in very different climates today than they did with the traditional nuclear family of thirty or forty years ago, where the father generally worked and the mother raised the children.

This societal upheaval in traditional roles and the place of love in modern society just might be the single biggest cultural challenge of this moment in human events. We know we can't go back to the way it was (and most of us don't want to), but we haven't quite figured out how to balance all of our needs and desires.

Simply put, what are our priorities?

In *Family Man*, Jack Campbell (Nicolas Cage) kisses his girlfriend Kate (Tea Leoni) goodbye after they graduate college, so he can go off to London for a year of work. She begs him to stay but he promises to come back. He never does.

Twelve years later, Jack is a wealthy, successful president of an investment house, lives in a New York high-rise, sleeps with women whose name he either forgets or never asks, and drives a Ferrari. Just before Christmas, he gets a call from Kate that he chooses to ignore.

One night, he is present at what he thinks is an attempted robbery, and makes a deal with the thief, whose name is Cash, (Don Cheadle) to thwart the "crime." He then tries to convince the thief to seek help. Cash looks at Jack with a mischievous look that says that Jack's life may not be as perfect as he thinks it is and warns him to remember "that you brought this on yourself."

The next morning, Jack wakes up in bed with Kate in New Jersey. They have two kids and a dog and he works selling tires "retail!" for his father-in-law. He races to New York to find that his old life there never happened. Cash finds him to tell him that he is getting a "glimpse" at a life he might have had, if he had made other choices. Cash then leaves Jack to deal with the discovery of the ramifications of the decision that he had made twelve years before.

Jack then discovers what his life would have been like if he had stayed and married Kate—a dead-end job, living in Jersey, no money (Kate's promising law career became pro bono work), etc. He also has two kids with whom he has no idea how to interact. Slowly, he learns more about the children, going from horrified to charmed. It is with Kate, however, that Jack discovers what he truly lost. He becomes aware of how much he loved her and that he never really stopped.

Trying to connive his way back into his old company, he discovers that the way he lived his life when he was totally focused on himself could not coexist with the family life he has found in this magical "glimpse." Just as he begins to realize that his love for Kate and his family is more fulfilling than his old obsession with another kind of success, he wakes up again in his old life.

Try as he might, he cannot go back to his previous lifestyle. He seeks Kate out and finds that she not only became a successful lawyer, she is now moving to Paris to head her firm there. She had called him originally to give him some old things that she had found while she was packing.

He follows her to the airport and, in a lovely, romantic scene, tells her about the glimpse he had of who and what they could have been. He apologizes for having been so wrong and begs her not to go. Ultimately, she relents, and we know that they are going to be together again.

The message of the power and preeminence of love is obvious but still very timely.

Today, people are searching for happiness in their lives and often are finding that all the things they thought they wanted—even needed—are not making them happy. We are finding that the message of Madison Avenue advertisers for the last forty years has indeed penetrated our psyches: you can't be too rich or too thin, and you'll be fine as long as you drive the right car, wear the right clothes, and at least appear to be "in."

The problem is, however, that we are finding that the realization of all those goals does not by itself bring happiness. In northern California, for instance, a whole psychiatric specialty has evolved from all the dot-com millionaires who thought that the pure advent of money would solve all their problems. Money helps, but it doesn't cure.

As to not being able to be "too thin" . . . well, we never had millions of young women with eating disorders until the last thirty or forty years. Just a "coincidence," I'm sure.

Movies like Family Man *emerge from the depths of our souls and challenge us to look at the issues they illuminate with different eyes. When a film can entertain us, stir our hearts, and, at the same time, gently empower us to re-examine our priorities, then that is the highest possible use of the art form we call movies.*

It's a Wonderful Life

Once upon a time, a wonderful director made a film that he thought was very special. Unfortunately, critics generally loathed it and ripped it apart. Audiences didn't respond much better, and the movie basically disappeared without a trace. Dejected and discouraged, the director thought that perhaps he should seek out a different line of work.

1946. Frank Capra. *It's A Wonderful Life.*

Hard to believe, isn't it?

It's a Wonderful Life is arguably the most beloved film of all time. If not the most, certainly in the top three or four. Every year, families gather together near Christmas time and watch it for the umpteenth time and get engrossed in it like it was the first viewing. I've seen it at least fifty times in my life, and I still cry when Clarence gets his wings. When it was first released, however, it was not embraced at all. Today, we see it for the classic that it is, but it was definitely not a movie for its time. Audiences needed to grow into the acceptance of the film as years went by, and it is not alone in that regard. *2001* was not appreciated for the classic it became when it was first released either. The true test of the power of a film is the way it is perceived by future generations. *Wonderful Life* and *2001* have aced that test in a manner that few other films ever have.

No film has given me more sleepless nights than this one in deciding where to discuss it. I decided to put it here because, at its center, it is the quintessential love story. Love of others. Love of self. Love of life.

While films like *Family Man* look at how our lives might have been different if we had made different choices, the story of *Wonderful Life* revolves around the intriguing question of what would the world around us look like if we had never been born? We've all wondered that in our darkest hours, and this film plays it out.

Wonderful Life also looks at our priorities as human beings and delivers a powerful message about the primacy of love.

As I know most of you have seen it, I'm not going to spend too much time outlining the plot here. George Bailey (James Stewart) lives in a small town that he yearns to leave so he can travel the world. He also falls in love with Mary (Donna Reed) but he doesn't want to admit it to himself. His father dies and, to prevent lonely miser Potter (Lionel Barrymore) from taking over the building and loan his father headed, he agrees to stay and run it. He also succumbs to his love for Mary and marries her. As he is leaving town for his honeymoon, there is a run on his father's building and loan and he actually distributes his honeymoon money to depositors to keep the building and loan open. Ultimately, he is framed for fraud by Potter and thinks he has destroyed himself, his family, and everyone around him. As he ponders throwing himself off a snowy bridge, a wonderful character named Clarence comes into his life (a guardian angel-in-training) and actually grants him the opportunity to see what his town and family would look like if he had never been born.

The revelations are terrifying to him, and he is brought back to his present existence.

In the meantime, his family, friends, and townspeople whom he has helped over the years have banded together and raised the money to keep him out of trouble.

For me, this is the most life-affirming, humanity-enriching movie ever. It was released in 1946, just as America was climbing out of the debris of World War II. The focus of the nation was on a newly found sense of self-respect and dignity. We had survived an enormous challenge and had prevailed. *Wonderful Life* revolves around the Great Depression of the 1930s, and America just didn't seem to want to embrace a movie about the last great challenge to our way of life. We had won the war and there was a desire to look forward, not back.

Timing is a critical ingredient in the success of most artistic ventures, and *Wonderful Life* was just not in tune with the tenor of that particular year; however, time has indeed allowed us to catch up with it.

George Bailey (and James Stewart who played him) is a perfect reflection of the idealistic young American-next-door of the times. He does the right thing because it is the right thing. No angles, no self-serving schemes. He falls in love and, try as he might, he knows that he would be a fool to walk away from that love, and so he gives up his dream of travel and stays home. What's critical here is that he does it with no sense of martyrdom—he just sees what he needs to do and does it.

When things sour for him, he descends into such shame and anger that he contemplates suicide. All Tom Hanks had in *Cast Away* to dissuade him from ending his life was a volleyball named Wilson—at least Jimmy Stewart had Clarence. When things got darkest in the outer world around him, he let himself forget what was truly important in his life—his wife, his family, his friends. That's when Clarence steps in and shows him what life would look like without him, and the experience reminds him of how important his life really is. (The character of Clarence was also a reminder of the "unseen friends" that we have around us during those dark nights of the soul that we all encounter. It is said that our souls never put us in situations that we cannot handle, and Clarence is a classic example of the help that is available to us when we need it most.)

The primary message was about the power of love. George may have given up his ideas of travel and adventure but he gained a loving wife, children, and friends who would steadfastly stand by him in his darkest hour.

In the last scene, a bell rings on the Christmas tree with George's daughter telling him that every time a bell rings, an angel gets his wings. The last image is of George saying, "Way to go, Clarence!"

The love that surrounds George Bailey reminds us that "no man (or woman) is a failure who has friends."

And family.

And the power of love.

"Life is a state of mind."

—*Being There*

CHAPTER TWELVE

This Time, We Win

Where do we go from here?

MOVIES

The studios will continue to make event-type, broad appeal films because, frankly, at this stage, it's really all they care about and think they know how to do. Most of these films open in May, June, July, November, and December to take advantage of both the summer and winter holiday seasons. As an audience, we often get our money's worth out of these movies, at least from a viewpoint of "pure spectacle." Whether you're paying matinee admissions or evening prices, there's an awful lot of movie up there on the screen and, some of the time, the films are escapist and fun. No one will ever supplant the studios in their expertise in this area.

The creative issues are, however, deeply troubling. Unfortunately, "sheer spectacle" is often all we get. Summer 2001 is generally acknowledged now (by studios, critics, and audiences alike) to be perhaps the worst season ever. One over-hyped, undernourished movie had promising opening weekends and then dropped with a thud as audiences realized that the hype was much better than the film. (Summer 2002 was better.)

Another challenge is that movie marketing practices have become blatantly aggressive, too often misleading, and, as it relates to "R"-rated films, inappropriately directed at younger audiences. There is real concern in the halls of power in Hollywood that Congress may indeed be considering legislation to restrict the studios' abilities to market "R"-rated films to children and younger teenagers. Although it is popular in Hollywood to scream "First Amendment!" at any attempt to infringe on creative freedom of expression, it is not the films themselves that are being questioned. The problem is the aggressive marketing to children for whom "R" movies are supposed to be just that—restricted. Kids don't read reviews, so their basic exposure to films is through their marketing campaigns.

Unlike teenagers, who are basically impervious to reviews, adults are much more discriminating when making their movie choices; consequently, studios have become almost fanatically obsessed with getting good reviews in their newspaper ads that target adults. This obsession has led to some pretty embarrassing situations. Critics often find that a few positive words in a generally negative review will end up being used by the studio in an ad, which makes the gist of the review seem much more favorable than the critic intended. Even worse, certain studios have recently been caught in the act of actually creating fictitious critics and quoting favorable reviews from them! Adults have caught on to all this and have, quite understandably, become very suspicious and even cynical regarding this kind of hype.

Adding fuel to the fire of suspicious practices, movie marketing campaigns have recently also been revealed to be utterly misleading as to the actual nature of the film. For instance, *A. I.* was marketed as a whimsical PG-13 adventure from Steven Spielberg, starring Haley Joel Osment. Trusting those elements, a lot of people showed up with their children for the opening weekend, only to be shocked at the violent and depressing nature of the film itself.

Another big challenge for the studios is that the costs of making and marketing these huge blockbuster projects are rapidly reaching the point of no return. Studios only get about half of the box office gross back from the exhibitors. It's good to remember when you read about "record box office grosses" that such figures are not terribly meaningful to the actual profit/loss calculations of a particular film.

The studios are playing an awfully high stakes game of what I call "Celluloid Russian Roulette." The gamble is that the worldwide marketplace will continue to expand, thereby making film libraries even more valuable and bringing new audiences (such as mainland China) into theaters. The big danger in this assumption, however, is that one mega-budget disaster can torpedo an entire studios' viability. This happened to United Artists because of *Heaven's Gate* in 1980, as it had previously happened to Fox in 1970 with *Tora, Tora, Tora,* and it's only a matter of time before it happens again.

The studios will also continue to churn out films for young people. Teenagers are the most reliable audience there is for movies and rightfully so. Where most adults choose to go out or not, teenagers *have* to get out of the house on weekends, don't they? That's after they have refused to be seen with a parent in a theater anymore. At one point, you just have to drop them at the mall, right? And not right at the entrance, either, because God forbid a "hot" boy or girl should see them being dropped off by a parent! We all remember (whether we want to or not) what it was like to be a teenager. You have to go hang with your friends, flirt with the boys/girls, and just "be seen." Movies are still a great financial bargain for kids, too, and, most important, there are those defining moments in a darkened theater when the arm that is draped over the back of your date's seat creeps down around his/her shoulders and that first touch is accomplished. If for no other reason than that, teenagers will remain loyal theatergoers until a suitable alternative is invented. As to what that might be, I shudder to even consider it. (Someone once told me that we missed a great opportunity to really show what true hell was like in *Dreams.* His suggestion was that it all should have been shot in a high school.)

Families will not be forgotten either because there's still a lot of magic in sharing the family experience at the movies; however, family films have certainly changed. There now must be something in these films for adults to enjoy as well and that has revolutionized even animated films. Adults will go to theaters on a regular basis with their younger children *if* the movie itself is fun for them as well. The studios have found that parents need to be entertained in these films, too, because younger children can't just be dropped off at the mall. Parents need to accompany them. The really breakthrough animated films also appeal to teenagers who usually reject animated films for kids once they reach puberty because they don't like to relate to themselves as "kids" anymore. When an animated film attracts kids, teenagers, and parents, you get a blockbuster. I laughed harder and more often than even my fifteen-year-old daughter Heather when we went to see *Shrek* together. (It was near Father's Day, so she decided to give Dad a break and deign to be seen in a theater with me. Rarely have I felt more honored—and those of you with teenagers know exactly what I mean.)

Big theatrical event films will continue to play in two thousand to three thousand theaters at a time and may even grow in scope and ambition. Films budgeted over one hundred million dollars used to be an extreme rarity, but not anymore. Regardless of the challenges previously discussed in this chapter, expect the studios to continue to try to up the ante with each other on these kinds of films.

The studios are already moving away from their traditional roles as both creator/producers and distributors. More and more films are being developed and produced with independent financing and then distributed by the studios so as to reduce the financial exposure as much as possible. In essence, the studios are primarily becoming distribution entities and that trend will only grow.

What about films other than events, family, and teenage films?

That's getting tougher and tougher to do in mainstream theaters. Art house theaters continue to survive in major sophisticated cities, but those kinds of films do not even generally play in most other venues in the country. Adults are very sophisticated nowadays and it's getting harder and harder to bring them into theaters with any regularity. Comedy is still a great experience in theaters because of the group response, but even adult comedies have become an endangered species.

Studios will not just surrender the production of films for adults, because there's still a lot of prestige and money to be garnered from Academy Awards . . . but the sledding has become much more treacherous.

Spiritual Entertainment, Technology . . . and Beyond

Although there is a lot of teeth-gnashing about the issue of ageism in Hollywood, the plain truth is that younger people are a much more reliable audience than people over forty; however, a valid argument can be made that adults might go more often if there were more movies made for them, and it is an argument that I personally embrace wholeheartedly. *Adults still love to go to see a movie if its subject matter appeals to them enough. There will, therefore, always be a place for niche films for adults if the costs are controlled and the subject matter is narrowly focused so that marketing can be very specific and less costly.*

If that sounds like a blatant plug for adult-oriented spiritual films, it certainly is. Just as sharing the laughter of a comedy and the thrills of a horror film are wonderful group experiences, so too is the group experience of inspiration and hope. People are yearning for connection. To each other and to self. We are not going to establish the recognition of this genre of spirituality and then just walk away. We have only just begun to pull back the veil. The full beauty of what lies underneath is just beginning to be revealed.

As to the subject matter of future films in this genre, and the delivery methods thereof, look for our new best friend—technology—to have a huge impact.

As noted previously in regard to *Final Fantasy*, digital filmmaking is already here and will rapidly supplant the use of film altogether. The latest *Star Wars* was shot digitally and there will be an avalanche of others to follow it.

Metafilmics conceived and produced the first Hollywood original movie designed for exclusive distribution over the Internet. We used a digital camera to shoot *Quantum Project* for Sightsound.com, and I can tell you from personal experience that none of us want to work with old-fashioned celluloid again. Shooting in digital format is much faster for a plethora of different reasons, and is so much easier in post-production that it's a joke. With film, you need to process it, edit it, etc. In digital, you can see the results of your shot immediately on a monitor as the finished product. You then just put in to your computer editing system, and that's it. It's all there instantaneously and takes half the time to edit. You can do multiple versions at the touch of a finger, etc. The only barrier to digital format completely replacing film is the aesthetic differences that still do exist. Film still has a richer, softer feel; however, that will be corrected soon, and film will have become an anachronism.

Theaters will also eventually be equipped with digital projection systems, and that will be a "win/win/win" bonus for the studios, theater owners, and viewers.

The studios will be able to save millions and millions of dollars on prints of films that now cost approximately $2,000 each. When one copy of a film can be digitally transmitted to thousands of theaters, the savings will be enormous.

For theater owners, film handling and the cost of projectionists, etc., will be reduced. Theater owners are now squealing about the expense of converting their theaters to digital projection, and studios are also paranoid about digital signals being intercepted, but that will eventually get worked out. While current forecasts for converting theaters to a digital format are in the range of $100,000 per screen, technology is being developed that will cut that estimate by more than half, perhaps more. For instance, the thinking has been that theaters will need to be retrofitted for satellite transmissions, etc. Microsoft, Panasonic, and Sightsound have already tested a technology that could bring the print onto the screen via the Internet. Exhibitors also will soon discover that digital technology in their theaters will allow them to use their theaters for international events, concerts, sporting events, and entertainment other than movies. As many theaters do very little weekday matinee business (except in major cities), these other events could turn out to be huge profit centers.

Digital technology is already available in certain theaters, and the studios are beginning to venture into this new form of exhibition. For us viewers, it's a huge bonanza. Picture quality is vastly better with digital technology, and the "print" will look as pristine after three months on the screen as it does on its first day. No more scratches or sound "pops" as there are today when prints have been run through the projectors for a couple of weeks.

Digital innovation will also lead to what I believe will be one of the new frontiers for entertainment—the Internet. We've spoken of the pendulum effect before in this book. The viability of the Internet as an immediate "cash cow" was tragically and drastically overrated in 1999 and early 2000. Internet companies with absolutely no metrics for success were selling for hundreds of dollars per share. The bubble had to burst, and indeed it did, causing the pendulum to swing in the exact opposite direction where the whole phenomenon is now being considered by some to have been a passing fad. Don't you believe it. The Internet will be an amazing market for entertainment just as soon as broadband technology becomes readily available.

Broadband is, in essence, about speed. People are used to turning on a television and getting an instant picture. Traditional 56k modems on computers are way too slow for the downloading of entertainment. *Quantum Project* is a thirty-two minute film that takes four hours to download on a traditional 56k hook-up. People just don't want to do that; however, broadband can download the film in fifteen minutes and soon it will be even faster. Once people can quickly download entertainment off the Internet and then hook their computers up to their television screens (which can actually be done now with a "monster cable"), a whole new marketplace will open up. The Internet will be to the entertainment industry in the years after 2005 what the videocassette was to the 1980s. This is not a question of "if." It's matter of "when."

While we are looking at home entertainment via computers, it's also important to note the explosion in cable technology and diversification. Homes in many major cities today already have the capacity to receive more than one hundred, or even several hundred, stations. The challenge obviously is going to be programming because, as of now, technology is way ahead of creativity. It's fine to have all those channels but what kind of programming will they deliver? The answer is already beginning to become apparent. Channels are going to be extremely specialized and focused on particular viewer interests. We already have several sports channels, including ones exclusively devoted to golf and fishing. We have cooking channels, history channels, religion channels, etc.

It's just a matter of time—and money—before there are twenty-four-hour-per-day cable channels that are exclusively devoted to spiritual entertainment. Talk shows, series, comedies, movies, documentaries, etc. Somewhere out there on the horizon is an entity that will become the HBO of this arena. After these channels become huge successes, people will look back and wonder why it took so long; moreover, we won't remember what it was like without such channels. Most teenagers today do not remember a television world without MTV, and such will be the case with spiritual entertainment channels.

What about the theatrical experience of spiritual entertainment?

I believe that the next "big thing" in the technological enhancement of the theatrical experience will be the advent of the virtual reality experience (which will probably be called "immersion") in specially equipped movie theaters. Today, one can only be immersed in a virtual reality experience by donning helmets that are attached to computer programs. Once you have experienced this adventure, you never forget it. You do not watch. *You are there.* You are literally immersed in whatever the adventure may be.

This technology already exists so it is only a matter of time before the geniuses who invent and then refine these quantum leaps devise a way to retrofit certain small theaters with the equipment that will enable viewers to sit in a theater and feel that they are actually inside the story that they are watching. Personally, I do not believe that interactivity is necessarily an appropriate goal, because I think audiences like to give themselves over to the visions they are seeing. It is, however, possible that both could be accomplished in the future.

If you think that's just a flight of fancy, just remember back to the modern dawn of the computer itself. When you see how the technology has streaked forward at the speed of light, I think anything of which we can conceive in the field of technical invention will be at our fingertips much sooner than we might think.

When "immersion" happens, the experience of dreams and the visions of our soul's experience will be possible in a breathtaking manner that we can today only just begin to imagine.

As to creative content, what adventures await us in this virtual world?

The first real movies about Atlantis and Lemuria, perhaps? What really *is* the secret of Oak Island? (Never heard of it? You will.) New versions of the story of Jesus seem inevitable. The entire world of our night dreams and what they signify will be available. Our inner visions of worlds past and future will take shape. What really is space and time travel all about? How did the universe begin? Where is it going? Aliens in a new light. Guided meditations in virtual space. Evolution itself.

Another exciting aspect of the future will come from the almost untapped reservoir of books that have been written on the subject of spirituality. Look at your bookshelves and imagine that all those books that you have loved in this genre will some day become filmed entertainment. Because they will. Movies, television shows, internet downloads, direct-to-consumer product—all will be available to translate the wealth of literature that already exists and that will be written by the thousands of volumes as the new millennium unfolds.

All these and worlds not yet imagined lie waiting for us at the dew line of the next era of spiritual entertainment

We have experienced thousands of years of evolution on this planet. We have seen civilizations rise and fall. We have been witness to the devastation of every manner of cataclysm, both from the forces of nature and also sadly from the results of our own weaknesses. Many of us know we have been here before. We have suffered the consequences of our own fears.

With all this as prologue, I want to go back to the question that we asked at the beginning of this discussion:

Why are we here?

It is my passionate belief that we have come back this time with a new vision. For us. For our children. And for our planet. A very different and unshakable commitment.

This time, we win.

"A producer can get rich,
but it's really hard to make a living"

—Producer Lawrence Turman

CHAPTER THIRTEEN

Producing 101

What in the world *is* a producer anyway?

What do we actually *do*?

And why does there always seem to be at least seven or eight different producing or executive producing credits on a film?

I know the stereotype: smoking cigars, wearing lots of gold jewelry, dishonest, scheming, chasing every underage woman in sight, stealing money from everyone, and totally full of bull. And that's on a good day, right?

Actually, I don't really know any producers who fit that entire description, although I do admit that certain aspects fit a small number of producers; however, mostly, there's a complete misconception of who we are and what we do.

The role of producer in the year 2002 is actually rather easily explained in general, although the specifics change on every film depending on how that film actually came into being. Generally speaking, it is useful to see films as a painting. The producer provides the paint, the easel, and the background so the director can paint the picture.

Film producers today fall into three general categories: financial, creative, and operational.

Financial producers are the ones who provide or find

access to the funding of a project. They may or may not have anything to do with the film other than this aspect, but this is a crucial contribution, and credit is almost always awarded to anyone involved in this process. Usually, these contributors get executive producing credits.

Creative producers are the ones who conceive of, develop, oversee the production and post-production of, and/or arrange the financing for a film (instead of or in conjunction with financial producers). These producers conceive a project or develop a book or put writers together with ideas. These producers are the real players in the process of putting a film together and are usually the only people who are around from "soup to nuts." They think of an idea, get a writer, develop the script, find the director, arrange financing, supervise casting (with the director), oversee the hiring of the crew, supervise the film from a creative standpoint, supervise editing (with the director having the principal authority), and consult with the distributor on the marketing and release of the film.

Creative producers are generally the most powerful category. The actual "produced by" credit is the most coveted producer credit for many reasons, not the least of which is the fact that only those producers with "produced by" credits get to accept Academy Awards. Being a prolific producer in the film industry today is extremely challenging and very few people succeed at becoming and remaining an "A" producer. To do so, one must be extremely bright and energetic. Seven days per week and twenty-four hours per day, you have to be working the phones, having meetings, working on projects, and keeping your eyes and ears on all the executive shuffling and gossip. You also have to be a very clever and savvy politician and have taste and courage. The major producers of today—Jerry Bruckheimer, Scott Rudin, Mark Gordon—are creative producers and they deserve all the credit in the world for being able to do what they do. Personally, I never quite figured out how to manage the whole process on a consistent basis. I had some of those qualities but not all by any means (I was *horrible* at the politics) and probably, on my best day, would have been considered by the industry to be a "B" or "B minus" player. (Today, as a result of my exclusively spiritual focus, I'm considered by most of the consensus industry to be a bit of a loose cannon—and some people would probably omit the "bit.")

The legendary producers of our industry (David O. Selznick or both of my former bosses, Ray Stark and Dino de Laurentiis) are considered creative producers, although the industry is so different today than it was in those halcyon years that exact connections are difficult to make.

Operational producers are called "line producers" in the industry, and they either receive that credit on screen, or "associate producer," or "co-producer," and sometimes "executive producer" or "produced by" as well. (Sometimes they only get "production manager" credit.) These producers are utterly indispensable to the whole process and the really good ones are as highly sought after as some directors. These producers are charged with the responsibility of making and then adhering to the budget of the film and supervising the day-to-day operations of the crew and the entire film. They are expected to know how and where the money is being spent and to alert the producer and/or financing entity if there is a problem looming. (Of course, that depends on the line producer's relationship with the producer, who may or may not want that information passed along in a timely fashion, but that's a whole other kettle of fish.)

Very, very few films are made today where one, or even two, people perform all these duties.

There are exceptions and corollaries to all these categories. Writers sometimes have the clout to get a producing credit, as do some personal managers and others.

(Television producing is different. In television, the executive producers are generally the writer/creative powers behind the show, and almost all power resides with them. Producers in television are most often writers and other creative personnel.)

The proliferation of film producing credits over the last decade or so has really blurred the lines of what a producer actually does, and it is not generally considered within the industry to have been a positive development. There is a cliché now in Hollywood and outside of it that even "hairdressers" can get credit. That observation was intended as a very unfair shot at Jon Peters, who was originally Barbra Streisand's hairdresser when he got into producing. Everyone has to start somewhere. Jon went on to become a hugely successful and wealthy producer, so he deservedly got the last laugh.

The challenge is that it is different on every single film that gets made. In most businesses, your set-up happens, and then you follow a proscribed procedure. In Detroit, for instance, you build a factory and an assembly line and then just retool and modernize as times dictate. In the film industry, you start over every single time. There are no set rules or infrastructures. That's what makes it so challenging, frustrating, fascinating, and rewarding.

You really have to know the particulars of the film to know who got what credit and why. Just as one personal example: On *What Dreams May Come*, Barnet and I got the "produced by" credits. The writer Ron Bass got an executive producer credit (well deserved because he did a lot more than just write the script). Ted Field, Scott Kroopf, and Erica Huggins all got "executive producer" credits as well. Ted owns Interscope and was the one guy who stood up and committed to get the film financed and also ran all the interference (in effect preventing real interference) from the financing entity Polygram. Scott and Erica are the creative heads of Interscope and were intimately involved with the entire process of the filmmaking. Alan Blomquist got a "co-producer" credit as the line producer.

To quote an old Harry Belafonte song . . . "it's as clear as mud, but it covers the ground."

So, why did I personally decide to be a film producer?

I love movies.

Sitting there in the dark in front of a massive screen, totally immersed in an alternate reality, identifying with the character you admire most (or maybe least), eating popcorn, drinking a Coke . . . spellbound.

I grew up with movies. Literally and figuratively. I live in and through movies. Always have. To me, movies often represent a better reflection of the "real world" than this illusion in which we walk around every day. I see at least sixty or seventy new movies a year and have done so ever since I was a teenager.

My oldest conscious memory is sitting in my father's lap at the age of three (1949) watching "dailies" (raw film footage shot every day) in our house. My biological father's name was

S. Sylvan Simon and he was a producer, director, and studio executive. He made movies with Abbott and Costello and Red Skelton, so there was always a lot of joy around our house on Sunset Boulevard in West Los Angeles, until the laughter abruptly ended with my Dad's sudden death from a cerebral hemorrhage at the age of thirty-nine in 1949. It was just before my fourth birthday. My sister Susie was twelve.

My mother remarried a year later to a wonderful man named Armand Deutsch, who became my Dad (that's why I referred to Sylvan Simon as my biological father) and raised me with all the love, generosity, and dedication he would have had he been my biological father. He was also a film producer, so I was really born into and raised in and around movies. No matter where I was, I always went to movies at least twice a week and watched every movie on television that I could find. Looking back, it was like learning everything I could glean from the language of film because I knew that filmmaking would be my path in life. Sure, I went through several different experiences—politics, college, and finally even a law degree—but I knew I would ultimately be in the film business. It was just a matter of when and how. There was no way I was going to be a lawyer for long. I didn't like it, and I knew I could never be good at it, either. (The late great George Burns was asked on the eve of his one hundredth birthday to reveal his secret of longevity. Without hesitation, he answered, "Love what you do.")

By the fall of 1975, I was twenty-nine years old and colossally bored. No offense to lawyers here. I love watching great lawyers at work. I just knew I could never be one of them. I had graduated Loyola Law School and passed the California Bar in 1974, but I had already dispensed with any thought of practicing law. I felt increasingly edgy. Remember the Phil Collins song that has this refrain?:

> *"I can feel it comin' in the night . . . hold on . . . hold on.*
> *"I've been waiting for this moment for all my life."*

That was me. The proverbial long-tailed cat in a room full of rocking chairs. I was ready. "It" was coming but I had no idea what "it" was, where it was coming from, or how to know it when it arrived.

I read a lot at that time. I had always loved reading, dating back from the years in which I had proudly read every single Hardy Boys and Tom Swift book that was published. There was a book store in Beverly Hills at that time called Martindale's (La Scala is in that location now), and I was there all the time, browsing, and getting to know all the clerks.

One day, I walked in, and a clerk who knew me well said that they had just received a book that he thought I would love. He knew I loved all fantasy and science fiction, so a new book by a renowned author in that field seemed perfect for me. He handed me a copy of *Bid Time Return* by Richard Matheson (*I Am Legend, The Incredible Shrinking Man,* etc.) and I took it home to read it.

My life changed forever that night.

I read the book in one sitting and was just mesmerized. Through my lifelong passion for movies, I was aware that the hallmark of any great love story is the obstacles between the lovers, dating back to *Romeo and Juliet. Bid Time Return* had the very barrier of life itself as that obstacle, so I knew there was something powerful at its core. I also knew that this was
183 the sign for which I had been looking. It was time to get out of law and into the film business, so that I could make this book into a film.

Three years later, in 1979, Matheson gave me the galleys of his new novel *What Dreams May Come.* I have had many requests over the years to chronicle the sagas of both *Somewhere in Time*, née *Bid Time Return,* and *What Dreams May Come.*

Although such detailed reminiscences are not a part of the primary narrative drive of the subject at hand, I am aware of how passionately millions of people feel about those two movies (me, too!); therefore, I have included the detailed histories behind both of those films in the next two chapters of this book.

As detailed in chapter 14, I got my first real break when Ray Stark hired me as his assistant in 1976, and that began my journey into the film world.

Over the past twenty-five years, I have been involved in about twenty-five films, either as a producer or as a film company president. The films have ranged from *Somewhere in Time* to *Bill and Ted's Excellent Adventure,* from *What Dreams*

May Come to *All the Right Moves,* from *She's Out of Control* to *Body of Evidence.* An eclectic mix, to say the least.

I got married in 1978 and became an instant father because my wife also brought into my life my oldest daughter, Michelle, who was then only one and a half years old. Over the next ten years, we also had Cari in 1980 and Heather in 1986, and my other adopted daughter Tabitha came into my life in 1989 when she was twelve.

Our marriage ended in 1988 in a very traumatic manner, the details of which I am not going to include here out of respect for my daughters and the privacy of my ex-wife and her family. The situation was so painful that I actually couldn't focus on work, so I also went through a bankruptcy at the same time. My very dark night of the soul.

I didn't work for almost two years, until I got back on my feet and was presented with a tremendous opportunity to work for another legend. Film producer Dino de Laurentiis almost single-handedly invented the Italian film industry. Dino is a remarkable man, a true legend, and I was lucky to work for him. Dino also pioneered the modern practice of financing films by bifurcating the rights; that is, by selling off the rights individually. Dino would sell domestic rights to a film to a studio, retaining all foreign rights, and then sell the foreign rights through his own sales company. The challenge was to try to lock in a profit up front by getting more in rights sales than the movie would cost. For instance, we could sell the domestic rights to a certain film for fifty per cent of the budget, and then hope to get sixty per cent of the budget from foreign sources, thereby locking in a ten per cent profit, no matter what the commercial results would be (assuming the film was on budget). Dino was just a genius at doing this; moreover, he had huge hits like *Serpico, Three Days of the Condor,* etc. so his profit participations were meaningful as well. It was like getting paid to learn from a master . . . and, in the mix, Dino is also one of the most engaging, passionate storytellers of all time. A thorough and complete original.

In late 1991, we had distributed Madonna's documentary *Truth or Dare* outside of the United States (where Dino, in his inimitable manner, re-titled it *In Bed with Madonna*). We had done very well with the film and wanted to make another film with Madonna. She told us that she wanted to do a very sexy thriller, and I found a script called *Body of Evidence,* which she agreed to do.

One aside here about working with Madonna. She was fantastic in every way. Very early on, she told me that we would get along great as long as I told her the absolute truth, no matter what. I followed her advice, and she was the consummate pro with whom to work. She was an absolute delight to be around, too. One brief story: She was in amazing physical condition. Worked out for hours a day. We shot the film in Portland, Oregon, and, of course, needed to hire security to be around her. She was, let's face it, probably the most famous woman in the world at that time. Taking no chances, we hired Pete Weireter as the head of security. Pete's "other" gig was training the Los Angeles Police Department's elite SWAT squad. (Also, interestingly, three years later, it was Pete who, as LAPD's top negotiator, talked O. J. Simpson out of the white Bronco after the infamous low-speed chase wound up back at O. J.'s Brentwood house.) Madonna had warned me to make sure Pete's detail was in good enough physical shape to stay with her when she did her morning exercise in the streets of Portland. Pete just smiled when I told him and I could see the thought process: "Sure, this little woman (Madonna is not tall) is going to give my guys a problem. Right." When I told Madonna that Pete seemed unconcerned, she just smiled a little knowing smile and told me to stand by after her first morning with the security detail. Well, sure enough, she took them on something like a ten-mile run and wound up coming back alone, with her security detail scattered behind her, struggling to find their way back. At that point, Pete brought up more guys and got a car to follow Madonna on her runs from that point forward. Madonna was totally good-natured about the whole episode, and Pete never forgot about it. When I saw him years later, his first words were about that moment and his chagrin at having Madonna leave his guys in her wake.

Body of Evidence was slated to open in late January 1993, and we took it to New York for its press screening on

January 12, 1993, another date on which my life would change forever.

Without going into extraneous detail, the film was received very poorly; in fact, people even booed. It was a defining and humiliating moment. I was dating a woman at the time who was with me in New York that fateful night. In the wee small hours of the morning, she told me to "get back to your heart, Stephen. The guy who started off making *Somewhere in Time* should not be making movies like *Body of Evidence.* Not that there's anything wrong with movies like that, it's just not you. It's not what you came here to do, and it's not who you are." She changed the course of my life that night and, even though we didn't stay together, we're still friends, and she knows how eternally grateful I am to her for guiding me back to the place that Enigma calls "the rivers of believe."

In that moment, I knew I couldn't go on with my life the way it was. Unfortunately, I didn't handle the next few months with Dino very well. I had changed and wanted to change the direction of the company accordingly. Dino had been doing things his way—very successfully—for fifty years. We fought. He finally got tired of the conflict. In August 1993, he fired me (more on that in chapter 15). I was no longer doing what was best for him and his company. I've always regretted that things ended that way. Dino is a fantastic man and I was very happy for him when he received the 2001 Thalberg Award at the Academy Awards.

I went into seclusion for a year, becoming, in fact, a complete recluse, interacting only with my beloved daughters, who by that time were living with me. During that year, I spent weeks browsing for metaphysical material, read voraciously on the subject, and began to meditate daily. The whole focus of my life shifted from an external view to an internal one. I found a particular spiritual path that resonated with me and dived in. I knew I could no longer do what I had been doing in my life. Even though I did try to find work, I knew that I couldn't stay in the mainstream movie life from which I had felt alienated for a long time anyway. Not that there is or was anything intrinsically wrong with that life. I just didn't fit into it and, in retrospect, never really did. To quote a wonderful old comedian named George Gobel, "I felt like the world was a tuxedo and I was a pair of brown shoes."

By this time, I wanted to make only metaphysical movies. I wanted to make *What Dreams May Come.*

In late April 1994, I attended a metaphysical seminar where I found myself seated behind a very tall man who had his arm around the shoulders of a very beautiful woman. Not only couldn't I see very well, but I also found myself feeling very jealous of the obvious love between them. I resolved that, at the first break, I would try to find another seat. During that break, I was talking to an acquaintance who saw someone walk up behind me. Smiling, she said, "Stephen, turn around, I want you to meet a writer who shares your interest in metaphysical films." You guessed it. The tall guy, Barnet Bain. We met. We shook hands, and instantaneously became best friends and partners. No exaggeration. We just knew at the moment that we had found each other and could begin our business.

Barnet and his wife Sandy had been absorbed in metaphysics for the previous ten years and had used a name for a corporation that handled their personal affairs. The name was Metafilmics. As soon as I heard it, I requested that we be able to appropriate it for the name of our new business. They graciously agreed, and the new Metafilmics was created—but the inspiration and original idea for it was theirs.

Barnet had been a writer for many years. The only film that had been made out of one of his scripts was the Royal Shakespeare version of *Jesus* which was released in 1980. Unbeknownst to many, *Jesus* is one of the most successful films ever released. Warner Brothers has a special division devoted only to the film; moreover, it's also fascinating that this amazingly metaphysical man wrote a traditional version of *Jesus.*

Barnet also developed several studio projects over the years and was way ahead of his time as a writer. His scripts were inventive and spiritual, and he was as frustrated as I was with the traditional business when we met.

In 1996, I decided to give myself a fiftieth birthday present and legally changed my last name from Deutsch back to my birth name of Simon. This was not a rejection of either my stepfather or anything else. It was, rather, an embracing of the name that my soul gave me in this life and a reawakening of the essence of the Stephen Simon who went into seclusion after my biological father died. As such, there was a deep spiritual significance in this decision for me, even though it meant a new name after my entire career up to 1996 had been spent as Deutsch. As a consequence, it has created a good deal of confusion and fortunately some humor as well. After the publicity started coming out for *What Dreams May Come* which also credited me with having produced *Somewhere in Time,* I got several concerned phone calls from fans of the latter to alert me that "some imposter" named Simon was going around claiming that he had produced *SIT,* not Deutsch. It also helps that I can now blame that jerk Deutsch for any mistakes that I do not want to own up to myself. Very spiritual, right?

With the synergy of Barnet's resonance, we finally found a way to get *What Dreams May Come* off the ground, and it became the first film to carry the Metafilmics banner.

So, twenty years elapsed between *Somewhere in Time* and *What Dreams May Come.* These are the two films of which I am the most proud, and the films that have struck the deepest chord in both myself and the audiences for whom they were made. Even though both films have generated a lot of interest, I have never really told the story of how I discovered both of them, nor have I discussed all the behind-the-scenes intrigue that marked both of them. Until now.

The next two chapters will detail, from my firsthand knowledge, how both films navigated the narrow shoals of Hollywood challenges and were born into the world.

"Is it you?"

—Somewhere in Time

CHAPTER FOURTEEN

Behind the Scenes: *Somewhere in Time*

I knew exactly where to go for my first movie business job.

Ray Stark was already a legendary producer. He had produced *Funny Girl* with Barbra Streisand (based on the life of Fanny Brice, whose daughter Fran was Ray's wife). He had also produced such films as *The World of Suzie Wong, Night of the Iguana,* and *The Way We Were,* another great love story with formidable obstacles between the lovers. Ray's company, Rastar, was one of the most prolific production companies in the business, and Ray was also a shrewd political power broker who had almost single-handedly resurrected Columbia Pictures under management he had recruited. Even more important, I knew Ray very well.

Ray was an agent when my Dad was the head of production at Columbia under Harry Cohn in the late forties. He was also somewhat of a protégé of my Dad. My mother and Ray's wife Fran were best friends. (There were actually four best friends at that time—my Mom, Fran Stark, Nancy Davis [Reagan] and Lee Annenberg, wife of legendary publisher and later Ambassador to England Walter Annenberg. Even though Fran passed away several years ago, the other three are still best friends after over fifty years—but that, as they say, is another story.) So, anyway, Ray was around a lot after my Dad's death, and I also became very friendly with Peter and Wendy, Ray's kids. Even after my mother remarried, Ray kept an eye on me, and I got a big kick out of him. Ray was and still is a fabulous guy to know. Funny, irreverent, bright, mischievous, outrageous, and perennially young. I always kept in touch with him as I grew up, both directly and through his kids.

Tragically, in the early seventies, Ray's son Peter died, and Ray was understandably devastated. I stayed in closer touch with him and a kind of quasi-father/son relationship evolved. My stepfather (to whom I also refer as Dad) was really wonderful to me, so neither Ray nor I wanted to do anything that would make him feel awkward, but the connection was definitely there, particularly after Peter's death. I teased Ray a lot that I was going to take over his company one day, but we both kind of knew that there was a lot of real intent in the kidding around.

So, I made my move. I went to see Ray and told him I was ready to start working for him. At first, he thought I was playing around, but it became very clear very quickly that I was really serious, and he kind of panicked, in a way. I mean, here I was, his mentor's son asking to become the protégé to him that he had been to my Dad. He had lost his son, there was no one else for him to teach the business to, and he knew I was bright, ambitious, and loved movies in the way he did. That was the good news. The bad news was that he adored my mother as a close friend (which lasts to this day), knew she was also his wife's best friend, and knew that he would be responsible for me leaving my law practice to work in the film business—a Jewish mother's nightmare! He also greatly respected my stepfather and didn't want to be seen as changing the course that he knew my stepfather thought I should pursue. So, he stalled. And stalled. And stalled.

I bugged him mercilessly, calling all the time, showing up at his office unannounced, becoming a really annoying pest. After about three months of this, he finally got exasperated and decided to put me to the test. I'll never forget that day in early February, 1976, in his office.

"Okay, Steve. You want to do this, we'll do this, but only on some very specific terms."

"Anything, Ray. You name it."

"First of all, I need someone right away so you have to start tomorrow."

"Uh, what about my law practice?"

"That's your problem. Also, you only get $200 a week and I have no office for you so you'll just have to sit on my couch in my office and listen. If you have to ask questions, you're not quick enough to do the job anyway, so don't start. That's it. Take it or leave it."

Now I know that sounds really tough but it wasn't meant that way at all. Ray admitted to me later that he designed the offer in such a way that he thought there was no way I could do it. My law practice being dealt with overnight. The cut in pay to $200 per week, etc. On the other hand, if I did accept it, then he knew I was utterly dedicated and he would give me a chance.

"Okay, Ray. Got it. I'll be here at eight tomorrow morning."

And so I started my career in the film business as Ray Stark's assistant in February, 1976. I disposed of my law practice over the first thirty days of my time with Ray, completing the work that I had committed to doing. Most of my practice was representing professional football players, and I actually negotiated my last contract huddled in a back office at Rastar, so Ray wouldn't know what I was doing. (That last deal was getting my friend Ron Jaworski away from the L.A. Rams and to the Philadelphia Eagles, so he could start as their quarterback. I concluded the negotiations with Eagles head coach Dick Vermeil, and together, he and Ron made it to the Super Bowl a couple of years later. Many more years later, Vermeil actually won the Super Bowl with the St. Louis Rams after they relocated from L.A.)

I didn't immediately tell Ray about *Bid Time Return*. I wasn't confident enough yet to discuss it, but I didn't want anyone else to beat me to it, either, so I had to make contact with the author, Richard Matheson. My very first phone call on the very first day of my job with Ray was to the Writer's Guild to find the agent for Matheson, which turned out to be a great guy named Rick Ray at the now defunct agency of

Adams, Ray, and Rosenberg. Using the name of Ray Stark got a lot of phone calls returned immediately, so I was very quickly on the phone with Rick, told him I was Ray's new assistant, and that I wanted to meet Richard Matheson about his book (which, to my relief, was still available as a film).

The next day, I had my first meeting with the legendary Mr. Matheson at a restaurant named Sorrentino's in Burbank. Richard Matheson is one of the most gifted storytellers in American fiction, and he's also one of the most engaging and delightful characters around. I loved him the minute I met him and also realized very quickly that, while Ray was going to be my professional mentor, Richard was going to be my spiritual guide. We became great friends at that first lunch. I told him how much I loved the book, and I committed to him that, although I didn't know how, when, or where, I would get the movie made. We shook hands, and that was it. My first movie deal.

It took three years.

I plunged myself into my job, and Ray was an amazing teacher. A producer named Mort Engelberg was working with us, and he came to me to champion a project he had acquired called *CB to Atlanta.* Ray had never done a road/action movie before, and it was a great challenge but we kept after him. The movie was eventually retitled *Smokey and the Bandit,* and it became a huge success. Even though I didn't produce the film (that was Mort's quite rightful claim to fame), Ray acknowledged my role in championing it by making me the head of production of his company. I was thirty-one years old. I lived in the Hollywood Hills, dated so-called fantasy women, and drove my convertible Jaguar to work every day blaring the Eagles' song, "New Kid in Town," convinced it was really about me. A stereotype's stereotype of a stereotype. I had no clue.

That was part of my life. The thrill didn't last long. I became very aware of how shallow my life had become and that I didn't really covet life in the fast lane. Ray was pushing me toward one way of life, that of a studio head. He was actively grooming me for that eventuality, and nobody was better suited to the role of kingmaker than Ray. He was an amazing force of nature within the business. I was "his guy." *Smokey* was a great calling card, and I could talk the talk; however, walking the walk was becoming increasingly difficult. While I knew Ray meant the best for me, and was doing what he felt that my Dad would have done if he had lived, I just couldn't quite stay with the program. Even if I had pursued the goal that Ray had mapped out for me, I would have eventually failed at it. As I have noted earlier, I did not have the requisite skill sets to either become or remain an "A" player in Hollywood. I think I instinctively knew that and, besides, there was something else beckoning me, and its call got louder and more insistent every day.

The siren's call was my growing interest in spirituality. It fascinated me. I couldn't get *Bid Time Return* out of my mind, and that drove Ray nuts. By now, I had talked him into optioning the book rights, but he just didn't see the commercial potential of the project. Ray had a fabulous sense of what was commercial, and he kept telling me that "the Matheson thing" was not a moneymaker.

In the meantime, Matheson was a ready spiritual tutor. He gave me reading lists and answered all my questions patiently and endlessly. He never got impatient with the passage of time and never pushed me to get his project moving.

We continued to have success at Rastar. We won a bidding war over the rights to a new script called *The Electric Horseman,* and that delighted Ray. The time was right for another "accident" and it came along in the guise of a fascinating director named Jeannot Szwarc.

Jeannot had just replaced the director on *Jaws 2* for Universal and had done a terrific job of getting the film back on track and in the can. I had forged a terrific relationship at Universal (which later saved my career) because of *Smokey,* so I heard how happy they were with Jeannot. I told Ray we should meet with Jeannot and see what he wanted to do next because Universal really wanted to pay him back for saving the day on *Jaws 2*. This was just the kind of maneuver that Ray loved, so he readily agreed.

Jeannot, Ray, and I met within days and began to talk about the kinds of projects that Jeannot wanted to do. Right off the bat, he said, "You know, what I'd like most to do is a really romantic fantasy, something like *Portrait of Jennie* back in the forties."

I quite literally jumped out of my chair! "Boy, have I got a project for you!" I rushed headlong into a rapt description of *Bid Time Return,* much to Ray's chagrin. I could see his eyes rolling back in his head, thinking I was going to corner Jeannot into championing what Ray felt was a commercial risk.

I gave Jeannot the novel, and he read it overnight, calling me the next morning to say that he was definitely "in" and that we should develop the script together. I called Richard, feeling relieved and excited, and the development process began.

To save time and space, I'm going to jump ahead here by one year.

Ray and I parted ways under very difficult circumstances that are not relevant to this narrative, and the only project I was able to take with me was our script of *Bid Time Return.* It was December, 1978. Ned Tanen was at that time the head of production of Universal Studios and one of the few straight-shooters in the business; that is, he always told you the hard truth, no matter what. The truth then was that he really didn't want to make *Bid Time Return* for the same reasons that Ray had always been opposed to it: Ned felt it was not commercial. (Let's remember that this was the late seventies—disco, etc. They were not wrong to conclude that we were a bit out of step with the times.) Ned's dilemma was that he really liked both Jeannot and me, and via both *Jaws 2* and *Smokey and The Bandit,* we had both done very well for Universal. He didn't want to say no, but he was hesitant to say yes.

A terrific woman named Verna Fields was our production executive. All studios have production executives who report to the head of production, and who are responsible for the day-to-day supervision of each project from development through release. The studio head makes the big decisions about casting, director, budget limits, and—most crucially—whether a project gets "green-lit" (approved to start shooting) or not. Production executives can torpedo a project if they are negative enough, and they can also be crucial allies if they are willing to stand up and push for a particular project in the staff meetings at which all decisions about films are made.

Verna was an amazing and revered woman in the industry. Winner of the Academy Award for editing *Jaws,* and editor for many years of several other high-profile films, Verna had moved into the executive suite at Universal. Jeannot had worked with her on *Jaws 2* so we were thrilled to get her to work with us. Affectionately known as "mother cutter," Verna was a living, breathing legend and commanded great respect everywhere, not just at Universal. (The "word" always was that she had "saved" *Jaws.* In her inimitably humble and yet brash way, she would always say—"Baloney! You can't make chicken liver out of chicken s . . . !") Fortunately, she was a passionate believer in our film and she fought tirelessly to get us in front of the cameras, so far, to no avail.

Christmas, 1978, saw the debut of *Superman 1* and the explosion onto the international scene of Christopher Reeve, who played the title role.

Just after January 1, 1979, we had a crucial casting meeting with Verna wherein we decided to make a run at Ned Tanen with a cast list to see if we could get him interested in pushing the film ahead in that way. Somewhat offhandedly—and not terribly seriously—I suggested that the best person for the role would be Chris Reeve, but that we could never get him, so we shouldn't even mention it to Ned. The minute the words were out of my mouth, I regretted them, not because it was a bad idea, but because I thought we had no chance to get Chris. He was the hottest young actor in the business, being offered mega-money and high-profile movies and we were definitely way under the radar. I also immediately saw Verna's expression and knew I had put my foot squarely in my mouth and halfway down my throat.

"Yes!" she cried. "That's it. Put him on the top of the list!"

"Please, Verna," I said. "If we put him on top of the list, Ned will say no to everyone else and tell us to get Reeve, which we won't be able to do, and then we'll be back to square one with a rejection that will only discourage Ned more."

"Yeah, well, maybe, but this is our chance, so put him on the list," she ordered me. And that was that.

We met with Ned the next day and sure enough, for probably the only time in my career, I predicted a studio head's response exactly.

"Chris Reeve?" Ned said. "Perfect. Get him and we'll make the movie."

"Ned, who else?" I asked.

"No one. Get him."

"What if we don't?"

"Stephen, don't ask questions that you don't want the answer for. You sure you want me to answer that question?"

"Uh . . . no, sir! We'll try to get Chris but, you know, he's going to be expensive. Probably $2 million (which was a huge salary at that time)."

"I'm only going to give you $4 million to make the movie, so you better get him for a lot less."

"So, Ned, we're supposed to get the hottest star in the business for a salary way below his price, for a movie you don't want to make and no one else understands?" I asked.

"Good, Stephen," Ned laughed. "Now you're catching on. You may have a future as a producer yet . . . if you get Reeve."

I thought Jeannot was going to kill me right there in the hall outside Ned's office. I had managed to get us in a predicament where we either produced a miracle, or we were out of luck and quite probably out of work.

We trudged back to Verna's office and worked out budget numbers. Jeannot had the brilliant idea that we should hire everyone on the crew at scale (the union minimum for each department). Crunching those numbers and making some other dubious wild guesses, we realized we could pay Chris no more than $500,000, a quarter of what he could command elsewhere. And that was the good news. The bad news was that I had to make the offer to his agent, knowing he would laugh me out of town.

Again, the only time I've predicted an agent's response correctly. He didn't just laugh. He howled. I cringed, and he howled again. He then refused to even consider the offer or pass the script on to Chris. The practice of law was beginning to intrigue me again.

Jeannot and I knew that desperate times called for desperate action by desperate people—us. We figured we had nothing to lose by taking a flyer on a wild long shot: Somehow we would figure out where Chris lived and slip the script to him. I knew that would put me on his agent's permanent hit list but, if it didn't work, I thought I'd be out of the business anyway, so who cared?

Through some clever skullduggery, we found Chris's address and literally slipped the script under his doormat with a note begging him to read it even if it seemed insane to him.

Fortunately, it didn't take long. Chris called us very quickly to come meet with him so Jeannot and I kind of floated (had our insane gamble actually worked?) up to Chris's rented house in the Hollywood Hills, whereupon Chris jumped in with both feet. He loved the script, the whole idea of the movie, and, most particularly, he loved the idea of doing a small intimate drama rather than all the action movies he was being offered. (Years later, Chris told me that he had just been offered the lead in a big Viking epic when we slipped him the script. The idea of him running around in one of those inverted "drinking gourd" helmets might have just pushed him right into our arms.) His only real concerns were how we would handle the time travel itself and whether we could actually get the audience to buy the notion that the actor who had just played Superman could actually waste away and die from a broken heart. Somehow, Jeannot allayed those concerns and we had our lead; furthermore, the salary was no problem. Chris was and still is a total and complete mensche. (By the way, his agent never did speak to me again.)

All the way back to the studio, I kept remembering the phrase that "even a blind squirrel finds an acorn once in a while."

So the two blind squirrels reported to Ned and Verna that we had Chris. Verna's mouth actually dropped open and Ned looked like a guy who had just realized his fly had been unzipped all day. I restrained myself from telling him that he "might have a future as a studio head," and off we went with our "green light" in tow and visions of making a classic love story firmly in our sights.

The next steps were finding our leading lady, a location, implementing the crew-at-scale concept, and coming up with a new title.

The search for the actress to play Elise McKenna did not take very long. Ensconced in our bungalow on the back lot of Universal in January 1979, we knew we had to start shooting in May, because that was our window of availability with

Chris. We didn't have a lot of time and, fortunately, we didn't need it. We started interviewing actresses, and Chris was very much a part of the process. He was totally game to read with anyone we wanted, so it was easy to gauge chemistry. Very early on in the process, we interviewed Jane Seymour who had just played a role in a James Bond film, but had not yet made an American film. She came into the interview in a beautiful period dress and was Elise McKenna from the time she walked in until she left. She just was the character. We watched her interact and read with Chris, and then she left. We all just kind of looked at each other and said, "Well, that was easy. We've got our lead. What's next?" She was so luminously beautiful and so perfect in her reading with Chris that I know there just couldn't have been another actress for the part. Elise is Jane and Jane is Elise.

The next step was location. The mantra of the restaurant business is that the three most important ingredients of a restaurant's success are location, location, and location. That was our mantra, too. To make our film for the budget we had, there was no way we could afford to build much—we had to find the perfect place that was pretty much intact for everything we needed.

First stop was a perfunctory visit to the grand Hotel del Coronado in San Diego where Matheson had set the book. Richard had been inspired to write the book while perusing an historic photo exhibit while staying at the Coronado. He saw a photo of the great turn-of-the-century actress Maude Adams and wondered what might happen if a writer fell in love with the portrait and willed himself back in time to meet her. (Richard's delightful and brilliant psychologist wife, Ruth, has enjoyed a couple of decades now of teasing him over *that* fantasy.)

We knew that the Coronado would not work for us because it had become too modern over the years. We knew we couldn't shoot period scenes around it, and we wanted to be much farther away from L.A. than San Diego. Filmmakers generally like to be as far away from daily scrutiny from the financing studio as possible. No offense here but, truly, studio executives on a shoot are much like dogs walking past a fire hydrant: they can't help but lift their leg. Enough said.

Jeannot's assistant was a bright young man named Steven Bickel, who became the associate producer of the film because of his terrific contributions (and, as the old joke goes, he was one of the few willing to "associate" with the producer). We gave Bickel (he became known by his last name so as to avoid confusion with me—rank does have some privilege) the assignment of researching great old hotels around the country. He got in touch with state film commissions whose job it is to lure shooting companies into their states. Photos of hotels and locations came flooding into our office. Nothing looked quite right until we saw photos of the Grand Hotel on Mackinac Island, Michigan.

The Grand was built in 1887 and has the longest porch in the world. The pictures were breathtaking, but the aspect that really grabbed us was that motorized vehicles were strictly prohibited on the entire island. On the one hand, that was very daunting because a movie crew has indispensable support vehicles (camera, power, props, etc.) that must accompany the shooting company; however, it also meant that they were trying to preserve the natural period feel of the environment and *that* was music to our ears. There was, however, the initial challenge of convincing them to let us come in the first place.

I contacted the owner of the Grand by letter and explained what we were doing. Fortunately, it was not a faceless corporation; rather, I was dealing with one man, Daniel Musser, whose father had owned the Grand for years and then passed it on to him. I got a very nice but perfunctory reply saying that a movie company just couldn't work. The Grand is seasonal (May to October) and they could not see accommodating us during that time. It was too cold to shoot in the winter (and our love story required sunshine and beauty anyway), and we couldn't bring vehicles on the island. So, in a nutshell, thanks but go away.

Undeterred, I decided to send Mr. Musser a copy of the script and a note beseeching him to read it. I told him that the movie would forever memorialize his hotel and that the hotel itself was a major character in the film. It worked. Mr. Musser contacted me, told me he loved the script, and that we could come visit if we wanted, although the challenges were still formidable. Elated, Jeannot and I planned our scouting trip. One small detail: it was February so the hotel and, indeed, the whole island were closed for the winter and it was about minus ten degrees in the Great Lakes at that time. We worked it out, however, that we could fly to Chicago, take a smaller plane to Pellston, Michigan, and then the hotel would provide us with a private single-engine plane to fly us to the landing strip on the island—so off we went.

We landed on the island and were met at the tiny landing strip by Dan Musser and Dan Dewey (who was to serve as our island guide and later became perhaps the most indispensable member of our crew). We climbed into a huge, horse-drawn sleigh, huddled under blankets, and began the snowbound journey to the hotel. Being a California native, I have very thin blood—and I had never been in cold like that. I was chattering and dying to get into the hotel. We pulled up in front of the massive building and it was almost completely dark. That's when it dawned on my California consciousness that, of course, they wouldn't heat an empty hotel in the dead of winter. Feeling a lot like Jack Nicholson in *The Shining,* I trudged up the steps into the hotel, where it was actually colder than it was outside. Dan Musser had been watching me all the time and I think, unwittingly, I won him over without saying a word. I think he figured that I had to want to do this pretty badly if I was willing to be that cold.

Aside from the temperature, Jeannot and I were absolutely enthralled. I could see his director's eye gleaming as he considered the visual possibilities of the hotel; however, the exteriors were going to have to be envisioned in the summer. Just then, everything was blanketed in snow. We got on snowmobiles to take our tour. Dan Dewey drove me and, at one point, I yelled at him "Where's the lake?" and he shouted back, "You've been on it for ten minutes." That's when I figured I should shut up and let Jeannot do the visualizing.

On a walking part of our tour, Jeannot and I talked about the possibilities and we were very optimistic but for the knowledge that we couldn't shoot the bedroom and other interior intimate scenes in the hotel itself. Nor could we stay at the hotel—both for the same reasons: the hotel was way too expensive, was very booked anyway, and the rooms did not lend themselves to what we needed. Rooms only look real in most films. Usually, they are constructed on a stage so walls can be moved around to accommodate camera angles and movement. Soon, we would find that the universe was indeed smiling on us and was about to take us into its arms.

We were shown a new "inn" that had just been completed on the other side of the island. Actually, it was a converted college dormitory for a long-defunct school. It was primitive, but it was cheap and it would do. Near the "dorms," there was a rather large building that we were ushered into next. Just as we were explaining to our hosts our dilemma of not having stage space, they flipped on the lights. We were standing in the middle of a completely equipped sound stage! On a small island in the Great Lakes! Huh? It turned out that The Moral Rearmament Crusade had built this stage to use as a television studio. They went out of business and just left the stage behind, completely equipped.

That was it. Everything we needed was on this island. Dan Musser had decided not only to allow us to shoot in his hotel—for no fee, by the way—but also agreed to smooth the way for us with the island government, businesses, etc. This was (and still is) tantamount to having the Pope tell you that he'll help you tour the Vatican. We were in.

Back in L.A., we put our crew together, cast the rest of the film, and prepared for our journey. There was one last thing to be done: a new title. *Bid Time Return* was too much of a tongue-twister for the marketing people and, hard as it may be to believe, there was some concern that it would sound like *Bedtime Return* and look like either a children's film or a porno. (You can imagine the discussions we would have later about *What Dreams May Come.*) Welcome to the bizarre world of "studio speak," where many a producer has lost his/her mind.

We all started the search for a new title. One night, I heard a Barry Manilow (hey . . . I liked Barry Manilow. . . . still do) song called "Somewhere in the Night." We had wanted to have time travel in our title so *Somewhere in Time* just popped up. Again, the universe gave us what we needed when we needed it.

So, in late April 1979, we took off for our adventure on

Mackinac Island. We arrived on the island, took our horse-drawn buggies (the island taxis) to our pathetic little "inn" and acclimated very quickly. Mr. Musser had smoothed the way with the local government so we could bring two trucks on the island. We had very strict rules about how and when they could move around, but it worked. In fact, it was the most seamless location shoot imaginable, due, in no small part, to our location manager Dan Dewey, who had been our guide on our first trip. Dan had lived on, and worked on, the island for many, many years so everyone knew, trusted, and loved him. We just told Dan what we needed, and he got it done. Never argued, never fussed. You just asked Dan and Dan did it. Without him, we might not have lasted a week. The other Dan, Musser, was our giant protector. He opened his hotel and his heart to all of us. Even in the height of his summer season, he closed off parts of his hotel when we needed it. Dan is one of those stalwart Midwesterners with utter dignity. Always impeccably dressed and implacable. Inside, he's a warm, loving man and his heart sustained us.

We had to go to Chicago to shoot the very opening of the film for two days. Verna Fields met us in Chicago to kick off the shoot, and I was thrilled to have our "mother cutter" there. At breakfast on our first day, Verna took me aside and, in her matter-of-fact way, calmly informed me that she had cancer and would not be able to be with us after that day. Talk about heaven and hell on the same day. Our first day was the heaven. Verna's news was something worse than hell. We all loved her and wouldn't have been there without her. I remember hugging her and breaking down crying. She just held me and comforted me. She was dying and she comforted me in those moments. That was Verna. (Verna lived to see the film completed, supervised the editing, and made it through the release in October 1980.)

The shoot itself was almost totally uneventful. After all those close calls with destiny, our cast and crew created our own Brigadoon for those two magical months. There were no ego problems. Chris Reeve was the most unassuming movie star that anyone could imagine. He was always there for all of us. Jane was an angel. Everything jelled.

Whatever tension there might have been was broken on the very first day of our shoot on the Island. We shot the opening sequence of the film where Susan French, who played "old Elise," finds young Richard at the performance of one of his plays and hands him the watch he left with her in the past. (Yes, the watch itself is a paradox. Where did it begin? We actually had crew T-shirts made which, referring to Richard Matheson, said, "Ask *him* about the watch." Richard's answer to the question was always a serene "Somewhere in time!") So we're shooting the scene where old Elise hands Richard the watch and says mysteriously, "Come back to me." After a couple of difficult takes, Susan walks meaningfully up to Chris in the next take, puts the watch in his hand, and purrs, "Get this fixed for me, willya?" That was the tension-breaker, and the weeks then just flew by.

Jeannot was a total and consummate pro the way he ran the show. During production, the director is the absolute boss of all that goes on. Think Tony Soprano in the Bada Bing. That's a director during production. By that time, you just have to hope you've chosen wisely because there's not much you can do except fire the director. Not that we had any of those problems. Jeannot knew exactly what he wanted, and he put it on film.

Things went so smoothly in fact that it almost seemed surreal. Everyone got along. We were all friends. It was so collegial, in fact, that a writer for the *Los Angeles Times* commented in print after visiting us that . . . "while it isn't completely true that the cast and crew skip to dailies, holding hands, it's not entirely wrong either." To that end, our talented, angelic set decorator, Mary Ann Biddle, told me something about halfway through the shoot that turned out to be utterly prophetic. One day, she said to me, "Stephen, this is your first film, so you have no frame of reference. You won't have any idea how truly special this experience is until you've been through a lot more films. This is total magic. We're creating a classic, and we all know it." She couldn't have been more right. I've been involved in about twenty-five films over these twenty-five years, as a producer and as an executive, and nothing compared to that summer on Mackinac.

☆☆☆

A film goes through many incarnations between its birth as an idea and its release. There is the original selling draft of the script that then gives way to the shooting script. Then the movie changes as the actors and director interpret it on screen.

Then the film is given to the editor and he/she puts it together with the supervision of the director and a new vision emerges. You can never really tell what you have as a film from watching "dailies" every day during the shoot. The only thing you really know is whether or not a performance is really bad. That you can see. Bad dailies never make a good movie. Good dailies—even great dailies—have, however, fooled and broken the hearts of many filmmakers and studios. You can be completely deluded by bits of film that seem to work on their own until they are put together. You just don't know. In fact, most directors will tell you that the moment they dread most in any film is when they see the first editor's assembly of the film. This is not a real cut, with timing and proper pacing. It is just a stringing together of the basic scenes so that the editor and director can have a starting point for the edit itself. It takes a strong stomach and constitution to sit through that first assembly. Many directors have been known to bolt for the bathroom and lose their lunches. Producers are basically prohibited from attending and, if you're smart, you consider yourself lucky to be excluded.

So our edit began. From all reports, the first assembly was almost three hours long and Jeannot went pale as a ghost. I wasn't worried. I trusted Jeannot, our bright young editor Jeff Gourson, and, of course, our "mother cutter."

Editing took the rest of the year of 1979. The studio was in no hurry. They didn't really know how to market the film yet anyway, and so they kind of forgot about us.

Finally, we were ready to show the film to the studio in early 1980. Now the director gets to share his nausea with studio executives. Another dreaded moment. Watching a rough cut is somewhat akin to seeing sausage get made: you might like the final product but the early steps are pretty hard to stomach. Studios want to see a film before all the final pieces are in place so they can have their input into the final product. ("He who has the gold makes the rules" is the mantra at Hollywood studios.) Rough cuts, however, require a great deal of experience and imagination to watch, because one has to be able to envision the final product from its rough components.

Rough cut screenings are also always preceded by a long disclaimer from the director—the edit isn't a fine cut yet, the music is temporary, the sound has not been smoothed out, no dubbing has occurred with the actors, the color is off, etc. All of which, by the way, is true; however, it's also an attempt to severely lower the expectations of the executives. The last thing you want in these kinds of screenings is for the film to begin with excited executive expectations (which will not be the title of the sequel to this book). You want to set the bar as low as possible so that a high crawl will get you over it.

Our expectation bar was very low. Still, we managed to crawl under rather than over it.

To say that the screening did not go well is like the apocryphal question: "Other than that, Mrs. Lincoln, how did you like the play?"

All the executives had blank stares on their faces until Ned Tanen finally said "It feels like I've just hiked through the Sahara Desert."

Not exactly a ringing endorsement.

Back to the editing room. About forty minutes were removed, the scenes were streamlined and, by the next time we showed the film, John Barry's extraordinary score was included.

If our executive expectations were low for the first screening, they were beneath the radar for the second screening. This time, it worked to our advantage. The film was remarkably better, and the executives finally understood what we had been searching for all along. All of a sudden, we were back on the radar, but with an asterisk. No one really knew how the film would play to an audience. It was time to find out.

Public previews are the next step in the sausage factory assembly line of nauseating movie experiences. You just never know how an audience is going to respond to the film as a whole or any of its scenes. Laughs in the wrong places, no laughs where you think they should be, people getting bored and walking out (and studios have people stationed outside the doors to ask why), a lot of rustling in seats that always signifies boredom, etc.

Previews in Los Angeles were and are pretty skewed because the movie audience in L.A. is so film-sophisticated that you wind up getting a lot of film-critic-like comments rather than just human responses. Universal scheduled our previews for Toronto and Minneapolis. One sophisticated big city audience and one more traditional Midwest audience. It sounded fair to us (not that it mattered to anyone if we had disagreed anyway) and off we went.

Toronto was first. I never remember being more nervous. Jeannot was trying to calm *me* down, even though he looked like he should have had an I.V. drip of valium himself. We were both wrecks. Until the film began. That's when the magic happened. From the very first scene, the audience was totally hooked. You could feel it sitting in the theater. They laughed in all the right places and in none of the wrong ones and, at the end, you could actually hear people crying. Even more important, there was applause as the screening ended. (On a purely personal note, I will never forget seeing my "produced by" credit for the first time on screen that night. The feeling that it generated was overwhelming. I just knew that this was what I had come here to do.)

At preview screenings, studios ask audiences to fill out preview cards where the audience can comment on a whole range of issues—from who they liked or didn't like in the cast, to their response to the story, the music, the pacing, etc. This is another moment most filmmakers dread because, again, you never know what an audience is going to say and what weight their comments will be given by the studio. That night, we had nothing to fear. Almost no one left until after the film was over—always a good sign that they were engaged in it.

As we exited the theater, many members of the audience had gathered outside and applauded again. When they found out that Jeannot was the director, they crowded around him, congratulating him and asking him for his autograph. They could have turned off the marquee lights and just used the reflection of Jeannot's beaming face. It was a wonderful moment.

We went back to our hotel and got the tally from the audience cards, and it was just extraordinary. They got it. They loved it. That simple. We were all thrilled and a bit stunned. None of us had expected it to go *that* well. I remember Ned Tanen getting on the phone to call his boss, Sid Sheinberg who, along with Lew Wasserman, ran the entire Universal business operation. Ned told Sid that Sid should get on an airplane the next morning and meet us in Minneapolis because "we may very well have a phenomenon on our hands here."

On to Minneapolis.

Now we were really holding our breath. If this screening went badly, it was very likely that the Toronto response would be considered by Universal to have been an aberration and then disregarded. And Sid Sheinberg showed up.

I decided not to actually sit in the audience for this screening. I stood off to the side of the theater so I could actually watch the faces of the audience, dimly illuminated by the reflected light from the screen. I'll never forget that experience. I actually watched the different waves of emotion that flickered across their faces as the film played. That's a rush that is hard to describe but impossible to forget.

If anything, the screening in Minneapolis was even better than Toronto. The audience not only applauded at the end, some of them actually stood and cheered. Again, Jeannot was mobbed out in the lobby when the audience realized that he was the director. Everyone was shocked, thrilled, and speechless—and that was us!

The original concept for marketing the film was to open the film in a few theaters in major cities and see if it could build an audience. This is the kind of release that films usually get in two different situations. The first such situation occurs when a studio has a special film that it thinks will get critical acclaim and build its audience from there. For example, films that open at the end of a calendar year, which are being projected by their studios as Academy Award contenders, often get this kind of release. That's a "good thing."

The other type of limited release is when a studio really doesn't believe in the film, doesn't know how to market it, and, most important, doesn't want to spend the money that a big national multi-theater release requires. That's *not* such a "good thing" and, until our previews in Toronto and Minneapolis, we were squarely in this second category of limited release.

The previews changed all that immediately.

Sid Sheinberg was totally dazzled and took me aside to confide in me that he thought what we had in *Somewhere in Time* was a 1980 version of the 1970 megahit *Love Story*. I'm surprised I didn't just pass out when I heard that comparison. Here I was, a young (thirty-three-year-old) producer with a film that I had championed and helped will into existence. We had faced all kinds of doubts and criticisms, and now the head of the studio was telling me we had a huge hit.

"Vindication" was the order of the day and my ego took the bit and raced off into the sunset. Talk about being "seduced by the dark side of the force." Rosalyn Carter once said that the reason her husband was so soundly defeated by Ronald Reagan was that "it is easy to lead people where they want to go in the first place." In a heartbeat, I abandoned all my previous convictions that the film had to be built slowly, find its audience, etc. Not anymore. My thoughts then were that I had just become a major producer in Hollywood and would be able to have the high-powered career that I had always thought I should have.

Oops.

Funny thing happened on my way to fame and glory. I completely forgot what had attracted me to the story in the first place. It was an intimate movie for lovers and dreamers, not a big studio film.

Among the many mistakes I regret as I look back on my life, this has always stood out like the proverbial sore thumb. Although I have been assured by everyone involved that I would have been overruled by the studio, even if I had objected to the new strategy, I wish I had at least tried.

The decision was made to do a major 1,000-theater national release in October.

To aid in the publicity, we scheduled a press junket for Mackinac Island, a big New York premiere, etc. Then the Screen Actor's Guild went out on strike and we lost our actors because they could not even promote the film. We went ahead with the press junket to Mackinac and Universal asked us if we would object if they also used that event to promote another film that they didn't quite know how to handle. The film was *Resurrection*, which was a perfect companion piece to our film and a beautiful, haunting experience itself.

As the fall rolled around, the reviews started to come in. They were almost universally dreadful, and that really hurt. I know we're not supposed to take things like that personally, but we do. At least most of us do. There may be some people who have become so inured to the process that those slings and arrows no longer find their mark—but it's not true for me. Bad reviews still hurt and they hurt like hell in 1980. In particular, I felt horribly for Chris. It was because of his courage and commitment that we got the film made at all, and I personally thought he was wonderful in the film. The critics were pretty merciless in their treatment of all of us, but seemed to particularly direct their ire at Chris, and it hurt him.

Without the publicity help of our actors, the film opened on October 3, 1980.

Basically, it bombed.

Stayed around for three weeks and then disappeared with a domestic box office gross of only $10 million.

We were all shocked and devastated. I felt like I had let everybody (particularly Richard Matheson) down by not fighting for a different distribution pattern. I was so depressed that I went into a deep funk for several months and grew the beard I have never shaved since that time.

The movie had come and gone, and barely anyone had even noticed.

Fade out.

☆☆☆

Three years go by.

I went ahead with my producing career and buried myself in other work.

Then, something interesting happened.

It was 1983, and there was a very adventurous cable channel

in Los Angeles known as the Z Channel. It was one of the first cable movie networks but it was very limited, particularly in light of how channels like HBO now operate. When Z premiered, it showed two movies a day, usually in the evening, and that was it. Z was programmed by a wonderfully eccentric film buff named Jerry Harvey, who had been one of the few people who had actually seen *Somewhere in Time* in its initial theatrical run and had just loved it. Jerry got the film from Universal and began to show it on a regular basis on Z. People who had never seen or ever even heard of it began to watch it. And then they wrote letters and made phone calls requesting that it be shown again and again. Word started to spread.

Eventually, the film began to be shown on another fledgling cable channel, this time a national one—HBO. Audiences all over the country began discovering *Somewhere in Time,* and they also began to seek out and buy the videotape of it, a development that came as no small surprise to Universal, who had basically written the movie off. All of a sudden, retailers were buying the videos, and record stores were requesting more and more copies of the soundtrack. This was truly a grassroots phenomenon, and none of us involved in the film really understood what was happening for a while.

Sales of videocassettes of the film were very strong by the mid-1980s and so were soundtrack sales. The film had begun to build a loyal following, and Universal continued to be pleasantly surprised. (Today, *SIT* is one of the all-time best selling videocassettes in the history of Universal.)

In 1990, we were contacted by Bill Shepard, who had been an engineer at Hughes Aircraft for many years. He had also been a devoted fan of *SIT* and informed us, to our amazement, that he wanted to form a fan club for *SIT.* I must admit that Richard and I were totally bemused by the notion, thought the guy was very sweet but very naïve to think he could start (let alone sustain) a fan club for a movie that so few people had ever seen in a theater. Undaunted, Bill went ahead and formed the club using the acronym INSITE (International Network of Somewhere in Time Enthusiasts). He began printing a quarterly newsletter and subscribers started writing in with their own stories about their passion for *SIT.*

In 1991, Bill convinced the Grand Hotel to hold an *SIT* Weekend for fans of the film. It sold out the very first year and every year since then. By its Tenth Annual Weekend (which occurs in late October every year as the final weekend of the Grand's season), the weekend was selling out as early as four to five months in advance. People come from all over the world to spend a weekend that is totally devoted to the film. Besides nightly screenings of the film, there are guided tours of the locations used on the Island, workshops, panels, and interview sessions with whomever from the cast and crew happen to attend. The highlight of the weekend occurs on Saturday night with a full costume ball. People come dressed in period 1912 outfits, and there is a promenade down the long hall of the hotel.

I had a very hard time with the idea of going back to the Island for one of the weekends. Richard and Jeannot have attended several weekends. Fortunately, Chris got to attend one weekend before his accident. Part of my hesitation was inspired by thoughts of Thomas Wolfe's *You Can't Go Home Again.* The experience had been so magical that I was afraid to revisit it for fear of it not being what I remembered. I also had personal misgivings because of the painful dissolution of my marriage to the woman with whom I had shared the whole original experience. My daughter Cari was actually conceived while we were filming the movie. For years, I demurred.

The decade of the nineties saw the film's popularity grow and deepen. Once INSITE constructed its own website, thousands of more fans from around the world discovered that they were not alone and began communicating with each other.

In 1999, Bill retired from his active leadership in INSITE, and a dynamic woman named Jo Addie took over. Jo had actually been an extra while we were shooting the film and had been one of the charter members of INSITE. It was Jo's burning passion to get *SIT* re-released theatrically and get it the premiere that it never had. This time, none of us doubted that resolve.

Sure enough, I got a call from Universal in the spring of 2000 saying that they had decided to do a documentary on the filming of *SIT,* to include a DVD release of the film in the fall.

A wonderful documentary filmmaker named Laurent Bouzreau conducted interviews with all of us that spring. The DVD of the film now contains that hour-long documentary and it seems to me that it is the perfect tribute to the spirit of the film.

As the fall approached, we were also informed that Universal was going to do a selected city by city theatrical re-release of *Somewhere in Time* and kick it off with a premiere in New York on October 24. Chris and Jane could actually attend the premiere of *SIT* twenty years after the original one was cancelled.

The evening of the premiere was just magical. I had not seen Chris since his accident, although we had corresponded. Barnet, Richard Bach, and I actually wanted Chris to direct the film version of Richard's classic novel *Illusions*. We knew that Chris had always loved the book and particularly related to the flying aspect of the story because Chris had such experience as a pilot. When I actually saw Chris in New York, the first thing he told me was that he wanted to direct *Illusions*.

A note here about Chris. Even when he was the hottest star in the business after *Superman,* he never took either the fame or himself very seriously. There was never any ego about him. He saw himself as an actor. Not a star. Just an actor. With great character.

His character as a human being has only flourished since his accident. Chris does everything he can to deflect attention away from himself and takes great pains to make everyone else around him feel comfortable. There is not a trace of self-pity in him. He looks only to the future day when he will be able to get out of his wheelchair and walk away. I'm absolutely sure that we will see that day come to pass.

I finally attended the Grand Hotel *SIT* Weekend right after the premiere in New York, accompanied by my daughters Cari and Heather. For me, it was an extraordinary opportunity to see first-hand the place that the film has won in so many hearts. To see six hundred people spend an entire weekend watching and talking about the film was a special experience that I will never forget.

In 1993, INSITE placed a permanent plaque on a rock at the site where we shot the now famous "Is it You" scene. I had never seen the plaque so I walked down there alone from the hotel in the very early hours of dawn of my first day back on the island after twenty years.

The plaque reads:

"Is It You?"

At This Site on June 27, 1912

Richard Collier Found Elise McKenna.

To see that permanent reminder of the moment in which Richard Collier and Elise McKenna first met was the final confirmation for me that, thanks to its loyal fans, all of my hopes and dreams for this beautiful love story have been completely fulfilled.

"Did anyone ever tell you that too much persistence can be kind of stupid?"

"Never give up"

—*What Dreams May Come*

CHAPTER FIFTEEN

Beyond the Camera: *What Dreams May Come*

Amen to both of those seemingly contradictory statements.

Little did I know what was in store for me when, in 1979, Richard Matheson asked me if I wanted to read the galleys of his new novel. We had just finished production of *Somewhere in Time* and Richard had become my spiritual teacher. I was so excited that I raced to his house to pick up the galleys.

I read the book that night. Twice. I cried both times. Reading *Bid Time Return* for the first time had propelled me into the film business. Reading *WDMC* propelled me into my spiritual journey in this lifetime.

I was just riveted. As I have previously mentioned, the hallmark of all great love stories is the obstacle between the lovers. The concept of a man who is willing to risk losing his soul by venturing through the very pit of hell to save his wife is, to me, about as romantic as a concept can be. I knew in my heart that *WDMC* had within it the power to become a cultural landmark in spiritual films and I knew that it was one of the main purposes of my career in movies to produce the film and get it out to the world.

The next day, I went to Richard's house and begged him to

let me try to get the film made. Richard was very pleased with the whole process of *SIT.* He spent a lot of time with us on Mackinac Island and Jeannot was very respectful of Richard's script. He also knew how deeply I believed in the subject matter so he was his usual wonderful self when I asked him to let me try to do the same thing with *WDMC* as I had done with *SIT*. He smiled and said, "Sure, Steve, it's yours." That simple. We shook hands and that was the only deal we ever had on the rights.

As I left him that day, I promised him that this time it wouldn't take three years as it had with *SIT*.

Well, I didn't lie. It didn't take three years. It took nineteen.

I thought it was going to be a cakewalk.

I told Richard we should just sit tight until *SIT* was released. I was sure that *SIT* was going to be a huge commercial success and that it would also launch (actually the word I used was "catapult") my career as an independent producer. It would also make Richard Matheson a hot commodity again and we would, therefore, be able to do whatever we wanted to as a team. The industry and the world would even demand that we do *WDMC* right away because of the worldwide fervor for "SIT."

Yeah. Right.

I was only thirty-three years old. That's the best excuse I can muster for my wild-eyed insanity. I guess it wasn't that bad. I was only wrong about every single assumption that I had made.

Even if I had been right, I would have been wrong. Let me explain that.

I knew Michael Douglas a little as I was growing up. Our parents were close friends so we saw each other a few times. That was it. When we were prepping *SIT,* I saw Michael one day at Universal and we talked for a little while. When he realized it was my first film as a producer, he told me the best cautionary tale that any producer could ever hear.

As you know, Michael produced *One Flew Over the Cuckoo's Nest*. The film was nominated for a slew of Academy Awards and Michael told me that he hatched what he was sure was an ingenious, foolproof plan. He was convinced that they were going to win at least one major award. He had a script for the next film that he wanted to do (which turned out to be *The China Syndrome*). Convinced that the subject matter might be a bit of a tough sell, he scheduled meetings at all the studios for the day after the Academy Awards. His reasoning was that they would win at least one award, and all the studios would want his next film as a producer. He would strike while the Oscar was hot, so to speak.

Sure enough, the night of the Awards comes along and *Cuckoo's Nest* wins *all* the major awards, including Best Picture, which Michael himself accepts.

The next day, Oscar firmly in hand, Michael goes to his meetings at the studios convinced that he is going to ignite a major bidding war for *China Syndrome*. One slight miscalculation there. Everyone turned him down! Every one!

The message that Michael clearly got out of that experience was the one he tried to communicate to me: a producer starts fresh every time. Actors may be hot—directors may be hot—but producers start new every time out. I heard it. I believed it. I was grateful for it—and I promptly forgot about it.

Anyway, *SIT* bombed out at the box office. There would be no Academy Awards.

The industry scoffed at it and me for thinking it was so special and nobody—*nobody*—understood *WDMC*. At least, most people recognized that *SIT* was a time travel movie and acknowledged the concept as a device that audiences could buy. *WDMC* was all set in the afterlife experience of the main character. How were we going to visually execute that? And, the conventional wisdom continued, the story was too depressing. Nobody wants to deal with that much death, I was told. Lastly, the wife in the book commits suicide after her husband dies while she has two young children at home. How do you sympathize with her when she leaves two kids without either parent? Now *that* one I got. Not only did I get it, but I also agreed wholeheartedly that we were going to have to figure that one out. I didn't know how but I knew we would have to do it. I just hoped and thought someone would trust us and a director to find the solutions to all those challenges.

Not only did no one care, my contemporaries started to

look at me as being a "bit weird" for caring about all that "crap." In this industry, the rule is that it's okay to be different, just not *too* different.

A note here about 1980 and spirituality. Shirley MacLaine's *Out on a Limb* was still three years away from being published. If you wanted a "new age" book, you had to go to a specialty bookstore.

Nobody was interested in *WDMC*. I sent the script to all the studios and production companies as well as a long list of directors. Again, nobody was interested.

This went on for about three years and around fifty or sixty rejections.

In 1982, I was at Twentieth Century Fox where I was prepping *All The Right Moves* with Tom Cruise. I had an exclusive producing deal at Fox at that time, a fact that would have a major bearing on what was about to happen.

Richard Matheson called to tell me that he was going to meet with Steven Spielberg. Richard had not only written many of the memorable *Twilight Zone* episodes, but he had also written *Duel,* the television movie that had really launched Spielberg's career.

We had sent a copy of *WDMC* to Spielberg, but had never received a response, and Richard asked me if he should ask Spielberg about it. I of course said he absolutely should because we had nothing to lose. (I had actually assumed that we had not heard from Spielberg because he was going to stick to his own idea of remaking *A Guy Named Mike* which was also an afterlife love story.)

Next thing I know, Richard calls me from Spielberg's office at Warner Brothers and tells me to come right over because Spielberg wants to talk about *WDMC*. I probably set the land speed record for travel between Century City and Burbank.

Spielberg was the hottest and most successful director in the world. *E. T.* had just become the biggest movie of all time and Spielberg was one of the few guys who COULD do whatever he wanted to do and, since I was not anywhere near that league, I just hoped he really was interested in *WDMC*.

"Interested" was not quite right—"fascinated and enthusiastic" are more appropriate. He was just terrific. He loved the book and complimented Richard on avoiding the one thing that had always seemed to him to be a real flaw in afterlife movies—no jeopardy. Drama requires jeopardy and, Spielberg said, the aspect of Annie's suicide and Chris's search for her was a brilliant conception. He went on to say that he really wanted to develop the script with us, and if the script went fine, he could make the film right after *Temple of Doom,* which he was going to direct next. He was very nice to me and told me that even though he couldn't commit that I would be the sole producer, I would definitely be one of the producers, along with his own people.

At that point, I thought I was the one who had died and gone to heaven. Steven Spielberg? So what if I had to share the job with his producers? "What dream *had* come!"

We then asked why he had not responded when he had first read the book, and he told us a very beautiful and touching story about having read it with Amy Irving (to whom he had then been married) and that they loved it and actually read it out loud to each other. Unfortunately, they had separated soon after that for other reasons, and the book had been too painful a reminder to him.

Spielberg then asked me whether I had any preference about going to either Warners or Universal. He was in business with both. At that point, I told him that I had an exclusive deal at Fox, and the temperature in the room plummeted about forty degrees. He very firmly told me that he would not, under any circumstances, do a film at Fox because of its vice chairman Norman Levy. Norman had been the head of marketing and distribution at Columbia when Spielberg had done *Close Encounters* there in 1977, and he refused to work with Norman again.

I not only had an exclusive deal at Fox, but Norman was my friend and mentor. When I started with Ray Stark at Columbia in 1976, Norman went out of his way to be nice to me and spent a lot of time teaching me aspects of marketing and distribution. When he left to go to Fox, it was he who recommended to Marvin Davis (who owned Fox at the time) that I be brought aboard. Marvin had been looking for a young producer to team with his good friend Gary Morton, who was married to Lucille Ball. Norman recommended me and I got my deal. So Norman was very close to me.

Even though I did my best to dissuade him, Spielberg was adamant that he would not even consider going to Fox.

I left in a daze. What was I going to do?

I went back to Fox (how I made it there intact, I don't know) and went right to see Norman to tell him what had happened. He turned pale as a ghost. He had no clue why Spielberg felt that way. To have the world's most sought-after director refuse to deal with your studio because of you is not exactly beautiful music to an executive's ears. Norman tried to call Spielberg but Steven wouldn't speak to him. Norman didn't want Marvin Davis to hear of this, and he asked me to sit tight for a while and let him work on it.

Sit "tight" is exactly what I did.

Norman called everyone he knew and finally discovered that he had earned Spielberg's enmity for having changed the ad campaign for *Close Encounters* three months *after* its initial release.

I called Spielberg again myself to plead Norman's case, but Spielberg remained adamant and told me I had to choose. Easier said than done. It seemed that I had no choice to make at that time other than to just let Spielberg do the movie without me. Richard then ruled out that possibility, because he wanted me to be involved for personal and business reasons of his own.

Finally, Norman agreed that we had to tell Marvin and we did. Fox was in the process of starting the ad work on the *Star Wars* sequel, so Marvin knew George Lucas and knew how close Lucas was to Spielberg. Marvin called Lucas and explained the situation to him. Lucas asked Marvin to send him the book, so Lucas would know what was at the center of the issue. Marvin had a copy flown up by private plane to Lucas in northern California.

A few days later, we were called to Marvin's office where he told us that Lucas had read the book and called Marvin to tell him what a "fantastic project" it was. (*This*, at least was very good news because—before the Spielberg interest—nobody at Fox had even thought the project was feasible.) Lucas had indeed called Spielberg and was told what I had been told—that there was no chance. Marvin had tried himself to call Spielberg but to no avail. Fox had a new head of production at that time named Joe Wizan, who read the book when Lucas did and became the first executive in Hollywood to champion it. In fact, he told Marvin that Fox would never get a better chance to make a historic movie. (I have always loved Joe for that courage, because he told that to Marvin right *before* they heard from Lucas.)

So there we all sat, and Marvin gave me a choice. They were kind enough to acknowledge that I should not be punished and deprived of being able to make a movie with Spielberg because of something Norman had done (or not done) years before. They told me that they would release me from my contract and let me go develop the film with Spielberg; *or,* I could say no to Spielberg, and they would buy the book and develop it at Fox with another director. They went on to assure me that they would give me great discretion in both choosing the director and developing the script.

I did not know what to say.

When the meeting ended, I went back to Norman's office with him and he was just crestfallen and humiliated. He didn't, however, try to influence me in any way, and just told me to listen to my conscience and my instincts.

I went to see Richard who, to my amazement, was totally unperturbed—even bemused—by the whole situation. He told me that I had obviously created quite a spiritual Hobson's Choice for myself.

"Myself?" I asked. "It's your book!"

"But I entrusted it to you. It's your decision to make."

Great.

We then talked about it for a couple of hours at the end of which, he asked me three simple questions.

One. Did I think Spielberg was being fair in his refusal? That was the easy part because I had already determined for myself that, while Spielberg had every right to feel and do whatever he pleased, his attitude towards Norman was, in my opinion, excessive.

Two. That being the case, what energy would then be attached to the project if I left Fox under those circumstances?

Only a spiritual guru could ask his protégé that kind of question. I told him that I thought Norman would suffer greatly if we left under those circumstances, and that would in turn make me feel awful because of the enormous support I had always received from Norman. In other words, some very questionable karma could be attached to a project that was deeply spiritual.

Three. And this one surprised me. Did I think that Spielberg would direct the film in the manner that Richard and I had always hoped it would be made? He told me to separate Spielberg's talent from what I thought he would do with *this* particular project. Something just clicked inside me. For reasons I did not quite understand consciously, I knew that we had to say no to Spielberg. I told Richard and asked him what he thought. He just gave me that enigmatic smile of his and repeated again that it was my decision to make, not his. No consensual validation, guru? No way. I was on my own. Out on my own limb, with apologies to Ms. MacLaine.

Years later, Richard and I went to see *Always*, Spielberg's remake of an MGM film called *A Guy Named Mike. Always* is an earthbound afterlife love story, with Richard Dreyfuss playing a daredevil firefighting pilot who dies in a crash and then "comes back" to help train his replacement and try to comfort his girlfriend (Holly Hunter). Walking out of the theater after the film, I knew I had made the right decision years before. *Dreams* might have become a wonderful adventure in the afterlife with Spielberg directing it in 1985, but it would not have had the soul it needed to have. I say 1985 because I believe that the Steven Spielberg, who later made *Schindler's List,* probably would have made an extraordinary film out of *Dreams.* We'll never know. And before anyone accuses me of "Spielberg-bashing," please note that he directed more of the movies listed in this book than anyone, and also please note my comments on *E. T., Close Encounters,* and *Raiders.*

I called Spielberg, who was surprised but tremendously gracious.

Norman was ecstatic and acted like a condemned man who had just received a last-minute pardon.

Everybody else told me I was completely insane. Yeah, so

what else was or is new? The truth about that is that I *am* "nuts" when you use a consensus barometer for such a reading and that is just the way it is.

Over the years, odd as it may seem (even to me), I have never regretted that decision. There was no guarantee that we ever could have developed a script that Spielberg would have liked, but that was never the point. I just know that the film was not meant to be made at that time under those circumstances. I never look back and I don't regret it (even though many of my friends tell me that my lack of regret is the surest evidence of my lack of sanity). As the great old baseball pitcher Satchel Page always said, "Don't look back. Someone might be gaining on you."

☆☆☆

Fox then purchased the rights to the novel from Richard Matheson and, in early 1984, we began to look for a director.

I went back to a number of directors who had passed on it before, and they passed again.

Fox was working on a film called *Enemy Mine* in Iceland with an inexperienced director. The film had to be shut down. They began looking for a new director and hired Wolfgang Petersen who had just burst on the international scene with the aforementioned *NeverEnding Story* (chapter 3). Everyone at Fox fell in love with Wolfgang's work on reinventing *Enemy Mine,* and with the man himself. Eventually, I was asked about him for *What Dreams May Come.*

At that point, I watched *The NeverEnding Story* for the first time and was just dazzled. We sent the book to Wolfgang, who was in Munich prepping *Enemy Mine* and received an immediate response. He loved it and came to L.A. for meetings on both *Enemy Mine* and *WDMC.* Wolfgang is a totally engaging and humorous man, and we all hit it off immediately. In an eerie reminder of Spielberg's experience with Amy Irving, Wolfgang also had read the book with his wife Maria and just loved it. He told me that the film was going to be his love letter to his wife. We made the deal to work on it together, but Wolfgang had to go back to Munich.

Richard quickly put a first draft of the script together, and we made plans to go to Munich during Wolfgang's Christmas hiatus from shooting *Enemy Mine.*

A week before we were scheduled to leave, I was hit by a severe attack of pancreatitis, which put me in the hospital for two days. The doctor wanted it to be longer and told me there was no way I could fly to Munich in less than a week. I told him I just had to go, and eventually he relented.

Even though I convinced the doctor, I have to admit I also had a bit of uneasiness about going to Germany. What if I relapsed on the plane? The doctor gave me a prescription for a sleeping pill called Halcyon, so that I could relax on the flight. Unfortunately, I took one before we boarded and forgot. Richard and I then toasted our voyage with some champagne and, absentmindedly, I took another Halcyon. Two Halcyons and some champagne after losing about ten pounds in a week after the hospital. Brilliant.

My next conscious moment scared the hell out of me. I was standing in the dark in the middle of a city that I did not recognize. It was very early in the morning, just past dawn, and I thought—no, I was sure—that I was dreaming. I finally saw someone and asked where I was, and his response was in German. I was in Munich. Thank God I remembered the name of the hotel where we had been booked to stay, and he directed me back there.

I had passed out on the plane, and Richard had had to get me off the plane in a wheelchair, drive me to the hotel, and put me to bed. I obviously awoke in the morning and, still semi-drugged, thought I was home and went out for a walk. I regained consciousness out in the street.

This probably was a strong omen of what was about to happen, but I chose not to pay attention.

The meetings with Wolfgang went okay but he was understandably very distracted with *Enemy Mine* issues.

We went back to L.A. and everything proceeded very quickly to totally fall apart in 1985.

Marvin sold Fox, and all of the executives were fired. This happens very often in Hollywood and is almost always a death knell for most of the projects in development at that time.

Incoming executives see projects that were developed by a previous regime as basically a no-win situation for the new executives. If they continue a project and it is successful, the old regime gets the credit. If they continue and the project fails, the new regime is blamed for not bailing out when they could; hence, no-win.

Bye-bye *WDMC*.

In addition, *Enemy Mine* failed at the box office and Wolfgang went from being perceived by the studio as a genius to being considered a pariah. This, of course, makes no sense at all. Ray Stark taught me very early on that a director should be judged on his/her best work. If they subsequently fail, it usually means that they just made a bad decision on the specific material. In this case, unfortunately, Wolfgang himself became depressed at his prospects and withdrew from the project at just about the same time that Fox told me to go elsewhere. (Wolfgang went on to have a fantastically successful career, directing such blockbusters as *The Perfect Storm,* among others.)

That wasn't the only body blow we got in 1985. Richard and I had also sold the concept for an eighteen-hour miniseries on psychic phenomena to ABC. Richard wrote an eight hundred-page "outline," and it was summarily dismissed by ABC at just about the same time Fox said goodbye to *WDMC*.

For us, Orwell had miscalculated *1984* by about a year.

We tried to interest other studios and other directors, but no one was interested. We had been put in "turnaround"(the industry's equivalent to someone saying they have been "let go" when they actually have been fired), our story was too weird, and we were the idiots who had turned down Spielberg. Actually, I was looked upon as the idiot who had turned down Spielberg, and Richard was the idiot who had allowed me to do it.

We were heartbroken and discouraged, so we decided to put *WDMC* aside for the moment and try to get back on our feet. We drifted apart for a while too, because it was just too painful for us to keep facing the sadness of what had happened.

I got very angry and somewhat bitter about it. I also felt like a total loser, to myself, to Richard, and to the universe.

A few years passed. From time to time, I would try to revive *WDMC,* but to no avail.

During that time, I sold *Bill and Ted's Excellent Adventure* (chapter 6) to a new production company called Interscope, headed and owned by Ted Field. As I never totally gave up on *WDMC*, I gave a copy of the book to Ted, who read it and was fascinated by it. We briefly discussed it but couldn't quite figure out how to proceed, and it slipped away again.

☆☆☆

A few more years passed, and from time to time, more directors would see and pass on *WDMC*.

It's now 1993, and Dino has just fired me. It was his company. I wanted to change directions, and he didn't. The specific incident that precipitated my firing, however, was another matter altogether.

We had hired Ron Bass to develop a script for us. Ron was and still is the most successful and prolific writer in Hollywood in the last twenty years. He won the Academy Award for *Rainman,* and he has written other such movies as *Sleeping with the Enemy, When a Man Loves a Woman, Stepmom, Snow Falling on Cedars, Entrapment,* etc. Ron had originally been a top entertainment lawyer, and we had met in 1979 because he negotiated Chris Reeve's deal on *SIT* for Chris. In the early 1980s, Ron started to write scripts, and we maintained a casual but friendly relationship. Dino desperately wanted a Ron Bass script, and I asked Ron to come pitch an original idea to Dino, and he did. Dino loved the idea, and we agreed to pay Ron $750,000 for an original script, the most that Dino had ever spent on a development deal. (If that seems a lot, know that today Ron gets $2 million for an original script and has projects backed up for a year. Is he that good? No. He's better.)

Ron turned in the first draft of the script, and it wasn't great. Not bad, just not great. Even Ron admitted that. It needed work, and he knew it. First drafts are *never* perfect. That's why they're called "first" drafts. Ron is the most professional guy around and he'll work on something tirelessly to get it right once he's received everyone's script notes.

I gave the script to Dino with those comments. He read it and just went ballistic. He screamed at me that Ron had not delivered the script that he had promised, which was completely inaccurate. Ron had delivered *exactly* the story that he had pitched us, but the execution of it wasn't great yet. I told Dino that Ron would take whatever notes we gave him and would do his usual Bass magic. Dino didn't want to hear it and continued to claim that Ron had reneged on the deal, but Dino was completely wrong. He told me that he did not want to pay Ron, and I told him that he had no legal grounds for so refusing. Undaunted, he called Ron in and told him what Dino had told me. Ron was taken aback but acted like a total gentleman, offering to do a complete rewrite for Dino, who would hear none of it. Dino just wanted out. Ron then offered to walk away and settle for half of what Dino was contractually obligated to pay him—a very generous gesture in light of the fact that Dino was completely groundless in his accusations. Dino refused that, too, and told Ron to his face that that he had not delivered the script he had promised. It's one thing to question quality and quite another to question integrity. I think Dino actually believed what he was saying but he was dead wrong. They both turned to me, and I told Dino flat out that he was wrong, and we owed Ron the money. Dino stood up, ended the meeting and walked away.

Ron left the office in a state of shock and, five minutes later, Dino called me into his office and fired me for not supporting him in the argument. And that was that. (To be completely fair here to Dino, he was pretty disgusted with me anyway, and this was just the proverbial last straw.)

When I told Ron, he felt awful and offered to try to talk to Dino again, which I knew was a waste of time. It was just over. Within a week, I had negotiated a settlement on my contract with Dino and was out of the office.

Ron called again to see how I was doing and said he wanted to try to do something together, so that we could get the bad taste of that experience out of our mouths. He then asked me if I had anything I wanted to do and—clang!—the red light went off in my head. I went to see Richard Matheson.

I told Richard that we might be able to get *WDMC* going again if we convinced Ron to write the screenplay instead of Richard. That was a rough moment. Richard and I had been through so much together that I sure as hell wasn't going to even mention it to Ron unless Richard consented. I explained to Richard that Ron had become the most sought-after writer in the business and that he was brilliant with writing scripts that studios understood and in which major actors wanted to star. I thought it was our best chance to get going again and, this time, I left it up to Richard. True to form, he understood completely and agreed with my reasoning. It hurt him, and he didn't like it. Neither did I. But we knew it made sense.

Ron read the book right away and called to tell me that he loved it, would love to adapt it but didn't think anyone would even begin to pay him to do it. He thought it was just too daring for any studio to be willing to pay him his (then) $1 million price. Knowing that an old friend of Ron's (Mike Marcus) had just taken over as the head of MGM, I asked Ron to at least be willing to talk to Mike. Ron agreed.

I then called David Ladd, who worked with Mike at MGM and who was an old friend of mine. (Remember the restaurant mantra of location, location, location? In the film industry, it is relationships, relationships, relationships.) David was aware of the history of the project too and was very supportive. I also sent David a copy of the book. The meeting was set.

I asked Ron if he had thought out the challenges of the book and, to a certain extent, he had; however, he had not thought of how to solve the dilemma of a mother committing suicide and leaving her kids without either parent. This was always the Achilles heel of the book, and I knew not only that Mike would ask about it, but also that we had to have an answer—and a good one. Ron felt that Mike would not ask and said that he was unprepared to answer if he was asked.

One interesting note here. As Ron and I waited outside Mike's office for the meeting in the waiting room at MGM, there was one other man there waiting for another meeting. As we walked to Mike's office, I asked Ron if he knew who the guy was and he said, "That's a New Zealand director named Vincent Ward."

The meeting went much better than we could have hoped until we got to the end and Mike Marcus said we had to solve the suicide problem or we could not proceed. As I thought we were about to go down in flames once again, Ron cheerily said, "*Oh*, I know how to do that. The kids are going to die *before* the husband in a tragic accident. The only reason Annie barely survives the trauma is her love for Chris. So when he dies, she really has nothing to live for. We'll understand completely. And I can use the kids as characters in the afterlife with different identities until Chris is ready to see them for who they really are. They can actually be his guides. Simple."

David later told me that my jaw literally fell open. Hell, I'm lucky I didn't pass out! It was a brilliant, inspired solution to a problem that I hadn't been able to even address in fourteen years. Mike loved it, said let's do this, and that was that. We had a deal.

As Ron and I walked out of Mike's office, I was just about to turn to him and ask how the hell that had happened. Ron just said, "Don't even look around. I know what you're going to ask, and I have no idea where that came from or how it happened. All of a sudden, I just knew that was it and said it. I didn't even know what I was saying until I finished."

Well, I knew at that moment what had happened. The universe had decided that it was time for this movie to get made and gave us an answer that we needed just when we needed it. It also introduced us to the man who would, a year and a half later, become our director. It was really like, "Okay, guys, the time has come. Here's the answer to your story problem and, oh, by the way, that guy you 'just happened' to see is going to be your director even though you don't know it yet."

Magic does happen. I saw it that day in November, 1993.

We then had to wait a year for Ron to write the script because of his other commitments.

I met Barnet in April, 1994 and we decided to form Metafilmics. Another helping hand from the Universe. I knew that Barnet was the last missing piece to the puzzle. I had been going it alone for too long and Barnet came in with fresh ideas and a whole new perspective on how we should proceed.

In November, 1994, Ron called to say that the first draft was ready, and he was sending it to us that day before anyone else saw it. I got so overcome by emotion that I had to stop reading it several times. It was and is the best first draft of a script I've ever read; moreover, that first draft wound up being basically the movie that was made, except for the huge visual changes inspired by our director later on. (Richard read and loved the script as well, even going so far as to call Ron and tell him that the adaptation was so good that Richard would have changed some things in the book if he had thought of them first. That kind of dignity is rare anywhere, particularly in Hollywood. Ron told me it may have been the greatest compliment he had ever received.)

We submitted the script to MGM, and they had a very interesting response. They seemed very pleased and also very detached. They had very few script notes because they too recognized that Ron had basically nailed it on the first draft. The question really became—again—who is going to direct this? How are we going to visualize it? So, for the umpteenth time in fourteen years, we set out on a director search.

Ron was represented by Creative Artists Agency (CAA) and they had some interesting director suggestions, including Vincent Ward, whom we had seen fleetingly at MGM a year before. When we were reminded of that, Barnet and I took one look at each other and knew the universe was guiding us. We immediately saw the last movie Vincent had directed—*Map of the Human Heart*. As soon as we saw it, we knew Vincent was our guy. *WDMC* required a director who knew how to create a whole new world on film, and Vincent was obviously a genius in that realm. We were thrilled.

Then Vincent turned us down. He said he liked the script, but could not figure out a way to visualize it. (It's important to note that the entire painting motif was not in the original draft of the script. Annie was a caterer.) Another director had said no. At that point, I felt like a kid who had asked every single girl in his class to go to the prom and been turned down by all of them. Was I going to have to stay home?

A week later, as we were still looking elsewhere, Vincent called back and said he had an idea. We met him for breakfast and he laid out the whole painted world concept. Annie would be a painter and work in a museum, so painting would be a huge connection between Annie and Chris. When Chris died, he would awaken in Annie's paintings and interact in that world of wet paint. It was a stunning and brilliant concept. We had known that the afterlife was going to have to look different from anything that had ever been seen before on screen and here it was. I remember asking Vincent if he knew how we could actually accomplish his idea, and he just smiled his impish grin and said, "No, but we'll figure it out."

A word here about Vincent. He is the most dedicated, hardworking guy that I've ever been around and he is just brilliant as a director. Very few directors can create a whole new world on screen and Vincent is one of the great visualists around. He is also one of those guys who will always be loyal and honest with you if you are loyal and honest with him. He and I became great friends right away. Over the next four years, we would have some huge, wall-shattering screaming matches, but it was always about making the movie better. For instance, I was troubled by the darkness of the hell sequences that he envisioned, and we would often argue about that until he would remind me that "the film is about a man who goes through *hell*, Stephen, to save his wife—he doesn't go through *heck!*" That's Vincent—a true and impassioned visionary director and a wonderful man. He is and always will be one of my most treasured friends.

Ron incorporated Vincent's ideas into the script, but MGM passed on making the film. It was just too expensive for them to make at that time and they were very gracious about letting us go.

We then submitted the script to more than fifty-five possible financing sources, and the first call we got was from my *Bill and Ted* friend Ted Field, who wanted to see us right away. Ted's president of production is Scott Kroopf, with whom I had also worked before. The third member of the Interscope team was Erica Huggins, the most amazingly resourceful and resilient executive/producer I have ever known.

They loved the script, and Ted committed right there in the room to getting Polygram, with whom he had a deal, to finance it. He also promised that he would never interfere with us creatively. Ted is a man of his word and he kept both promises. He is definitely one of the major heroes in this saga.

Polygram demanded that we get a major star to play Chris. (To this day, I don't believe that any of the major Polygram production executives wanted to make *Dreams*. They never understood it—thank God!—and I think the way we sneaked through was due to the pure will of the universe and Ted Field's persistence.) Anyway, they wanted the "insurance" of a major star. When we really went through the list, we came down to two people: Tom Hanks and Robin Williams. We needed a major star who was sympathetic with the audience and could lead them into the afterlife. He had to be believable and credible as a human being, not just as an actor. He also had to have the tenderness for the love story. In the "major star" category, that left Hanks and Williams.

Robin said yes right away. In fact, he graciously volunteered to play "all the parts" if we wanted him to do so. This was in May 1996 and it began a one-year pre-production period, where Vincent and our brilliant production designer Eugenio Zannetti began to design the film, and we began the detailed work of getting a film of this size and scope ready for filming. That story could fill its own book, but is way too detailed to describe here.

As to casting, Cuba Gooding Jr. actually came in to talk about playing the tracker, but wound up getting very excited about playing Ian, Robin's afterlife guide. We actually met Cuba the week after he had won the Academy Award for Best Supporting Actor in *Jerry Maguire,* and he is exactly that guy you saw do a somersault on stage. He is an absolute delight to be around. After we cast Cuba, we cast Rosalind Chao to play the adult version of Robin's daughter, and that really pleased us because of the obvious underlying theme of diversity. We jokingly suggested to some executives that perhaps we should then cast Cheech Marin as the tracker. They didn't laugh. And we got the legendary Max Von Sydow, so we had Swedish diversity anyway.

Annabella Sciorra was cast as Annie after having graciously agreed to do a screen test with Robin. She was so obviously perfect with him that the decision was, for us, very easy; however, we had to go through some machinations with Polygram about considering a major "name" female star, but we all wanted Annabella and finally we were allowed to offer her the part. (A few words about her performance here. I think that Annabella had one of the most amazingly difficult parts to play in any movie in many years and, to me, she gives a truly perfect performance. She never missed a beat or a note throughout and she never received the credit that she so richly deserved. Now that she's got a special relationship with Tony Soprano, maybe he can do something about that.)

On June 23, 1997 (my daughter Heather's eleventh birthday), we started shooting in Glacier Park, Montana. To that point, I had been trying to get the project filmed for seventeen years. I will never forget the feeling of that day, and three of my four daughters were there to share it with me.

Remember how idyllic I said the shoot was on *Somewhere in Time?* Well, if that was heaven, *Dreams* surely was Hell. For myriad reasons, again too detailed for a chapter which has to detail the whole history of the project, the production period seemed to all of us to be a four-month-long nightmare. When it ended in October, we all felt that we had experienced the journey through the nightmare alongside Chris.

Our editor David Brenner had won an Academy Award for *Born on the Fourth of July,* and in typical genius fashion, he had a rough cut of the film ready to show us by December. We were all excited and dumbfounded by the power and scope of the film. The first cut was edited just as it had been written, so the first act was as disorienting as Chris's senses.

In January, we recruited an audience solely on the basis of their interest in the subject matter of the film. They weren't even told who was in the film until they agreed to come. That is a very key distinction. No hype, no dazzle. Just subject matter. And they loved the film, even in its rough cut form. And I mean they loved it. It was a fantastic response; however, Polygram didn't buy it. They argued that this audience was too specialized in their interest and they insisted on recruiting an audience on the basis of cast and a broader storyline. What a difference. The second audience didn't accept the film at all and was actually hostile about the confusing nature of the first act. We had to go back and re-edit the film with a much simpler and cleaner through-line in mind.

There was a lot of teeth gnashing over that. We had all loved the first cut, and, in my opinion, it is still the best version of the film—*for me*. Not for a broad, mainstream audience and therein lay the dilemma. To get the film made, a lot of money was spent. The sets and effects were extremely expensive, as was the cast; therefore, Polygram had a huge investment, and they needed to have the film appeal to the widest possible audience. Another excruciating paradox. They were absolutely right, and I completely agreed with what we needed to do, but making it a more mainstream film took some of the power of the experience away from those who were deeply interested in the subject matter. Such are the compromises of mainstream filmmaking. Ted Field was the catalyst for getting the film re-edited in a much more accessible way, and he proved to be an extraordinary diplomat in his balancing of all the competing interests at hand.

The creation of the visual effects for the painted world sequence was a slow and unbelievably expensive process. As the budget of the film required that we do something spectacular for a broad audience, it was imperative that the visual effects be ground-breaking. Thanks to Vincent and our entire effects crew, they were. They all did a magnificent job.

We previewed the film about seventeen times, I think. Polygram kept hoping that we could do something to really impress a mainstream audience, but the results of the previews were pretty generally the same (after we made the film more linear and less confusing). People who were attracted to and interested by the subject matter really loved it. People who were brought to it by the star power or the promise of the adventure generally wound up being disappointed—or worse. It became extremely obvious that the film was going to work great for the audience attracted by its story, but not for the casual viewer.

Dreams is not a walk in the park. It challenges audiences to look within themselves and, as such, it is not a movie where you can just check out and go along for the ride. (This is not to criticize those films where you can just enjoy the ride. I *love* those movies. It's just that *Dreams* is not one of them.)

There was a lot of "buzz" about *Dreams* in Hollywood, as we moved closer to our October 1998 release date. Academy Award buzz. Huge commercial hit buzz. And it was all wrong. There was no way that this intensely challenging and metaphysical movie was ever going to be a critical or box office bonanza.

Fortunately for me, I didn't totally blind myself this time. Yes, I was very hopeful that we could break out beyond our core audience but, deep inside, I knew doing so would be a very difficult task. I was not, however, prepared for some of what happened next.

First, the film was absolutely excoriated by most of the critics. They hated it and took great glee in listing all their reasons: corny, not believable, overwrought. And those were some of the nicer words. One magazine actually called it "metaphysical crap." That hurt me very badly. I took it very personally. I felt like *Dreams* was one of my children and I watched helplessly as it went out into the world and was attacked. I know that sounds really melodramatic, but it's what I felt. Fortunately, Siskel and Ebert both loved it, so we got the "big two" and a few others. It also helped a bit when I remembered how poorly both *2001* and *It's a Wonderful Life* had been originally treated by the critics.

Next, the film did not become a major commercial success. It grossed $55 million in the U.S. and another $45 million foreign, so it hit around $100 million in worldwide box office but, because of its cost (almost $85 million plus another $30 million in U.S. marketing alone) it was going to lose money for Polygram—and we knew it on the opening weekend.

The film went on to garner two 1999 Academy Award nominations, for Eugenio's brilliant design and for the visual effects. It won the latter (and should have won the former). On video and DVD, the film has been a tremendous success. The video retailers are talking about it in the same terms as *Somewhere in Time*; that is, it is on its way to becoming a perennial "evergreen" title. It has found its audience, and it is my proudest professional accomplishment.

As for me, the quest to get it made was over. After twenty years.

Interestingly, it was an event that occurred the week after the film opened that crystallized the entire experience for me and taught me once and for all, on a deep cellular level, why I love what I do so much.

Instead of focusing on the accomplishment of a twenty-year dream and the introduction of a purely metaphysical movie into the Hollywood mainstream, I focused a bit too much on bad reviews and disappointing grosses. For about five days. The universe then stepped in, and I was once again taught about perspective.

We got a call from a theater owner in the Midwest who said he had been contacted by a man in Milwaukee who had a terminally ill seventeen-year-old daughter. She had seen the previews for *Dreams* on television and wanted desperately to see the film but was too ill to get to a theater. The father was asking if there was any way that we could send a videocassette of the film to him. You can imagine how difficult a call that is for a film company like Polygram, with so much money invested in a film. To put a video out into the world is a big business risk; however, when I called to ask for their help, they immediately agreed, and a video was sent by courier to Milwaukee. I found out the man's phone number and left a message for him on his answering machine that we all hoped the film would be what his daughter hoped it would be.

A few days later, I got a call from a friend of the family in Milwaukee to say that the film had arrived and that the young woman passed away two days later. I left another message of condolence.

Two weeks later, the father called me. His name is Chuck Weber and he is a contractor in Milwaukee. He told me that his daughter Amanda had contracted a rare form of incurable cancer and had been ill for a year, during which time she had been very brave. At the end, she got a bit frightened, and that's when she started seeing TV ads for *Dreams,* and that in turn motivated Chuck to find a way to get a video copy.

Chuck told me that he watched Amanda while she watched the movie and that he saw her entire demeanor change when she saw the painted world sequence. She just seemed to relax. The next day, she asked to be taken out to a park where she could see the fall colors. Chuck thought that she might just pass away outside in the peace of the park, but she asked eventually to go home. On the way home, she told her Dad not to worry about her because, as a result of *Dreams,* she had a frame of reference for where she would go. The next day, she died peacefully in her home with her Dad and her friends.

Chuck's words that day to me forever changed my perspective. He told me that he didn't watch the film so he couldn't comment on it per se; however, he did watch the effect it had on Amanda. He told me that "no matter what, Stephen, this film gave peace to me and my daughter in the last two days of her life. Never lose sight of that. Nothing else is that important, is it?"

I will never forget those words. To this day, I carry a picture of Amanda in my wallet. Chuck has become a dear and close family friend. Chuck was a single father and we have a deep connection spiritually as well. My daughter Cari is the same age that Amanda would be now, had she lived. After getting to know Cari, Chuck gave a lot of Amanda's clothes and other personal effects to Cari and some to my youngest daughter Heather. It's been four years now since Amanda's passing, and we feel her presence with us often.

Personally, she reminded me again of what really is important in my life.

To touch and affect deeply even one human life in the profound way *Dreams* affected Amanda is the greatest satisfaction I could ever receive from my work. Not recognition. Not the trappings of a traditional definition of "success." It's the work itself and the empowerment and inspiration that can flow into the hearts and minds of those whom the work touches.

A brave seventeen-year-old girl and her loving father taught me that.

Thank you, Amanda and Chuck.

I will never forget.

"God is a comedian playing to an audience that's afraid to laugh."

—Oh, God

CHAPTER SIXTEEN

Your Turn

In the wonderful comedy *Tootsie,* Bill Murray plays the part of a playwright who is most intrigued, not by the people who come up to him to say how much they loved his play, but by the ones who say, "Hey, man, I saw your play . . . what happened?"

It is my hope that you will have been one of those in that audience mentioned in *Oh, God* that has laughed with us and maybe even been inspired. On the other hand, you may think that I am several tacos short of a combination plate and should be committed to some facility, where they keep me away from sharp objects . . . and my computer. One way or the other, I hope your feelings are strong ones. That kind of response provokes passionate debate and, to me, that's one of the things we're here to do. Ask questions. Form opinions. Engage. And, above all, *feel something!* Volunteer for and participate in this great adventure we call life. As far as I'm concerned, that is the prototypical "win/win" scenario.

We have established a website for you to make your feelings known:

www. Mysticalmovies.com.

We look forward to receiving your comments on the films we might have omitted, particularly the ones that have contained important messages for your life. You will also be able to chat with other people who are interested in this genre, exchange ideas with others on all the films we have listed, and even purchase the films we have discussed. We will also be posting updated comments on new movies and other forms of entertainment that relate to spirituality.

It is my hope and plan to compile your comments and publish a sequel to this book that will include those observations.

Let the games begin.

Afterword

Before commenting on the subject matter of Stephen's book, I would like to quote from a section of my foreword to the 1995 Dream Press edition of my novels *Somewhere in Time* and *What Dreams May Come.*

What I wrote is this:

"I am pleased that these two novels have been joined together in one book. Both are love stories, one romantic, one metaphysical; in a way I believe that *What Dreams May Come* augments *Somewhere in Time.*

Somewhere in Time is the story of a love that transcends time. *What Dreams May Come* is the story of a love that transcends death.

I never planned that they should be so joined at the psychic hip but I think they are . . . "

Clearly, Stephen has also thought they are. How else to explain the many years and dedicated effort he expended in bringing both of them so beautifully to the screen.

Which brings up another point I would like to make before commenting on the rest of Stephen's book.

In addition to its avowed content, I found the book to be fascinatingly educational in the multiplicity of details from today's film business. Literally—despite my years in the industry—I knew none of them. Many I find dauntingly challenging, making me almost grateful (but not quite) for the existence of ageism in the business. I am a simple storyteller.

As to the book itself, it is very clear that Stephen has accomplished—and that to a fare-thee-well—what I for one am increasingly incapable of: that is, delving into every aspect of the metaphysical realm. The details of metaphysical realities are probably beyond number—beyond, at least, any number conveniently available to our observation. That Stephen has approached them head-on, directing a bright light of psychological investigation on them is remarkable enough. That he has succeeded in explaining them so well goes beyond the remarkable to the awesome.

Stephen's observations and judgments are far beyond my ability to explore. As I have said, I am a simple storyteller. I have long been aware of this.

What I have not been aware of is the extraordinary growth and discerning skill of my friend Stephen Simon.

The Force Is with You is beyond question a landmark book. I visualize it on the shelves of film schools, bookstores, universities, and public libraries for years to come.

If I have been, in any way, a contributing factor to the genesis of the book, I am not only intensely gratified but, as noted, intensely overwhelmed as well.

How does one cope with the sudden, eye-widening discovery that the young man you have known for decades as a consummate film producer is, in addition (or has *become* in addition) a man of considerable spiritual insight and sheer writing ability?

His penetrating comprehension regarding the metaphysical content of so many Hollywood films was truly striking and unexpected to me. His ability to create carefully phrased breakdowns of these films was (and is) extraordinary.

Where did this young (well, he was young when I met him) man come from? I do believe that when the time is propitious, we invariably meet people we are destined to meet.

How marvelous that Stephen was in the wings all my life, waiting to appear, to help, to enrich my existence and, now, to astonish me with his wisdom.

I feel as a man might feel who, playing catch with a pleasantly capable baseball player, discovers, in a burst of amazement, that this self-same man may well be voted into the Hall of Fame on the first ballot.

—Richard Matheson
Hidden Hills, California

About the Author

Stephen (Deutsch) Simon has been a film producer and executive for twenty-five years. He has produced such films as *Somewhere in Time, All The Right Moves,* and *What Dreams May Come.*

Stephen has also been the president of production of two major production companies, where he supervised development and production for legendary producers Ray Stark and Dino de Laurentiis. In this capacity, Stephen was involved with such diverse films as *The Goodbye Girl, Smokey and the Bandit, The Electric Horseman, California Suite,* and *Madonna's Truth or Dare.*

In 1995, Stephen and Barnet Bain formed Metafilmics, a production company that exclusively develops and produces spiritual projects.

Stephen teaches seminars in several major U.S. cities entitled "Metaphysical Movie Messages" and authors a monthly column "The MovieMystic," which runs in dozens of magazines and Internet newsletters.

Stephen is a single father of four daughters—Michelle, 27, Tabitha, 25, Cari, 22, and Heather, 16.

A more complete professional and personal history is included in chapters 14 and 15—behind-the-scenes looks at both *Somewhere in Time* and *What Dreams May Come.*

Walsch Books is an imprint of Hampton Roads Publishing Company, edited by Neale Donald Walsch and Nancy Fleming-Walsch. Our shared vision is to publish quality books that enhance and further the central messages of the *Conversations with God* series, in both fiction and non-fiction genres, and to provide another avenue through which the healing truths of the great wisdom traditions may be expressed in clear and accessible terms.

Hampton Roads Publishing Company
. . . for the evolving human spirit

Hampton Roads Publishing Company
publishes books on a variety of subjects including
metaphysics, health, complementary medicine,
visionary fiction, and other related topics.

For a copy of our latest catalog,
call toll-free, 800-766-8009,
or send your name and address to:

Hampton Roads Publishing Company, Inc.
1125 Stoney Ridge Road
Charlottesville, VA 22902
e-mail: hrpc@hrpub.com
www.hrpub.com